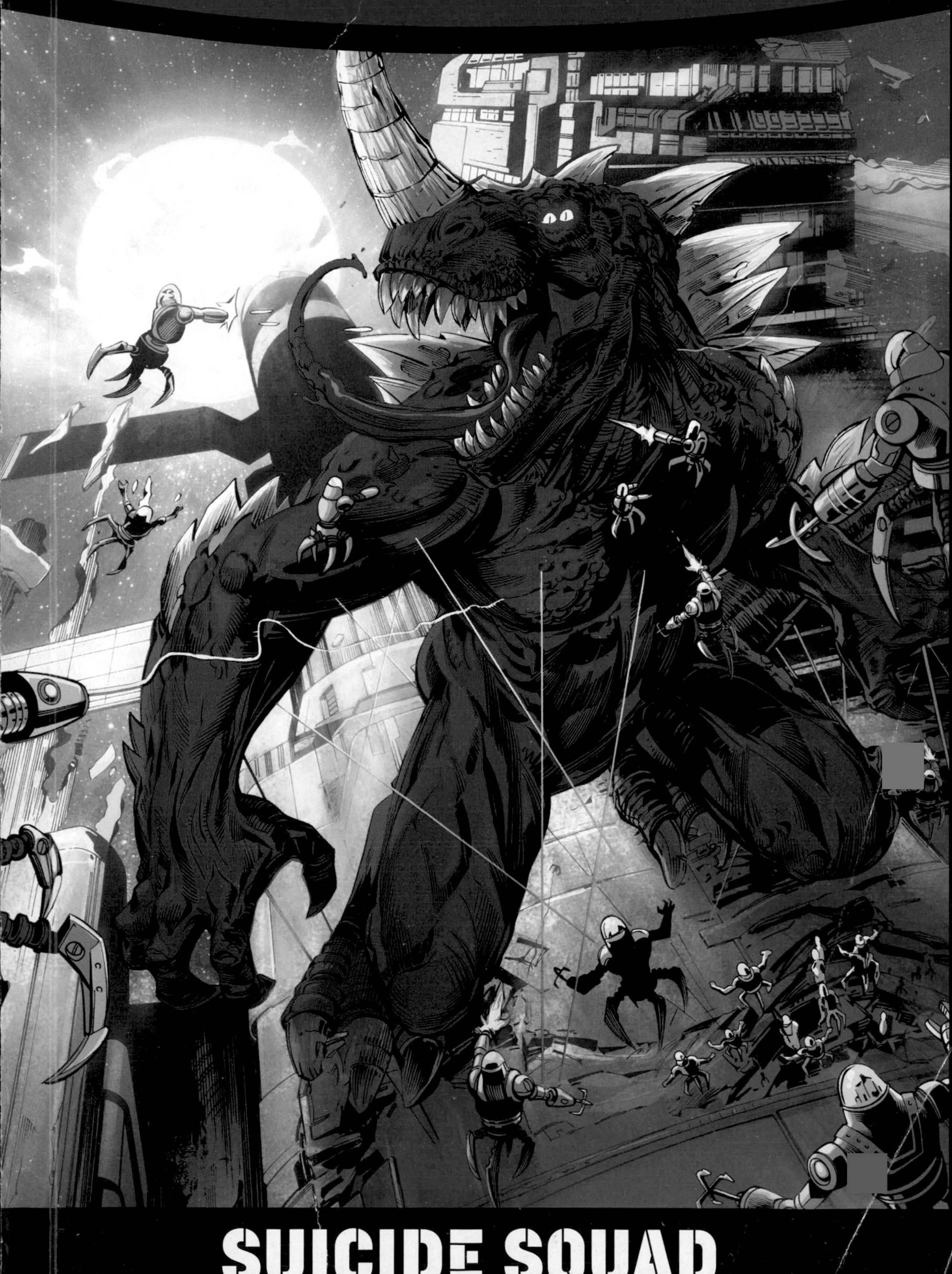

SUICIDE SQUAD

VOL.6 THE SECRET HISTORY OF TASK FORCE X

SUICIDE SQUAD

VOL.6 THE SECRET HISTORY OF TASK FORCE X

ROB WILLIAMS
writer

BARNABY BAGENDA
ELEONORA CARLINI * **PHILIPPE BRIONES** * **SCOT EATON**
JAY LEISTEN * **WAYNE FAUCHER** * **WILFREDO TORRES**
artists

ADRIANO LUCAS
colorist

PAT BROSSEAU
letterer

STJEPAN SEJIC
collection cover artist

TONY S. DANIEL, DANNY MIKI and **TOMEU MOREY**
EDDY BARROWS, EBER FERREIRA and **ADRIANO LUCAS**
STJEPAN SEJIC
original series cover artists

SUPERMAN created by **JERRY SIEGEL** and **JOE SHUSTER**
By special arrangement with the Jerry Siegel family

ALEX ANTONE Editor - Original Series ✳ **DAVE WIELGOSZ** Assistant Editor - Original Series
JEB WOODARD Group Editor - Collected Editions ✳ **ROBIN WILDMAN** Editor - Collected Edition
STEVE COOK Design Director - Books ✳ **MEGEN BELLERSEN** Publication Design

BOB HARRAS Senior VP - Editor-in-Chief, DC Comics ✳ **PAT McCALLUM** Executive Editor, DC Comics

DIANE NELSON President ✳ **DAN DiDIO** Publisher ✳ **JIM LEE** Publisher ✳ **GEOFF JOHNS** President & Chief Creative Officer
AMIT DESAI Executive VP - Business & Marketing Strategy, Direct to Consumer & Global Franchise Management
SAM ADES Senior VP & General Manager, Digital Services ✳ **BOBBIE CHASE** VP & Executive Editor, Young Reader & Talent Development
MARK CHIARELLO Senior VP - Art, Design & Collected Editions ✳ **JOHN CUNNINGHAM** Senior VP - Sales & Trade Marketing
ANNE DePIES Senior VP - Business Strategy, Finance & Administration ✳ **DON FALLETTI** VP - Manufacturing Operations
LAWRENCE GANEM VP - Editorial Administration & Talent Relations ✳ **ALISON GILL** Senior VP - Manufacturing & Operations
HANK KANALZ Senior VP - Editorial Strategy & Administration ✳ **JAY KOGAN** VP - Legal Affairs ✳ **JACK MAHAN** VP - Business Affairs
NICK J. NAPOLITANO VP - Manufacturing Administration ✳ **EDDIE SCANNELL** VP - Consumer Marketing
COURTNEY SIMMONS Senior VP - Publicity & Communications ✳ **JIM (SKI) SOKOLOWSKI** VP - Comic Book Specialty Sales & Trade Marketing
NANCY SPEARS VP - Mass, Book, Digital Sales & Trade Marketing ✳ **MICHELE R. WELLS** VP - Content Strategy

SUICIDE SQUAD VOL. 6: THE SECRET HISTORY OF TASK FORCE X

DC Comics, 2900 West Alameda Ave., Burbank, CA 91505
Printed by LSC Communications, Kendallville, IN, USA. 6/15/18. First Printing.
ISBN: 978-1-4012-8098-7

Library of Congress Cataloging-in-Publication Data is available.

PEFC Certified

Printed on paper from
sustainably managed
forests, controlled
sources

PEFC/29-31-337   www.pefc.org

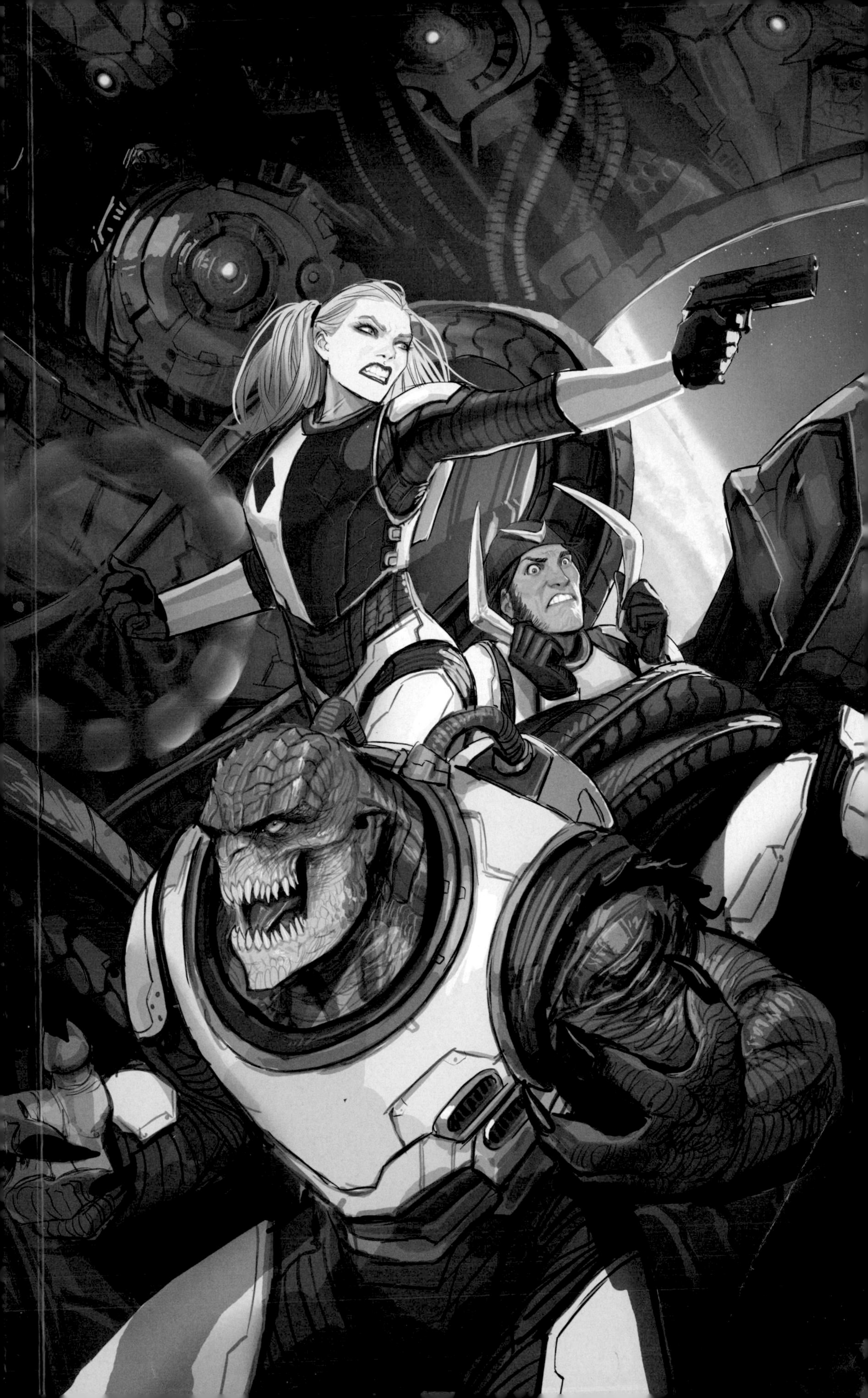

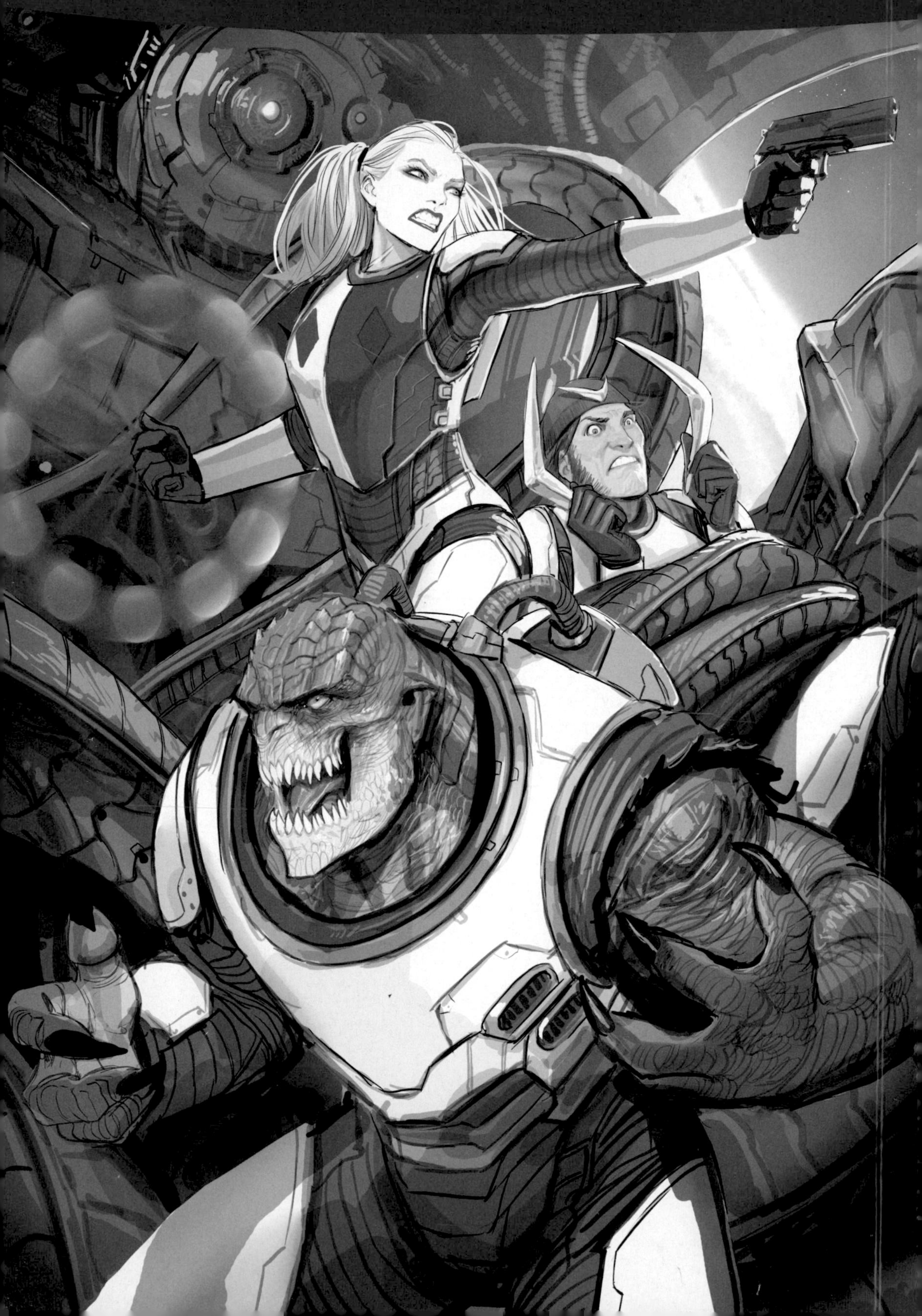

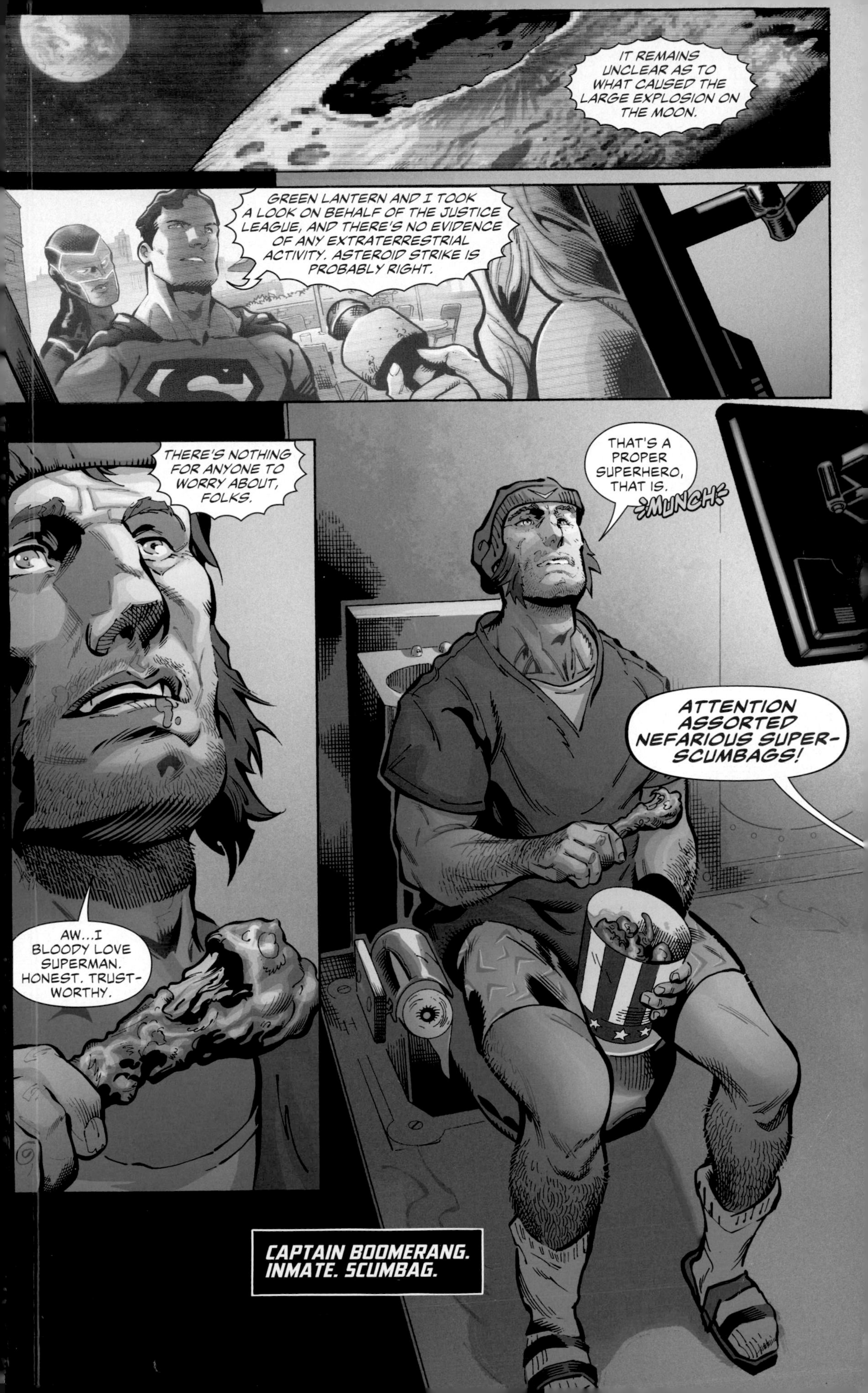

IT REMAINS UNCLEAR AS TO WHAT CAUSED THE LARGE EXPLOSION ON THE MOON.
GREEN LANTERN AND I TOOK A LOOK ON BEHALF OF THE JUSTICE LEAGUE, AND THERE'S NO EVIDENCE OF ANY EXTRATERRESTRIAL ACTIVITY. ASTEROID STRIKE IS PROBABLY RIGHT.
THERE'S NOTHING FOR ANYONE TO WORRY ABOUT, FOLKS.
AW...I BLOODY LOVE SUPERMAN. HONEST. TRUST-WORTHY.
THAT'S A PROPER SUPERHERO, THAT IS.
MUNCH
ATTENTION ASSORTED NEFARIOUS SUPER-SCUMBAGS!
CAPTAIN BOOMERANG. INMATE. SCUMBAG.

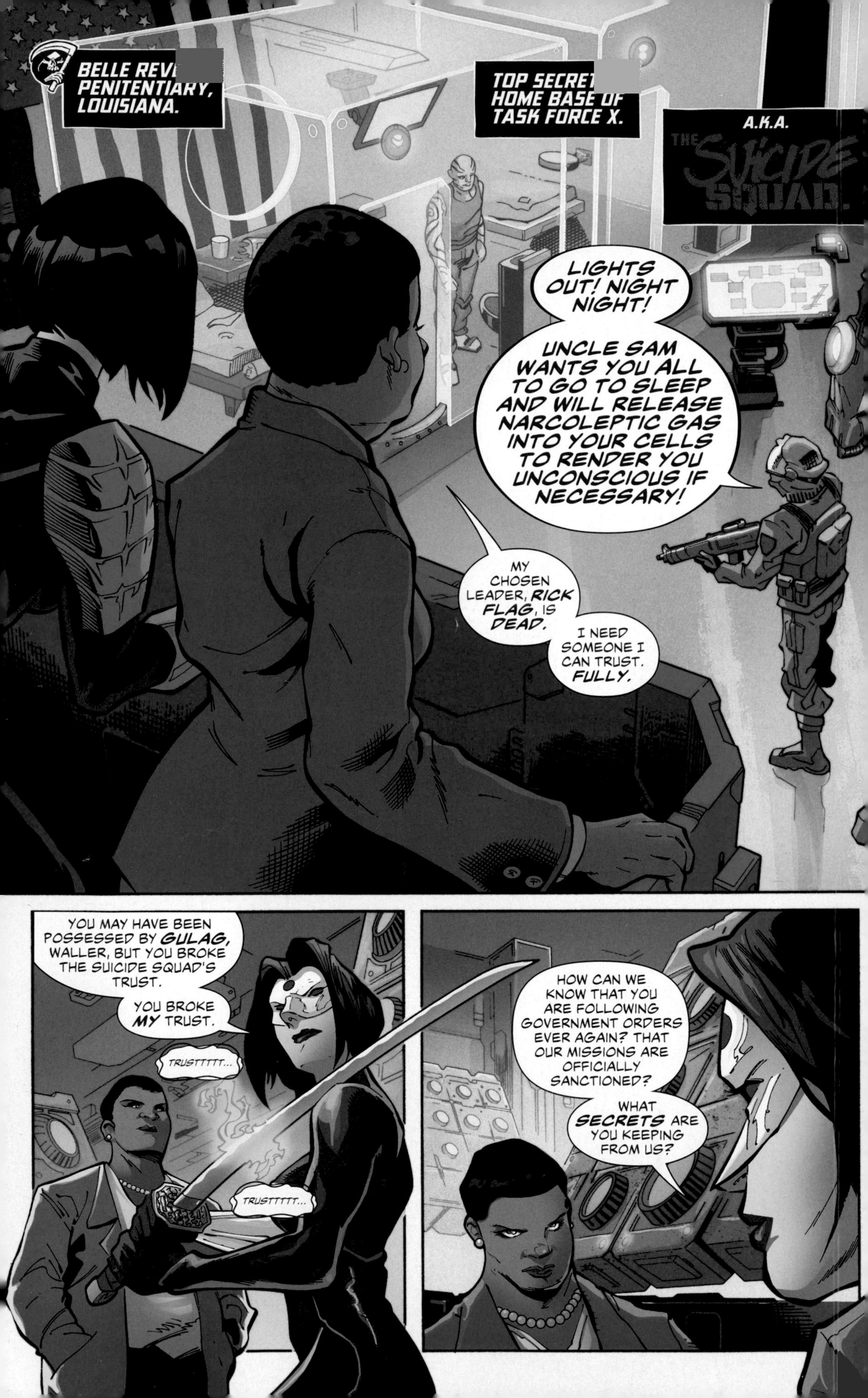
BELLE REV[redacted] PENITENTIARY, LOUISIANA.
TOP SECRET[redacted] HOME BASE OF TASK FORCE X.
A.K.A. THE SUICIDE SQUAD.
LIGHTS OUT! NIGHT NIGHT!
UNCLE SAM WANTS YOU ALL TO GO TO SLEEP AND WILL RELEASE NARCOLEPTIC GAS INTO YOUR CELLS TO RENDER YOU UNCONSCIOUS IF NECESSARY!
MY CHOSEN LEADER, RICK FLAG, IS DEAD.
I NEED SOMEONE I CAN TRUST. FULLY.
YOU MAY HAVE BEEN POSSESSED BY GULAG, WALLER, BUT YOU BROKE THE SUICIDE SQUAD'S TRUST.
YOU BROKE MY TRUST.
TRUSTTTTT...
TRUSTTTTT...
HOW CAN WE KNOW THAT YOU ARE FOLLOWING GOVERNMENT ORDERS EVER AGAIN? THAT OUR MISSIONS ARE OFFICIALLY SANCTIONED?
WHAT SECRETS ARE YOU KEEPING FROM US?

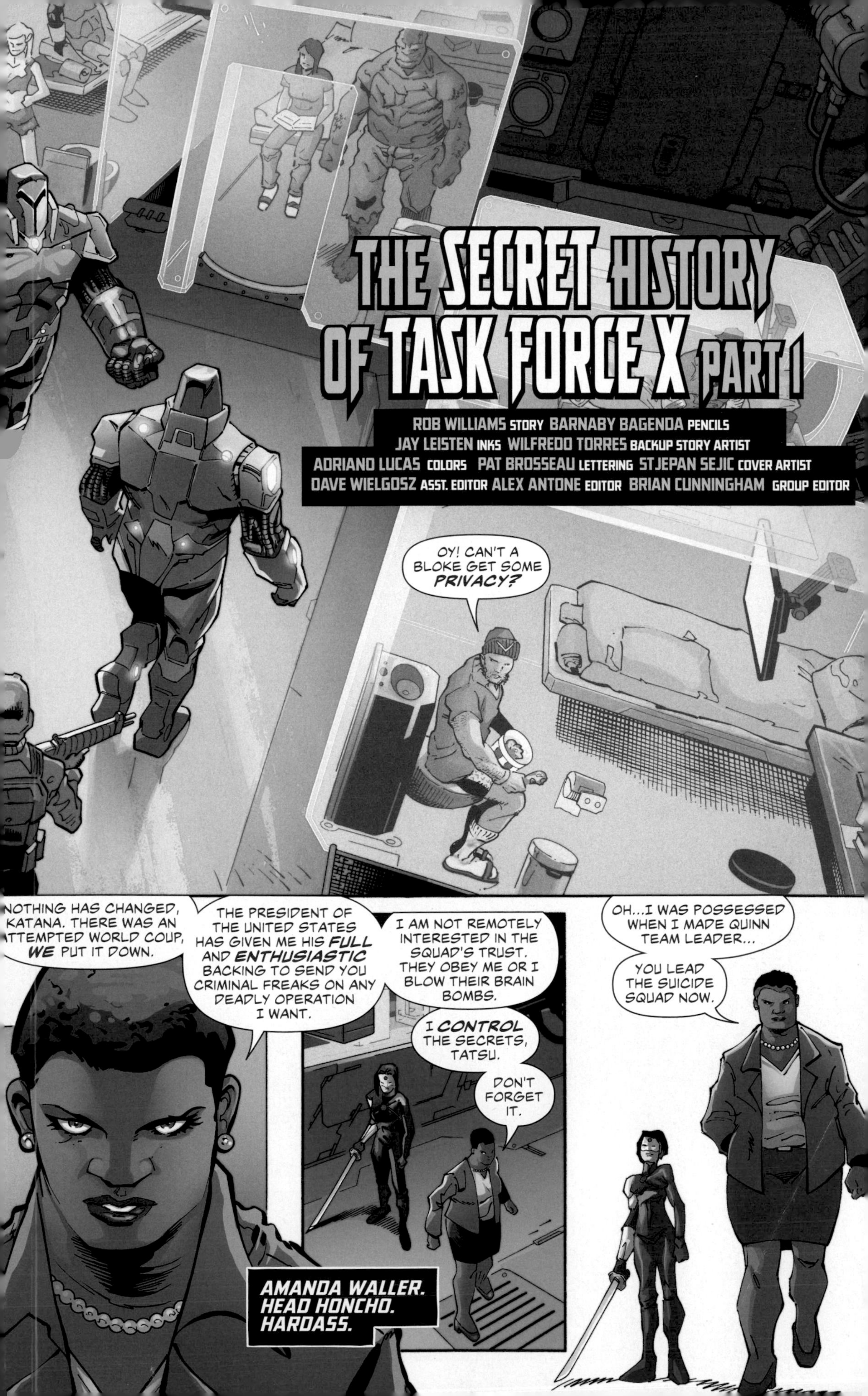
THE SECRET HISTORY OF TASK FORCE X PART 1
ROB WILLIAMS STORY BARNABY BAGENDA PENCILS
JAY LEISTEN INKS WILFREDO TORRES BACKUP STORY ARTIST
ADRIANO LUCAS COLORS PAT BROSSEAU LETTERING STJEPAN SEJIC COVER ARTIST
DAVE WIELGOSZ ASST. EDITOR ALEX ANTONE EDITOR BRIAN CUNNINGHAM GROUP EDITOR
OY! CAN'T A BLOKE GET SOME PRIVACY?
NOTHING HAS CHANGED, KATANA. THERE WAS AN ATTEMPTED WORLD COUP, WE PUT IT DOWN.
THE PRESIDENT OF THE UNITED STATES HAS GIVEN ME HIS FULL AND ENTHUSIASTIC BACKING TO SEND YOU CRIMINAL FREAKS ON ANY DEADLY OPERATION I WANT.
AMANDA WALLER. HEAD HONCHO. HARDASS.
I AM NOT REMOTELY INTERESTED IN THE SQUAD'S TRUST. THEY OBEY ME OR I BLOW THEIR BRAIN BOMBS.
I CONTROL THE SECRETS, TATSU.
DON'T FORGET IT.
OH...I WAS POSSESSED WHEN I MADE QUINN TEAM LEADER...
YOU LEAD THE SUICIDE SQUAD NOW.

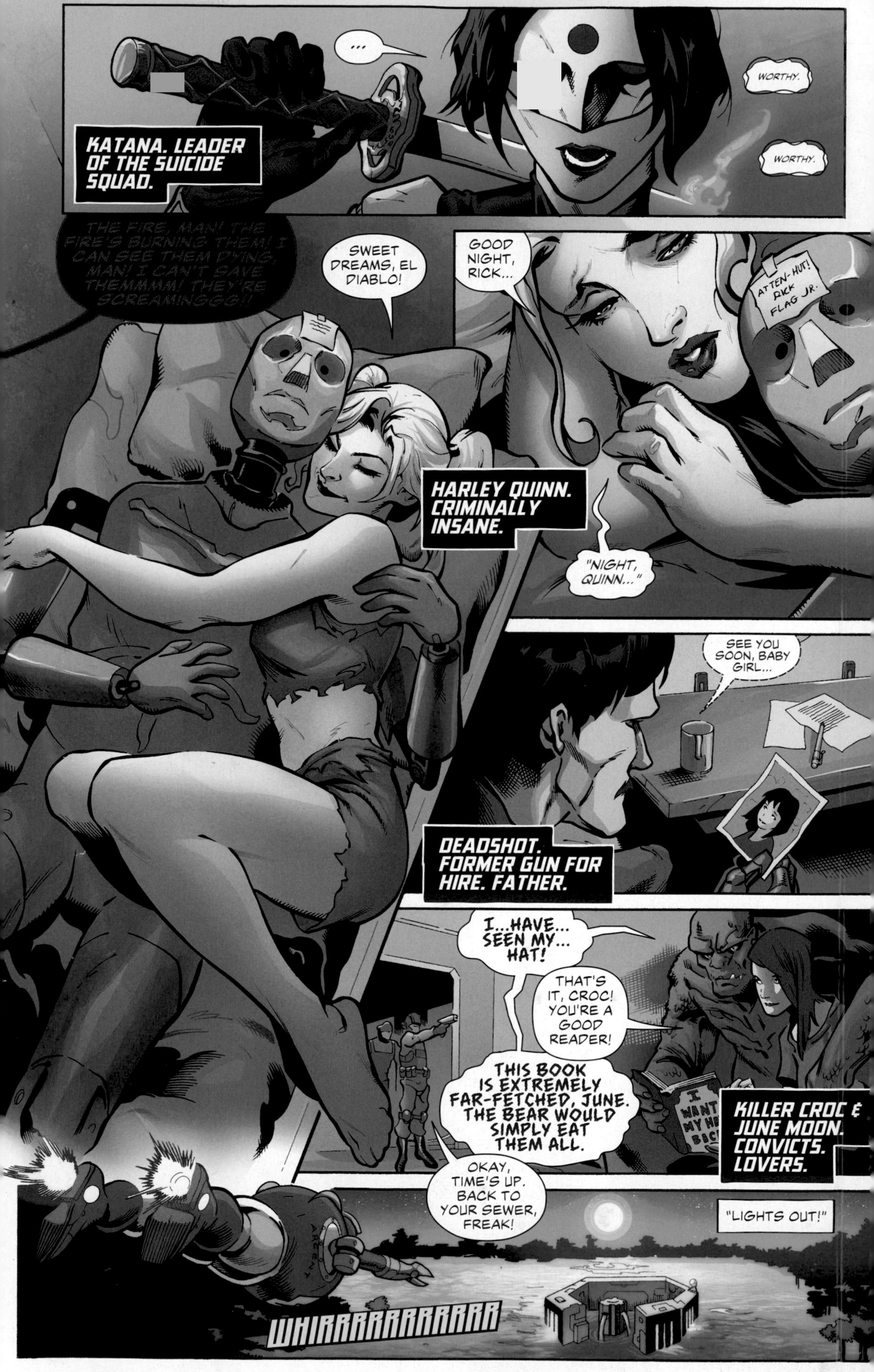
...
WORTHY.
WORTHY.
KATANA. LEADER OF THE SUICIDE SQUAD.
THE FIRE, MAN! THE FIRE'S BURNING THEM! I CAN SEE THEM DYING, MAN! I CAN'T SAVE THEMMMM! THEY'RE SCREAMINGGG!!
SWEET DREAMS, EL DIABLO!
GOOD NIGHT, RICK...
ATTEN-HUT! RICK FLAG JR.
HARLEY QUINN. CRIMINALLY INSANE.
"NIGHT, QUINN..."
SEE YOU SOON, BABY GIRL...
DEADSHOT. FORMER GUN FOR HIRE. FATHER.
I...HAVE... SEEN MY... HAT!
THAT'S IT, CROC! YOU'RE A GOOD READER!
THIS BOOK IS EXTREMELY FAR-FETCHED, JUNE. THE BEAR WOULD SIMPLY EAT THEM ALL.
KILLER CROC & JUNE MOON. CONVICTS. LOVERS.
OKAY, TIME'S UP. BACK TO YOUR SEWER, FREAK!
"LIGHTS OUT!"
WHIRRRRRRRRRRRR

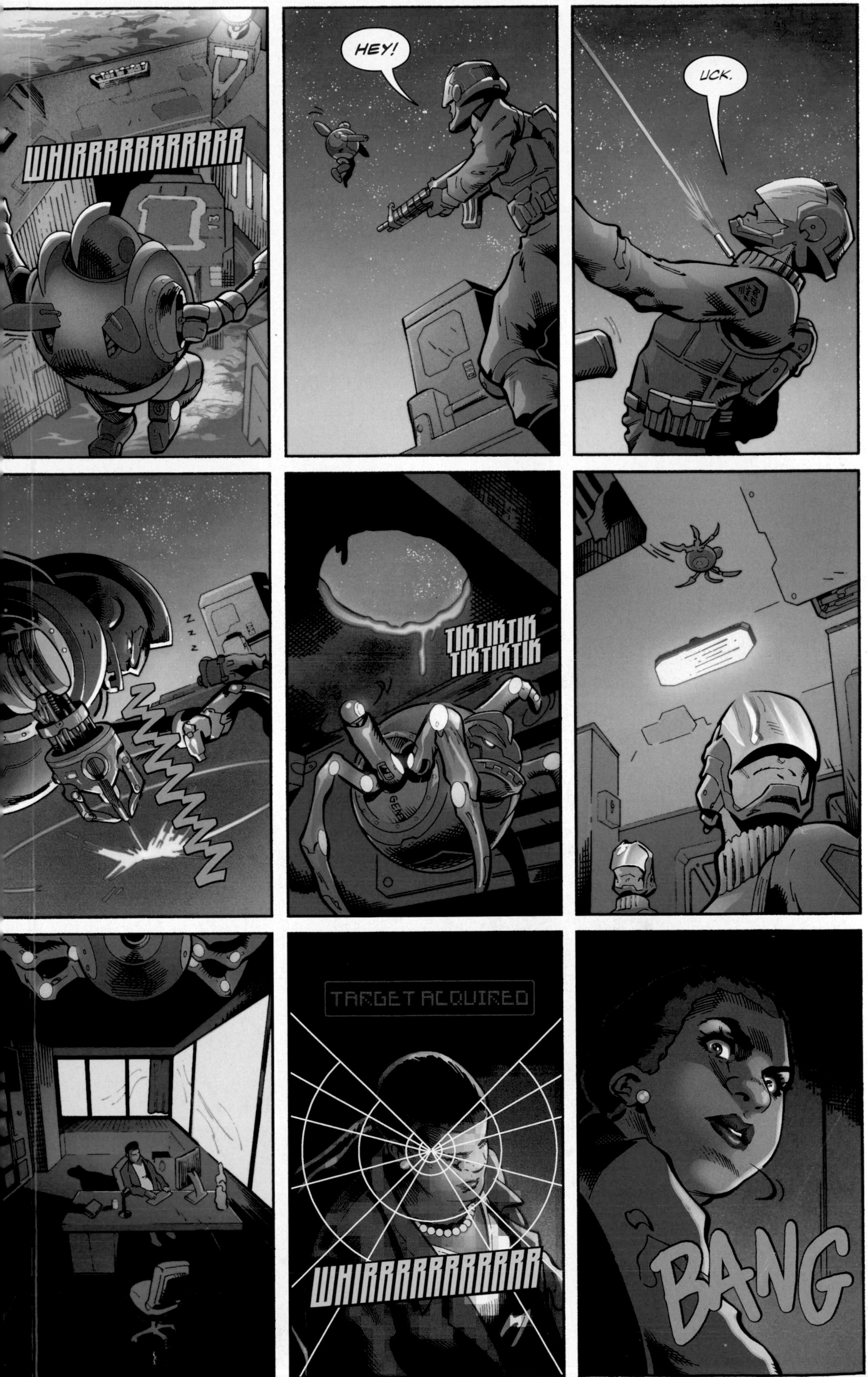
WHIRRRRRRRRRRR
HEY!
UCK.
TIKTIKTIK
TIKTIKTIK
TARGET ACQUIRED
WHIRRRRRRRRRRRR
BANG

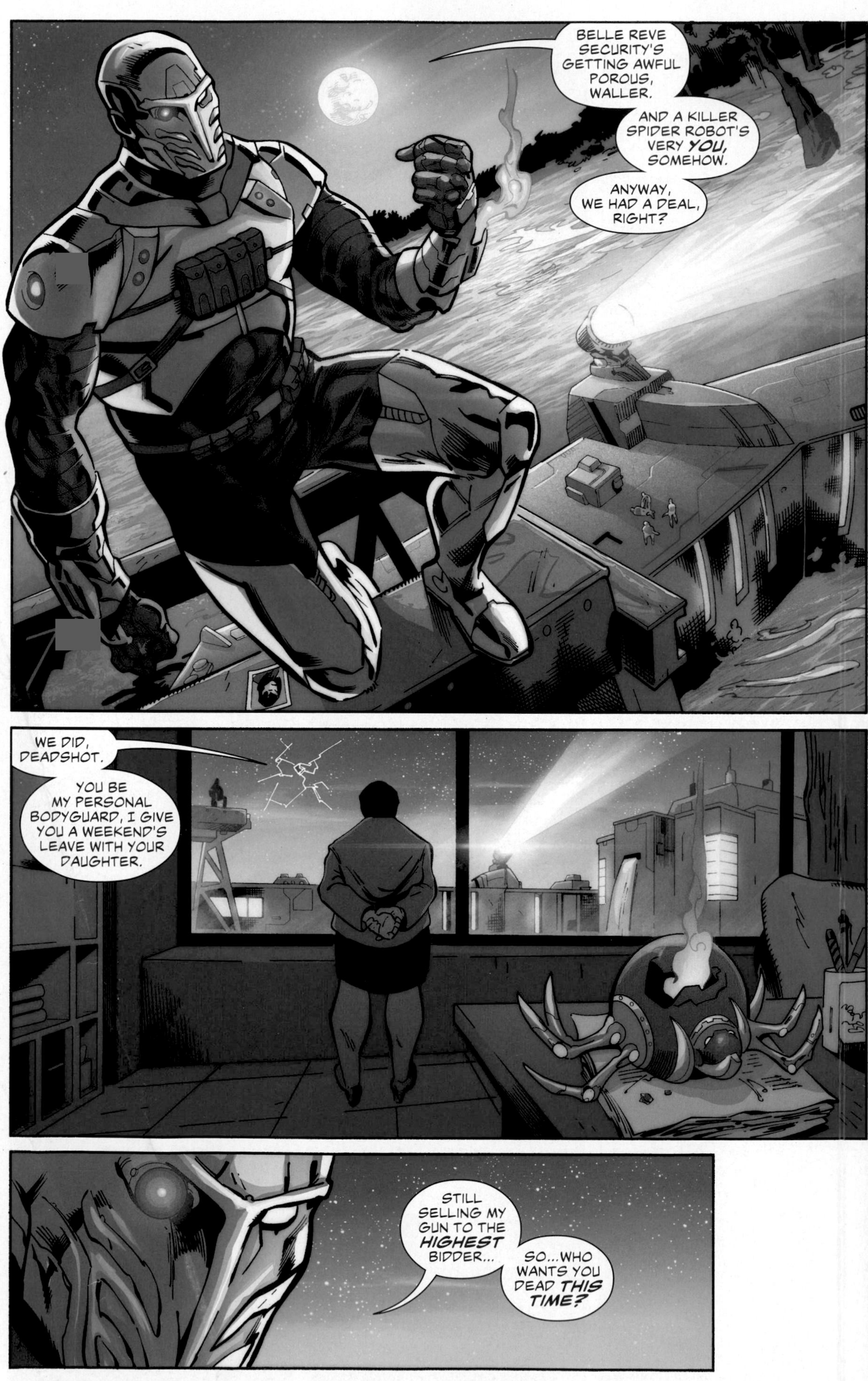
BELLE REVE SECURITY'S GETTING AWFUL POROUS, WALLER.
AND A KILLER SPIDER ROBOT'S VERY YOU, SOMEHOW.
ANYWAY, WE HAD A DEAL, RIGHT?
WE DID, DEADSHOT.
YOU BE MY PERSONAL BODYGUARD, I GIVE YOU A WEEKEND'S LEAVE WITH YOUR DAUGHTER.
STILL SELLING MY GUN TO THE HIGHEST BIDDER...
SO...WHO WANTS YOU DEAD THIS TIME?

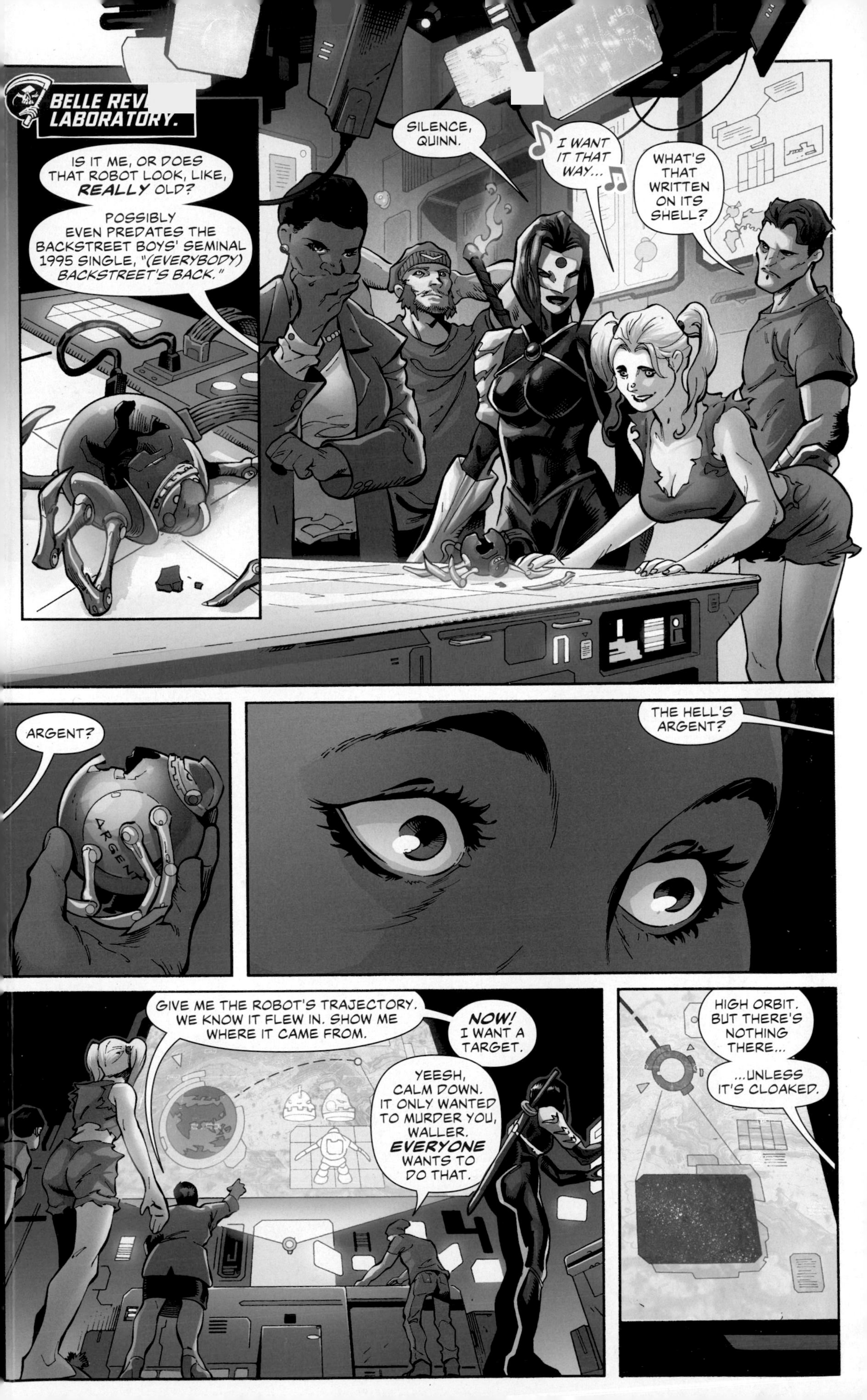

BELLE REV
LABORATORY.
IS IT ME, OR DOES THAT ROBOT LOOK, LIKE, REALLY OLD?
POSSIBLY EVEN PREDATES THE BACKSTREET BOYS' SEMINAL 1995 SINGLE, "(EVERYBODY) BACKSTREET'S BACK."
SILENCE, QUINN.
I WANT IT THAT WAY...
WHAT'S THAT WRITTEN ON ITS SHELL?
ARGENT?
ARGENT
THE HELL'S ARGENT?
GIVE ME THE ROBOT'S TRAJECTORY. WE KNOW IT FLEW IN. SHOW ME WHERE IT CAME FROM.
NOW! I WANT A TARGET.
YEESH, CALM DOWN. IT ONLY WANTED TO MURDER YOU, WALLER. EVERYONE WANTS TO DO THAT.
HIGH ORBIT. BUT THERE'S NOTHING THERE...
...UNLESS IT'S CLOAKED.

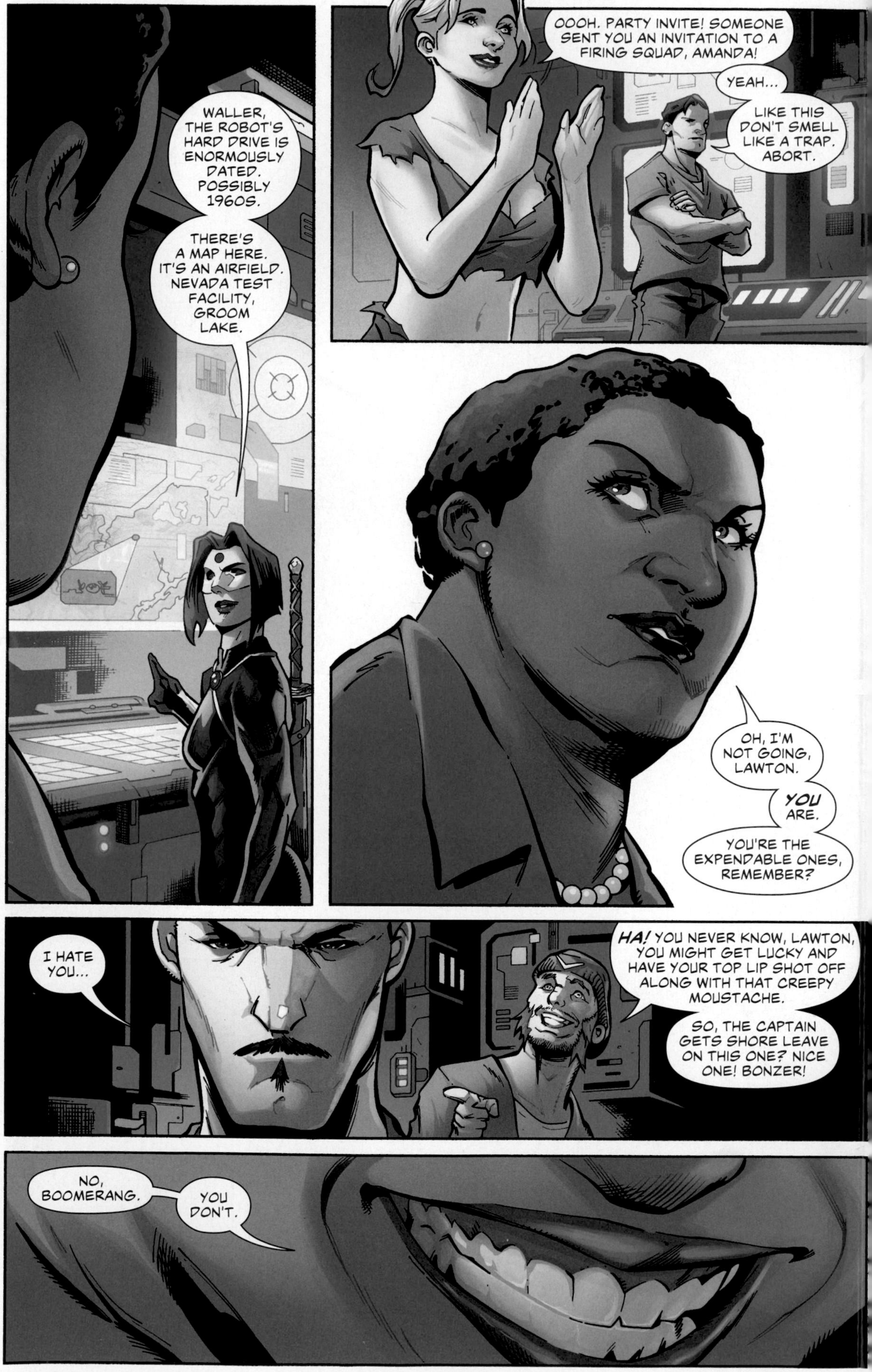
WALLER, THE ROBOT'S HARD DRIVE IS ENORMOUSLY DATED. POSSIBLY 1960S.
THERE'S A MAP HERE. IT'S AN AIRFIELD. NEVADA TEST FACILITY, GROOM LAKE.
OOOH. PARTY INVITE! SOMEONE SENT YOU AN INVITATION TO A FIRING SQUAD, AMANDA!
YEAH...
LIKE THIS DON'T SMELL LIKE A TRAP. ABORT.
OH, I'M NOT GOING, LAWTON.
YOU ARE.
YOU'RE THE EXPENDABLE ONES, REMEMBER?
I HATE YOU...
HA! YOU NEVER KNOW, LAWTON, YOU MIGHT GET LUCKY AND HAVE YOUR TOP LIP SHOT OFF ALONG WITH THAT CREEPY MOUSTACHE.
SO, THE CAPTAIN GETS SHORE LEAVE ON THIS ONE? NICE ONE! BONZER!
NO, BOOMERANG.
YOU DON'T.

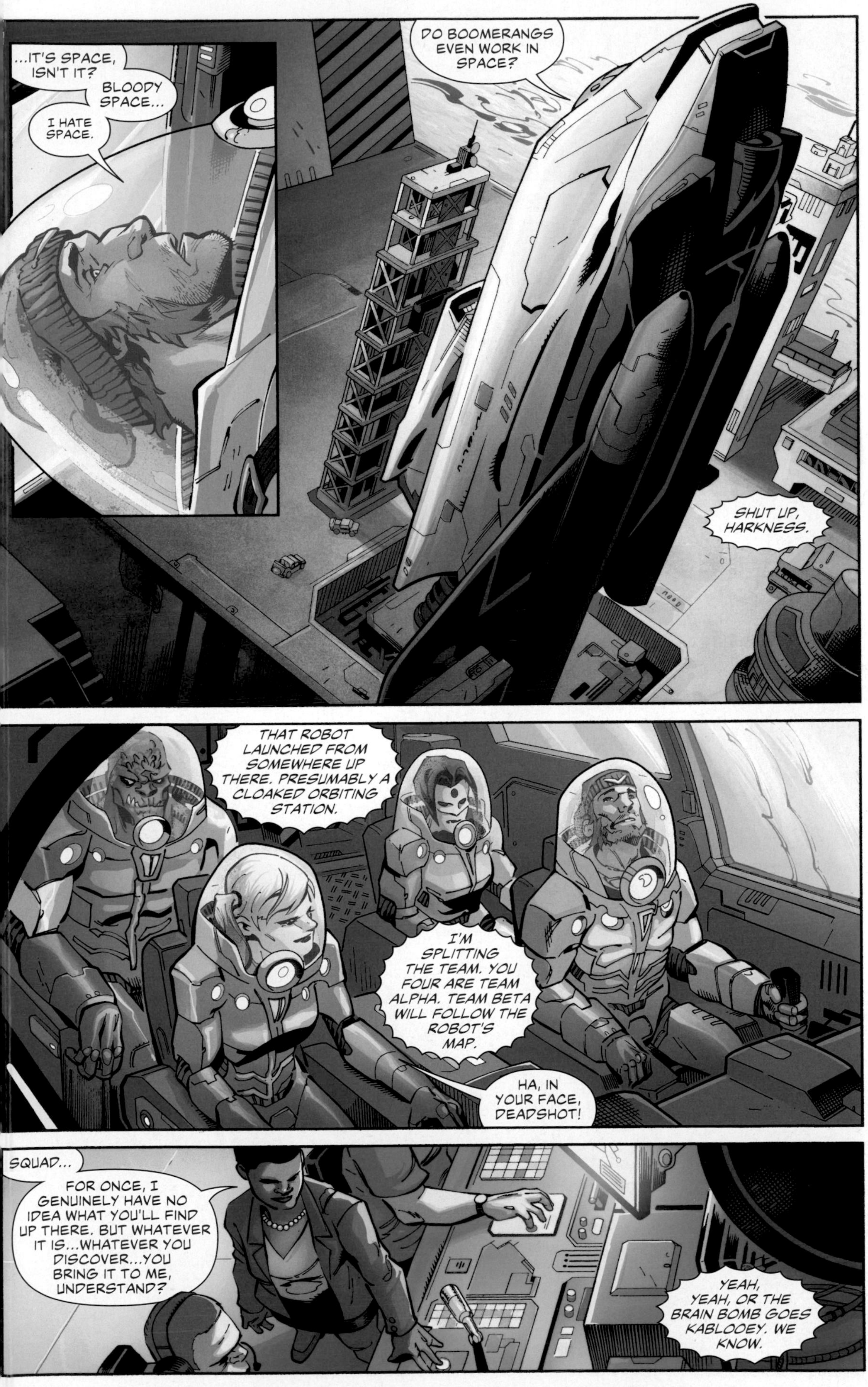
...IT'S SPACE, ISN'T IT?
BLOODY SPACE...
I HATE SPACE.
DO BOOMERANGS EVEN WORK IN SPACE?
SHUT UP, HARKNESS.
THAT ROBOT LAUNCHED FROM SOMEWHERE UP THERE. PRESUMABLY A CLOAKED ORBITING STATION.
I'M SPLITTING THE TEAM. YOU FOUR ARE TEAM ALPHA. TEAM BETA WILL FOLLOW THE ROBOT'S MAP.
HA, IN YOUR FACE, DEADSHOT!
SQUAD...
FOR ONCE, I GENUINELY HAVE NO IDEA WHAT YOU'LL FIND UP THERE. BUT WHATEVER IT IS...WHATEVER YOU DISCOVER...YOU BRING IT TO ME, UNDERSTAND?
YEAH, YEAH, OR THE BRAIN BOMB GOES KABLOOEY. WE KNOW.

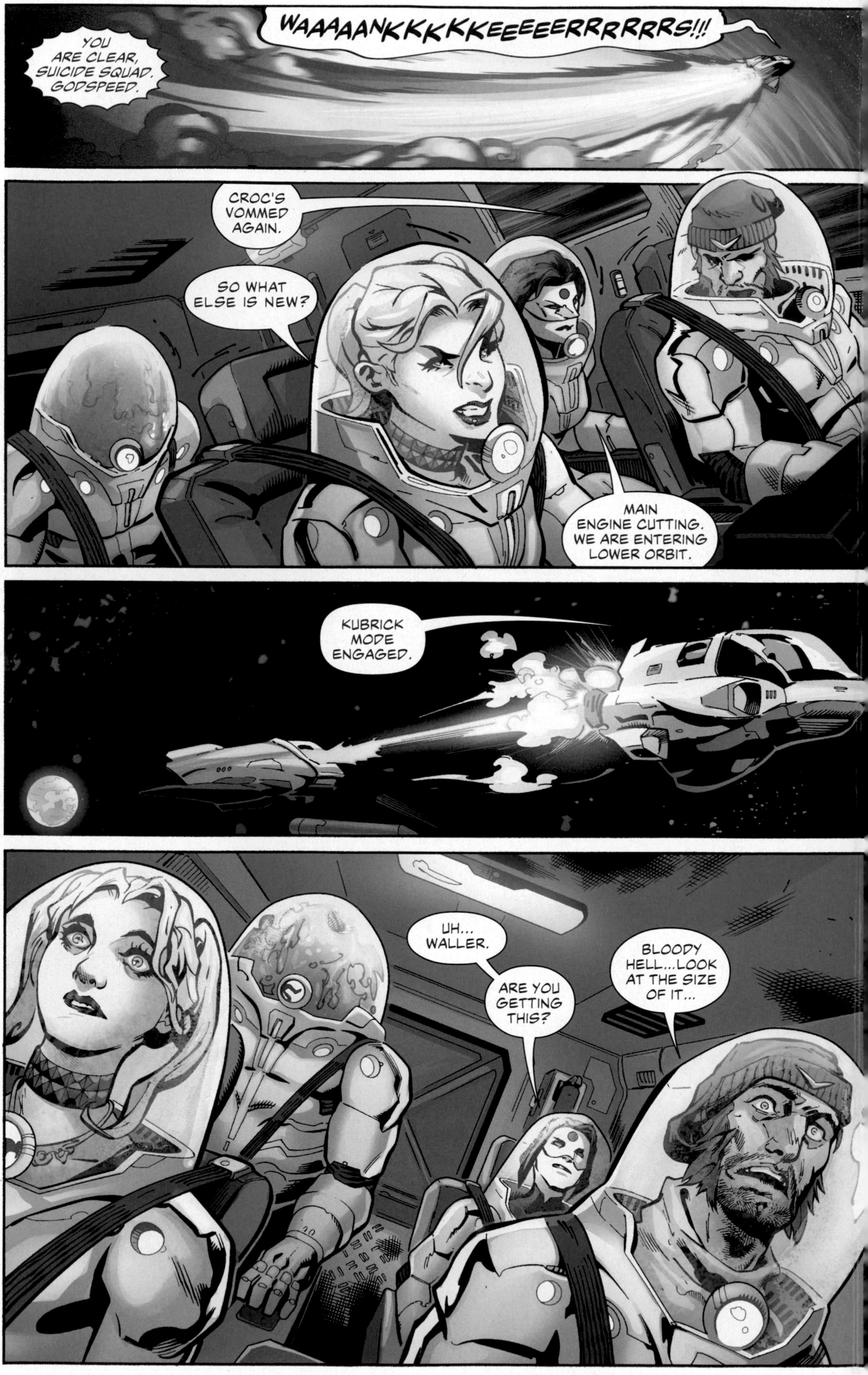
WAAAAANKKKKKEEEEERRRRRS!!!
YOU ARE CLEAR, SUICIDE SQUAD. GODSPEED.
CROC'S VOMMED AGAIN.
SO WHAT ELSE IS NEW?
MAIN ENGINE CUTTING. WE ARE ENTERING LOWER ORBIT.
KUBRICK MODE ENGAGED.
UH... WALLER.
ARE YOU GETTING THIS?
BLOODY HELL...LOOK AT THE SIZE OF IT...

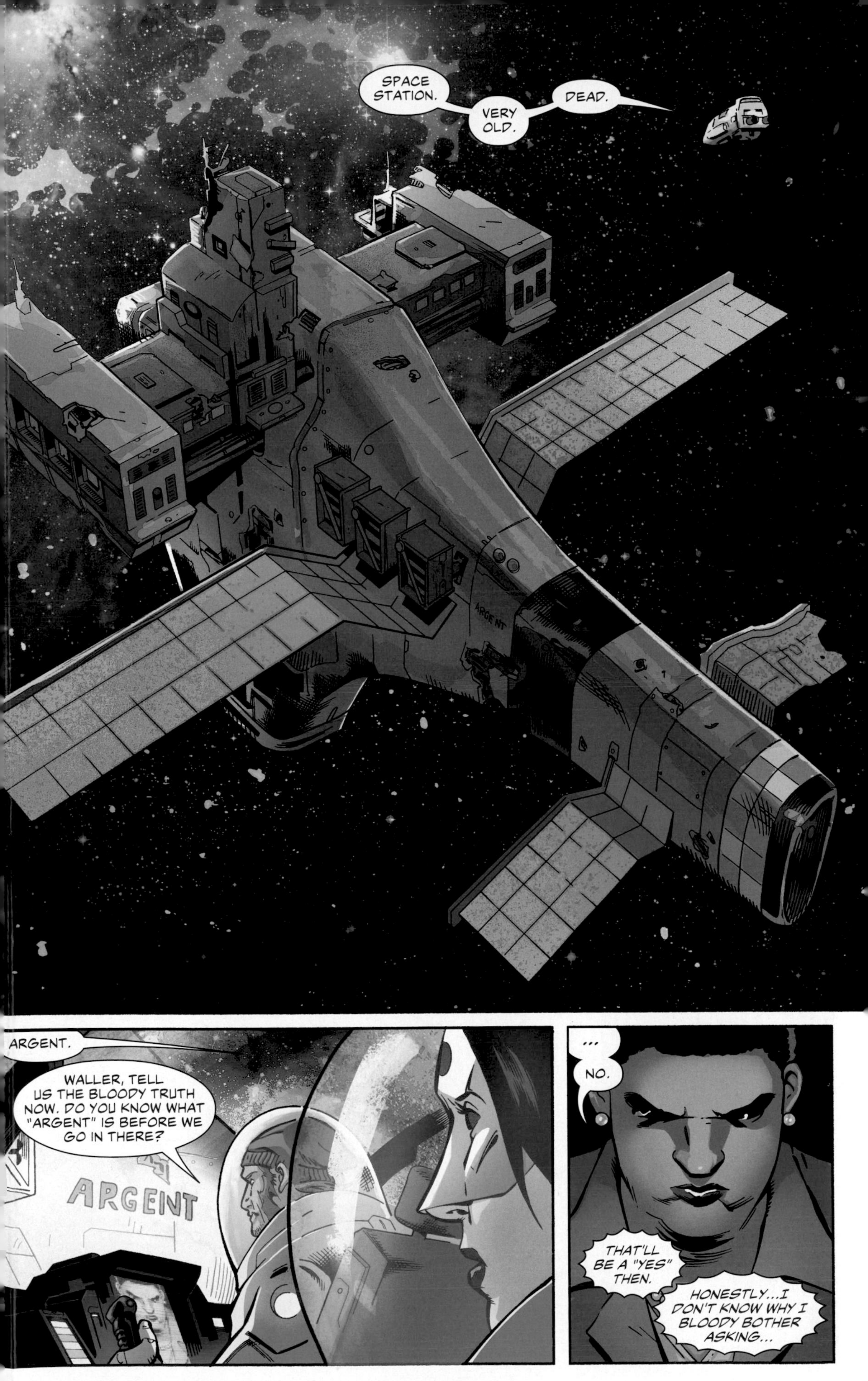
SPACE STATION.
VERY OLD.
DEAD.
ARGENT
ARGENT.
WALLER, TELL US THE BLOODY TRUTH NOW. DO YOU KNOW WHAT "ARGENT" IS BEFORE WE GO IN THERE?
ARGENT
...
NO.
THAT'LL BE A "YES" THEN.
HONESTLY...I DON'T KNOW WHY I BLOODY BOTHER ASKING...

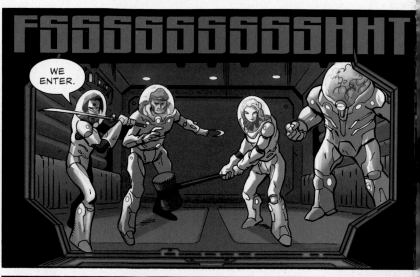

FSSSSSSSSSSHHT

WE ENTER.

DOCKING.

CLUNK

OW.

UH-UH. NO WAY, MATE. NO CHANCE. I MEAN, HAVE YOU LOT BEEN LIVING IN A CULTURAL VACUUM FOR DECADES OR WHAT?

DESERTED SPACE STATION, MATE! DESERTED £$%&£%$ SPACE STATION AND ALL THE DIGESTION-RELATED DEADLINES THAT IMPLIES!

YOU WILL ENTER, CRIMINAL.

OR DIE.

THERE YOU GO, CROC...

≷SNIFF≷

ARE YOU...CRYING? WAS IT THAT BAD?

...NO...

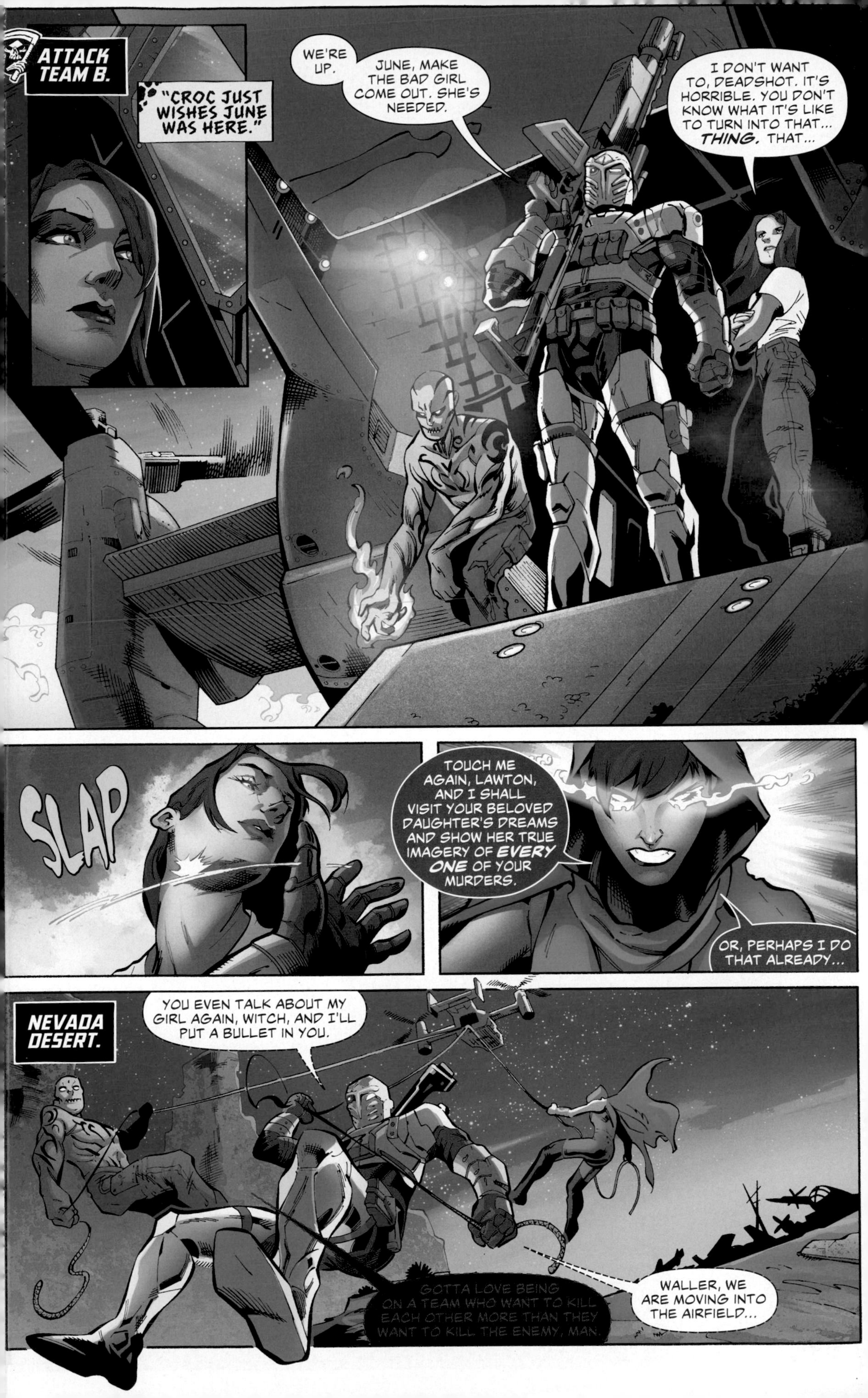
ATTACK TEAM B.
"CROC JUST WISHES JUNE WAS HERE."
WE'RE UP.
JUNE, MAKE THE BAD GIRL COME OUT. SHE'S NEEDED.
I DON'T WANT TO, DEADSHOT. IT'S HORRIBLE. YOU DON'T KNOW WHAT IT'S LIKE TO TURN INTO THAT... THING. THAT...
SLAP
TOUCH ME AGAIN, LAWTON, AND I SHALL VISIT YOUR BELOVED DAUGHTER'S DREAMS AND SHOW HER TRUE IMAGERY OF EVERY ONE OF YOUR MURDERS.
OR, PERHAPS I DO THAT ALREADY...
NEVADA DESERT.
YOU EVEN TALK ABOUT MY GIRL AGAIN, WITCH, AND I'LL PUT A BULLET IN YOU.
GOTTA LOVE BEING ON A TEAM WHO WANT TO KILL EACH OTHER MORE THAN THEY WANT TO KILL THE ENEMY, MAN.
WALLER, WE ARE MOVING INTO THE AIRFIELD...

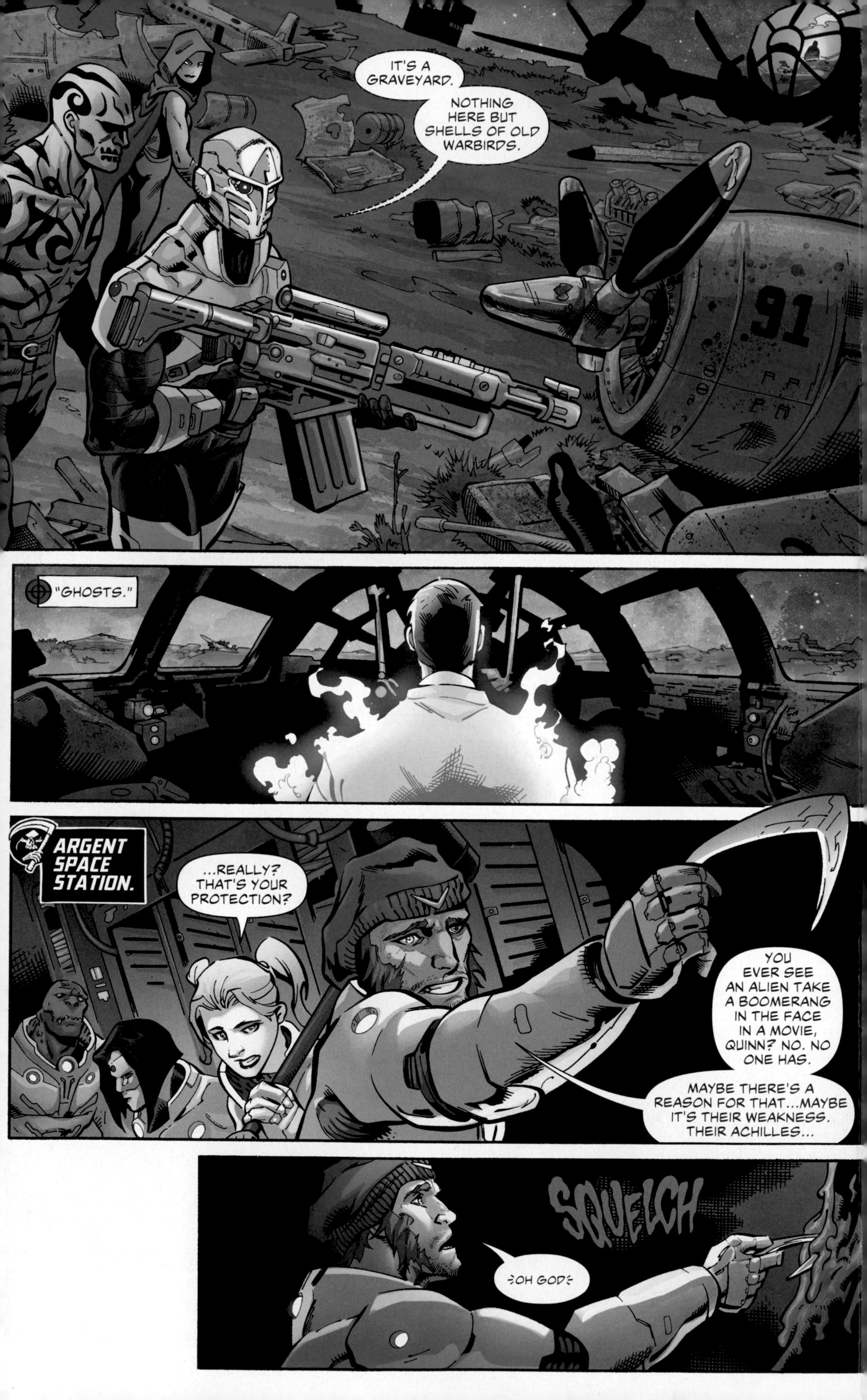
IT'S A GRAVEYARD.
NOTHING HERE BUT SHELLS OF OLD WARBIRDS.
"GHOSTS."
ARGENT SPACE STATION.
...REALLY? THAT'S YOUR PROTECTION?
YOU EVER SEE AN ALIEN TAKE A BOOMERANG IN THE FACE IN A MOVIE, QUINN? NO. NO ONE HAS.
MAYBE THERE'S A REASON FOR THAT...MAYBE IT'S THEIR WEAKNESS. THEIR ACHILLES...
SQUELCH
OH GOD

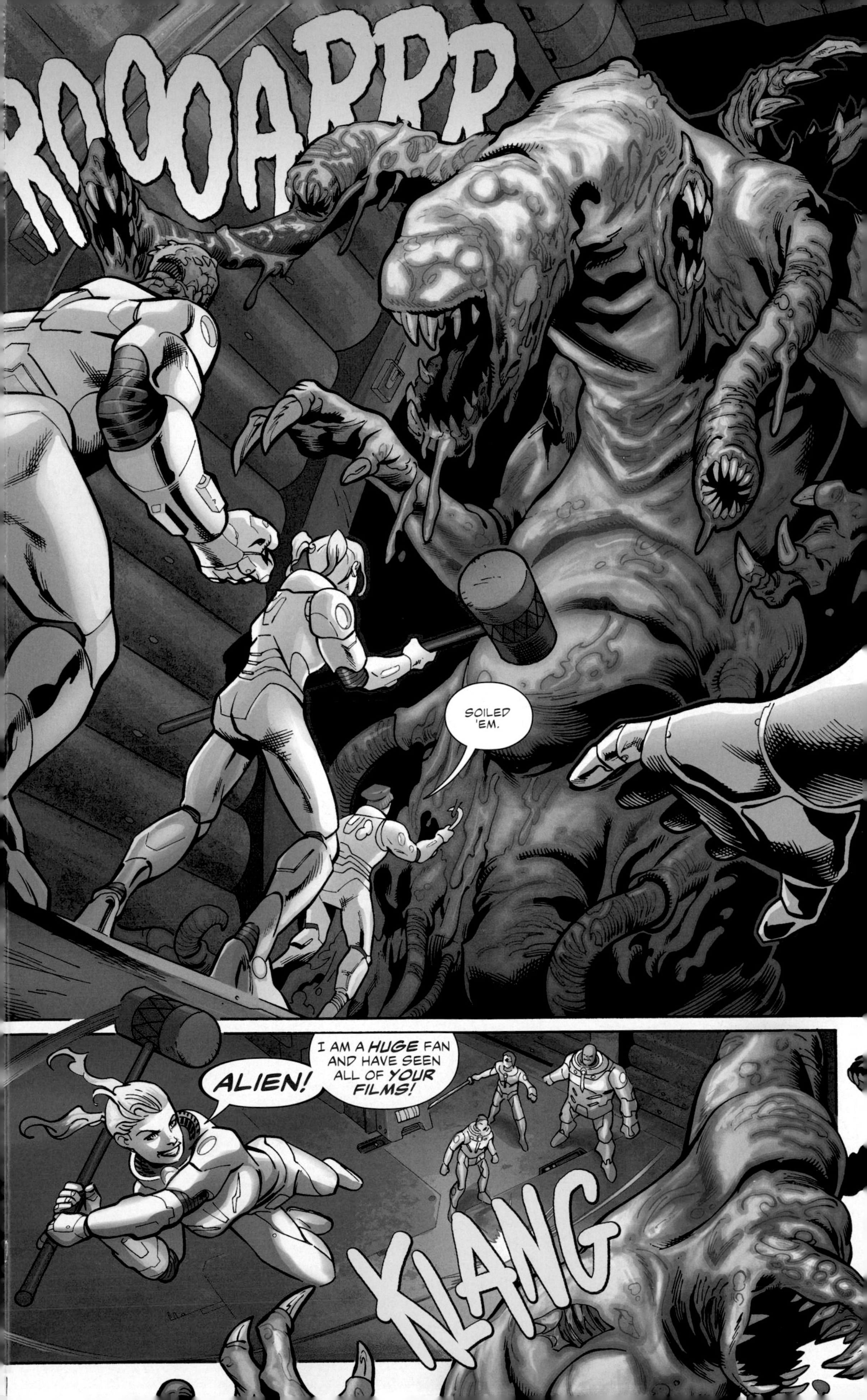
ROOOARRR
SOILED 'EM.
ALIEN!
I AM A HUGE FAN AND HAVE SEEN ALL OF YOUR FILMS!
KLANG

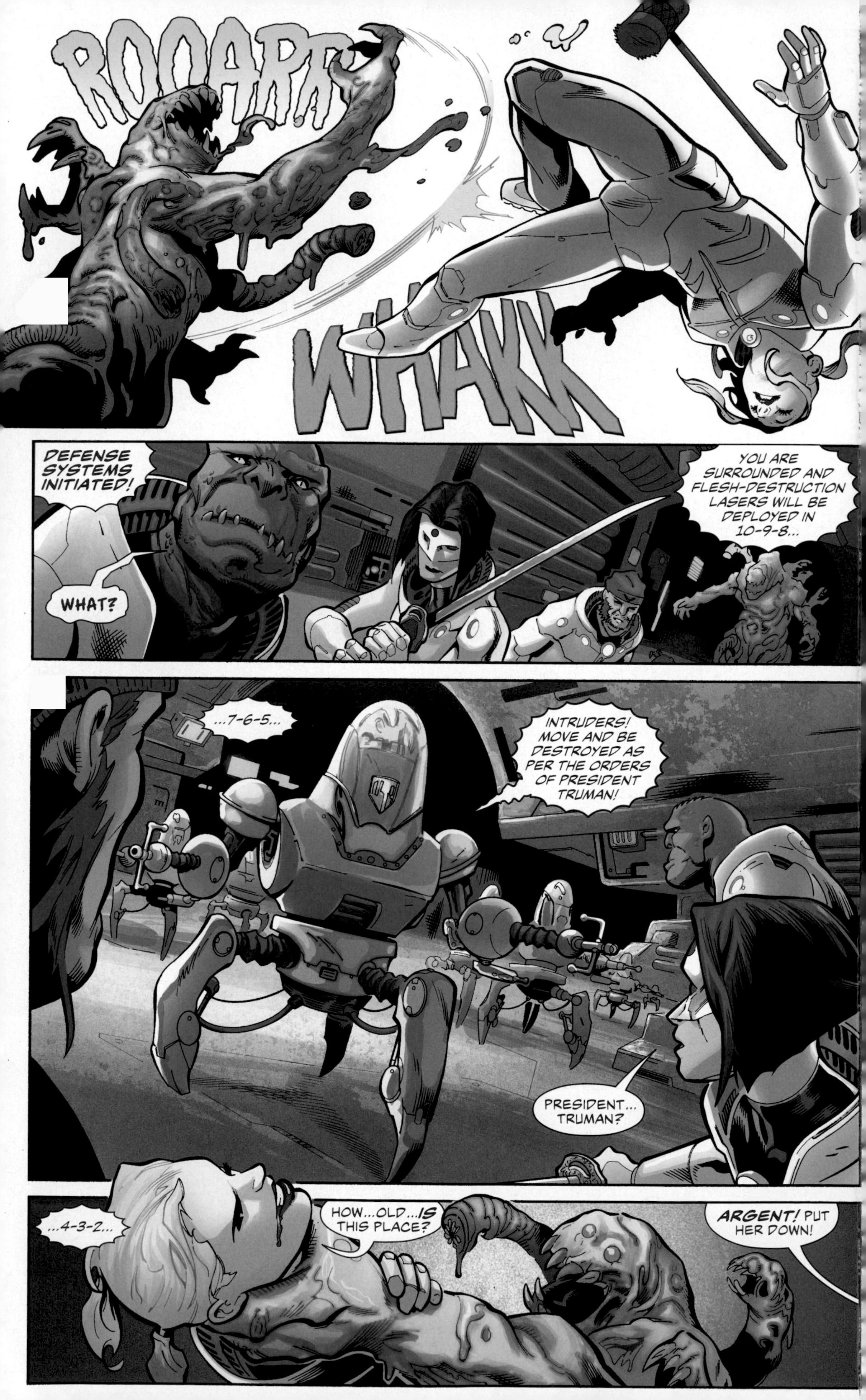
ROOARR
WHAKK
DEFENSE SYSTEMS INITIATED!
WHAT?
YOU ARE SURROUNDED AND FLESH-DESTRUCTION LASERS WILL BE DEPLOYED IN 10-9-8...
...7-6-5...
INTRUDERS! MOVE AND BE DESTROYED AS PER THE ORDERS OF PRESIDENT TRUMAN!
PRESIDENT... TRUMAN?
...4-3-2...
HOW...OLD...*IS* THIS PLACE?
ARGENT! PUT HER DOWN!

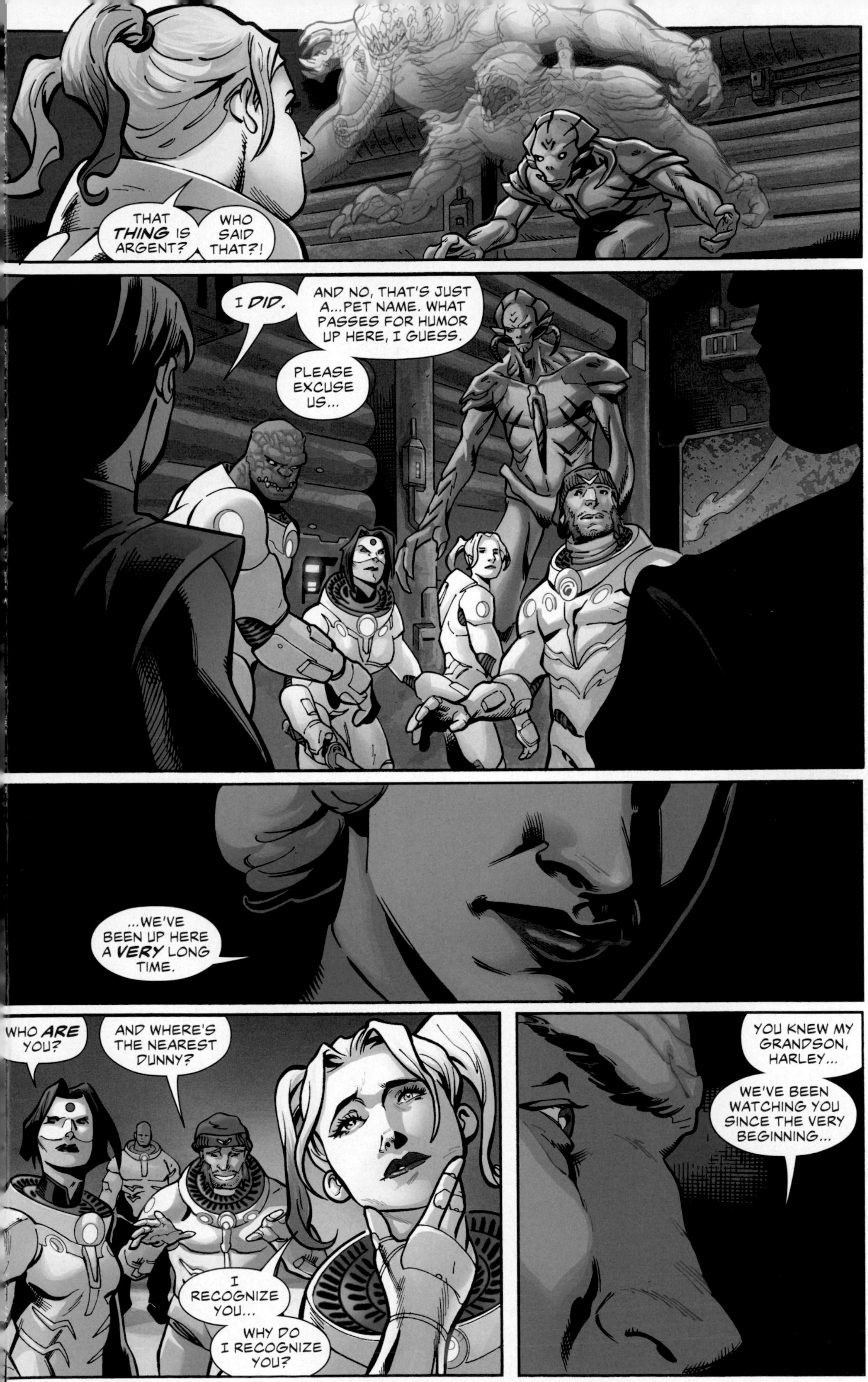
THAT THING IS ARGENT?
WHO SAID THAT?!
I DID.
AND NO, THAT'S JUST A...PET NAME. WHAT PASSES FOR HUMOR UP HERE, I GUESS.
PLEASE EXCUSE US...
...WE'VE BEEN UP HERE A VERY LONG TIME.
WHO ARE YOU?
AND WHERE'S THE NEAREST DUNNY?
I RECOGNIZE YOU...
WHY DO I RECOGNIZE YOU?
YOU KNEW MY GRANDSON, HARLEY...
WE'VE BEEN WATCHING YOU SINCE THE VERY BEGINNING...

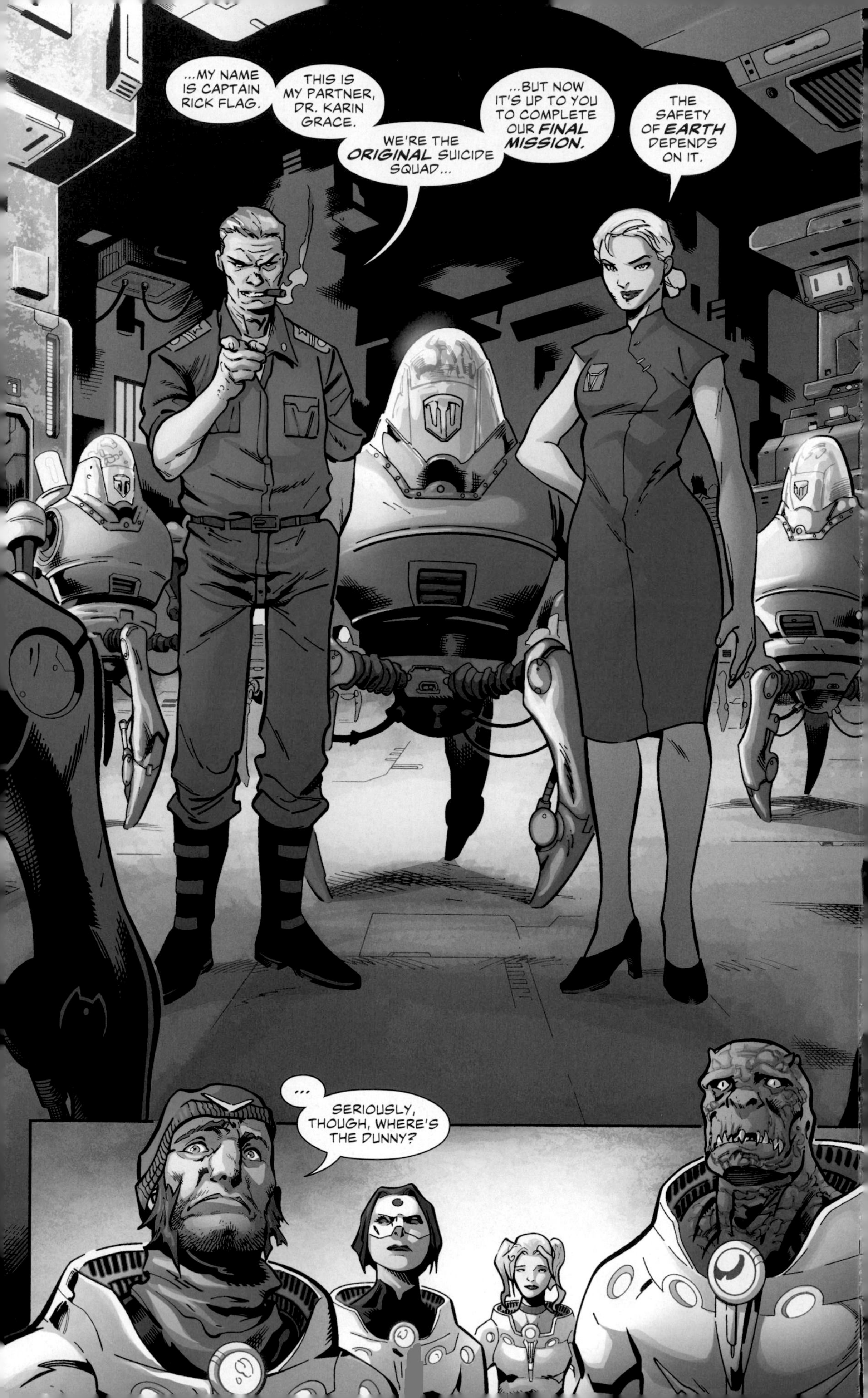
...MY NAME IS CAPTAIN RICK FLAG.
THIS IS MY PARTNER, DR. KARIN GRACE.
WE'RE THE ORIGINAL SUICIDE SQUAD...
...BUT NOW IT'S UP TO YOU TO COMPLETE OUR FINAL MISSION.
THE SAFETY OF EARTH DEPENDS ON IT.
...
SERIOUSLY, THOUGH, WHERE'S THE DUNNY?

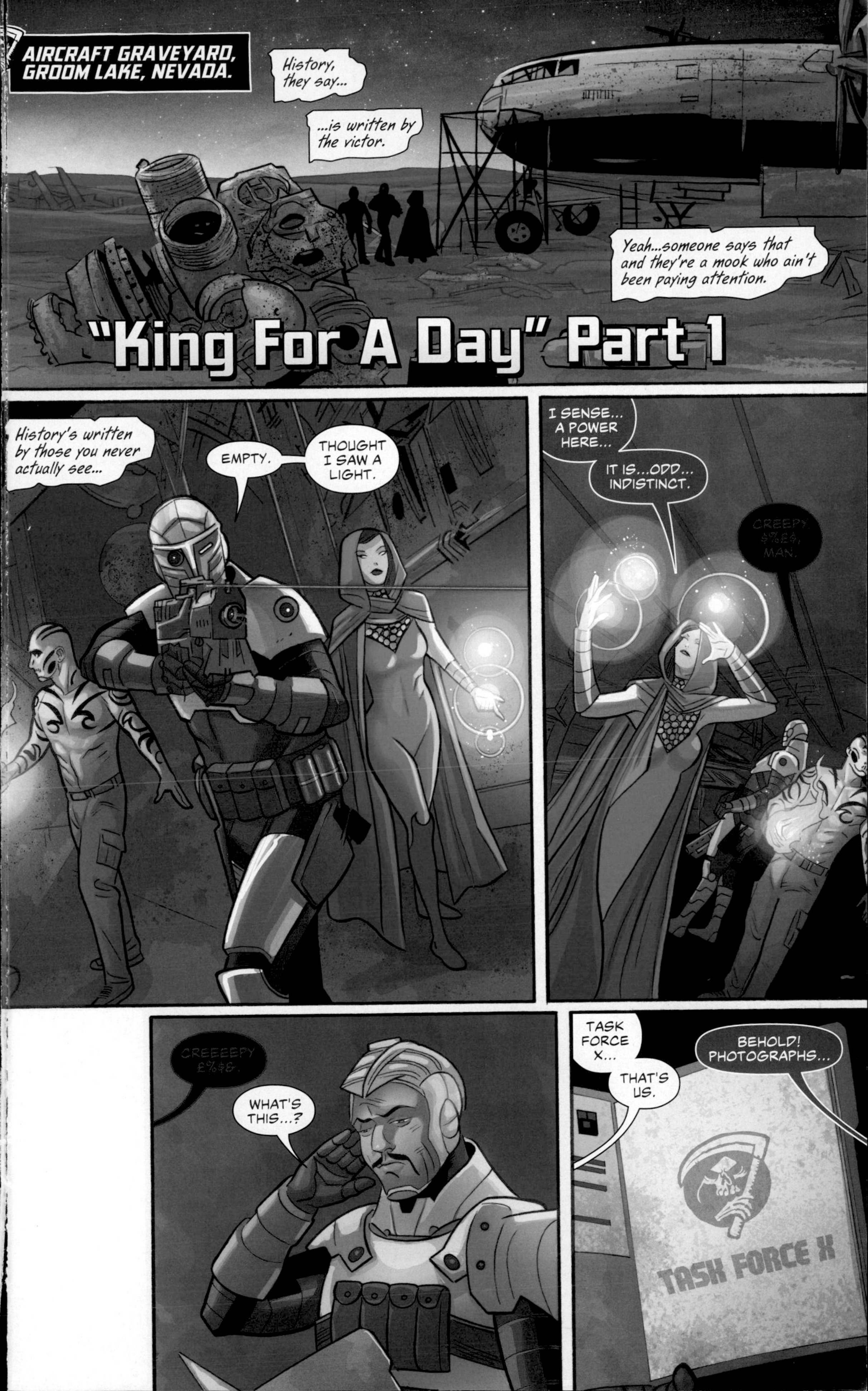
AIRCRAFT GRAVEYARD, GROOM LAKE, NEVADA.
History, they say...
...is written by the victor.
Yeah...someone says that and they're a mook who ain't been paying attention.
"King For A Day" Part 1
History's written by those you never actually see...
EMPTY.
THOUGHT I SAW A LIGHT.
I SENSE... A POWER HERE...
IT IS...ODD... INDISTINCT.
CREEPY $%£$, MAN.
CREEEEEPY £%$&.
WHAT'S THIS...?
TASK FORCE X...
THAT'S US.
BEHOLD! PHOTOGRAPHS...
TASK FORCE X

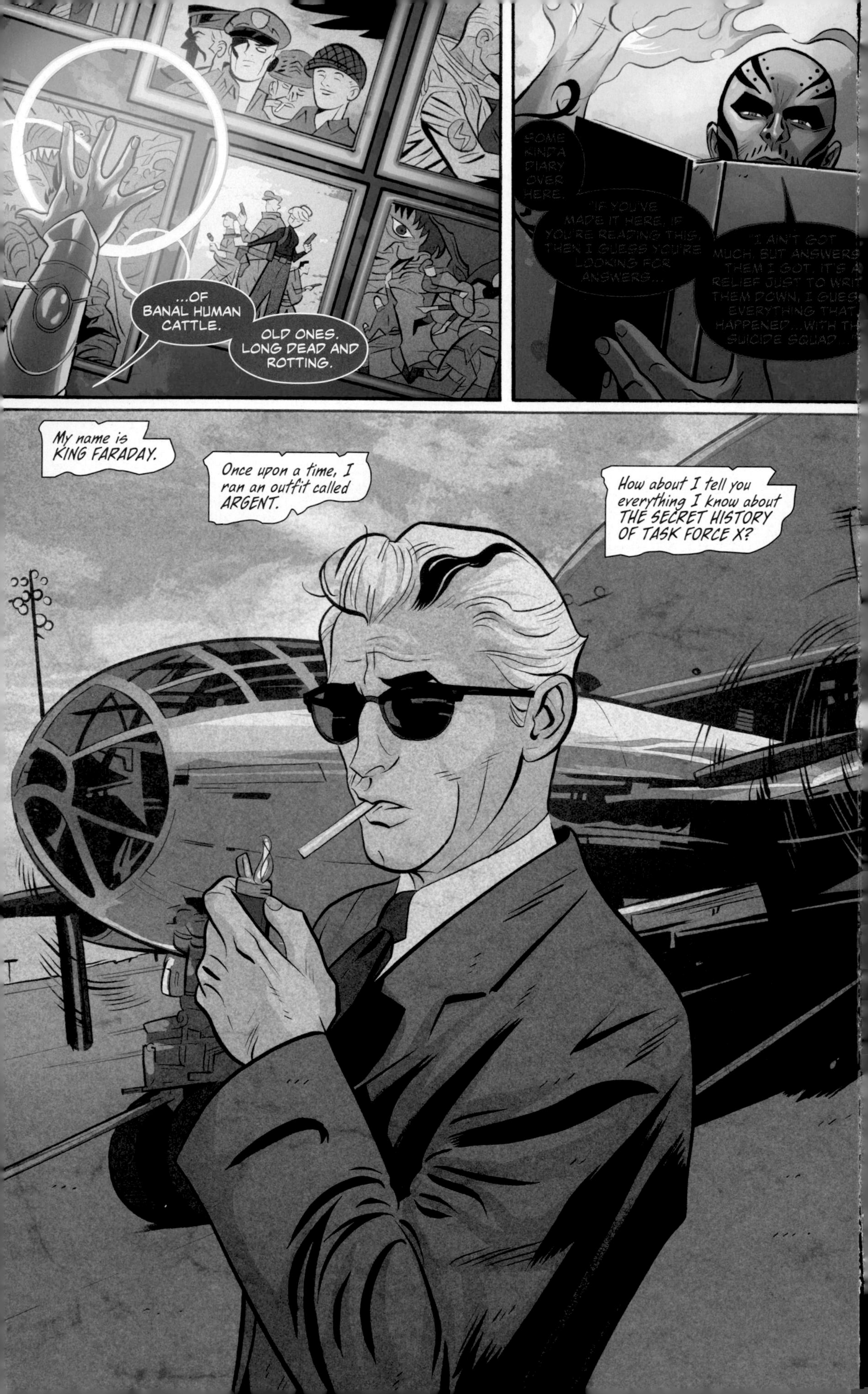
...OF BANAL HUMAN CATTLE.
OLD ONES. LONG DEAD AND ROTTING.
SOME KIND'A DIARY OVER HERE.
"IF YOU'VE MADE IT HERE, IF YOU'RE READING THIS, THEN I GUESS YOU'RE LOOKING FOR ANSWERS...
"I AIN'T GOT MUCH, BUT ANSWERS THEM I GOT. IT'S A RELIEF JUST TO WRIT THEM DOWN, I GUES EVERYTHING THAT HAPPENED...WITH TH SUICIDE SQUAD...
My name is KING FARADAY.
Once upon a time, I ran an outfit called ARGENT.
How about I tell you everything I know about THE SECRET HISTORY OF TASK FORCE X?

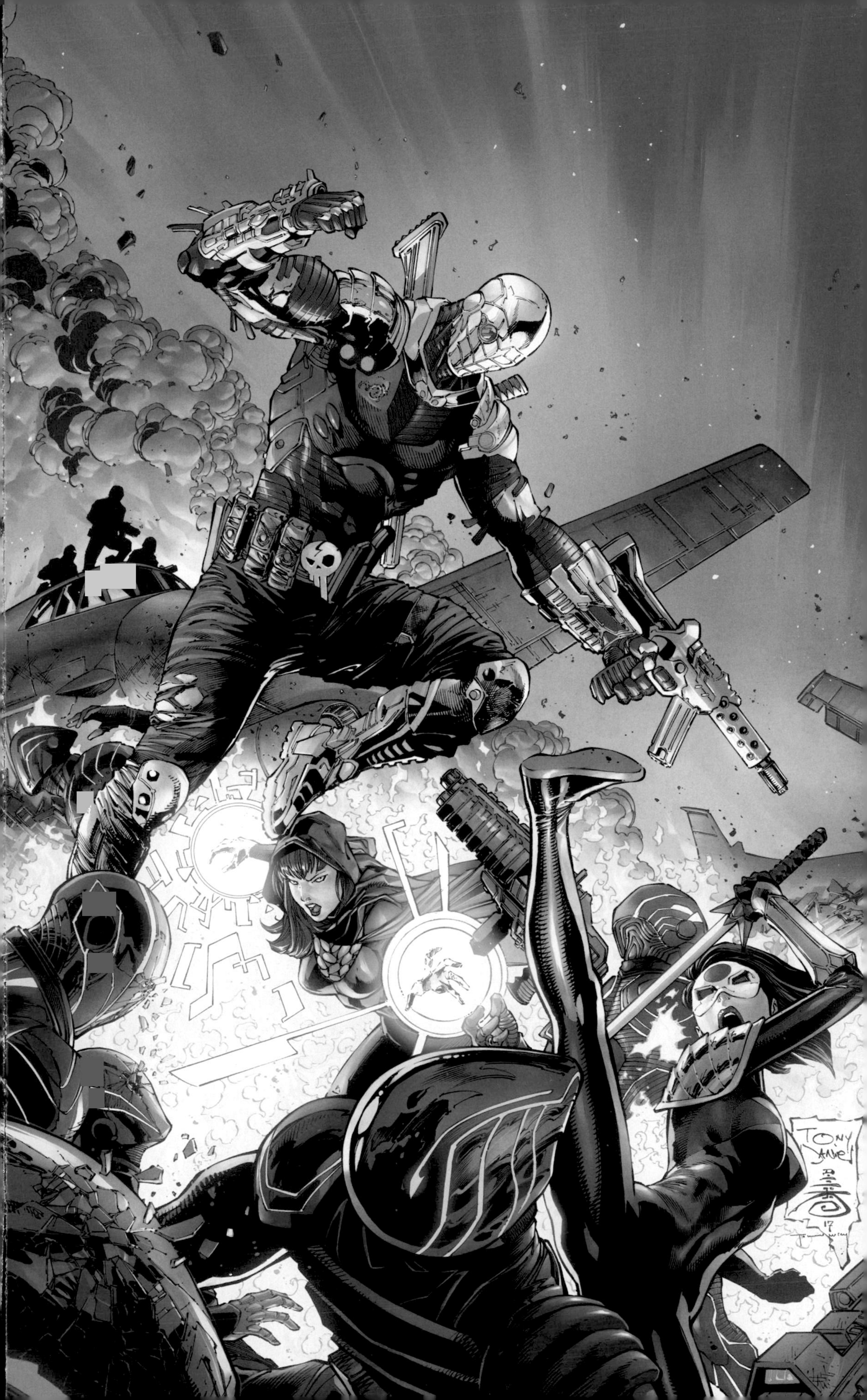

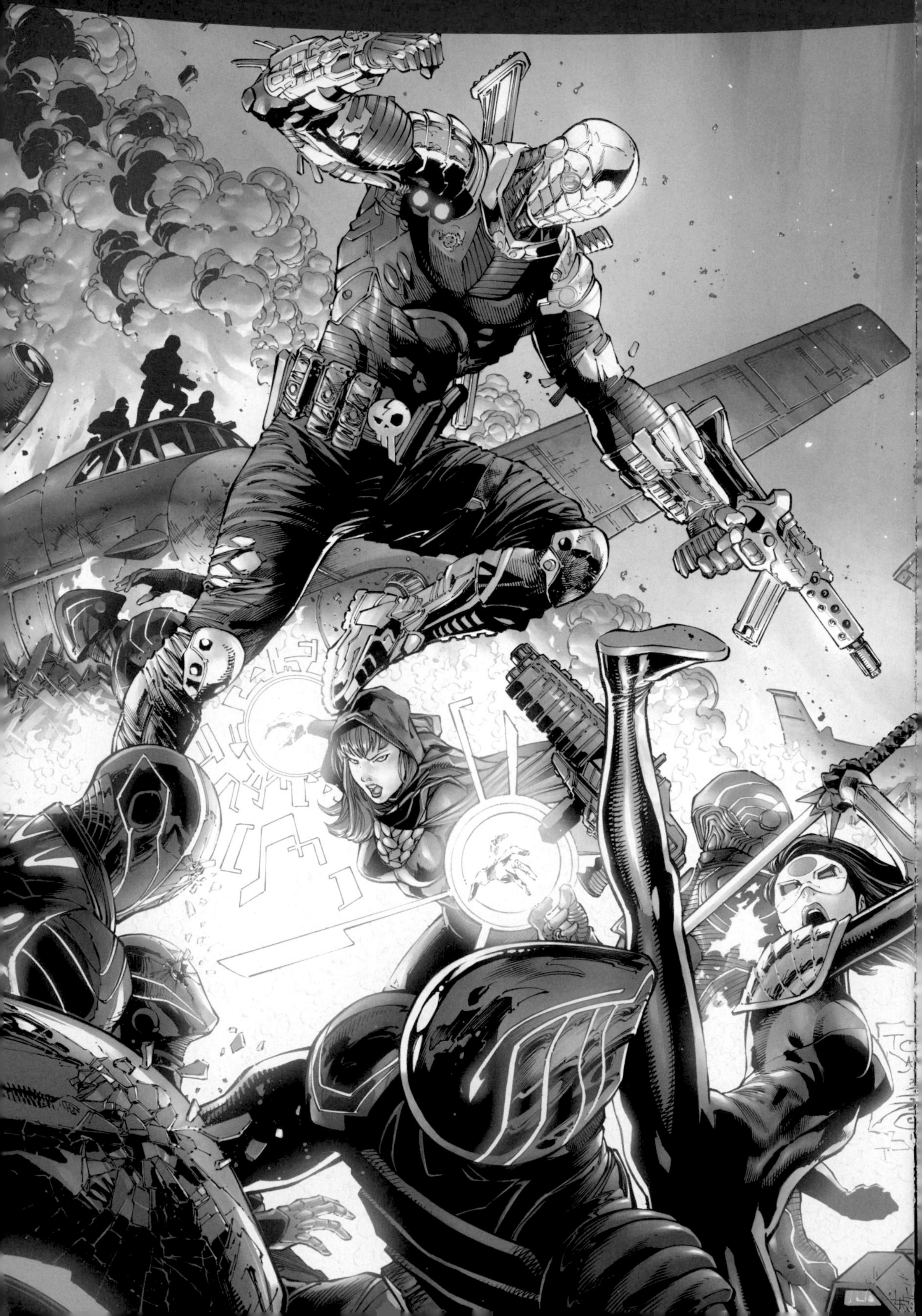

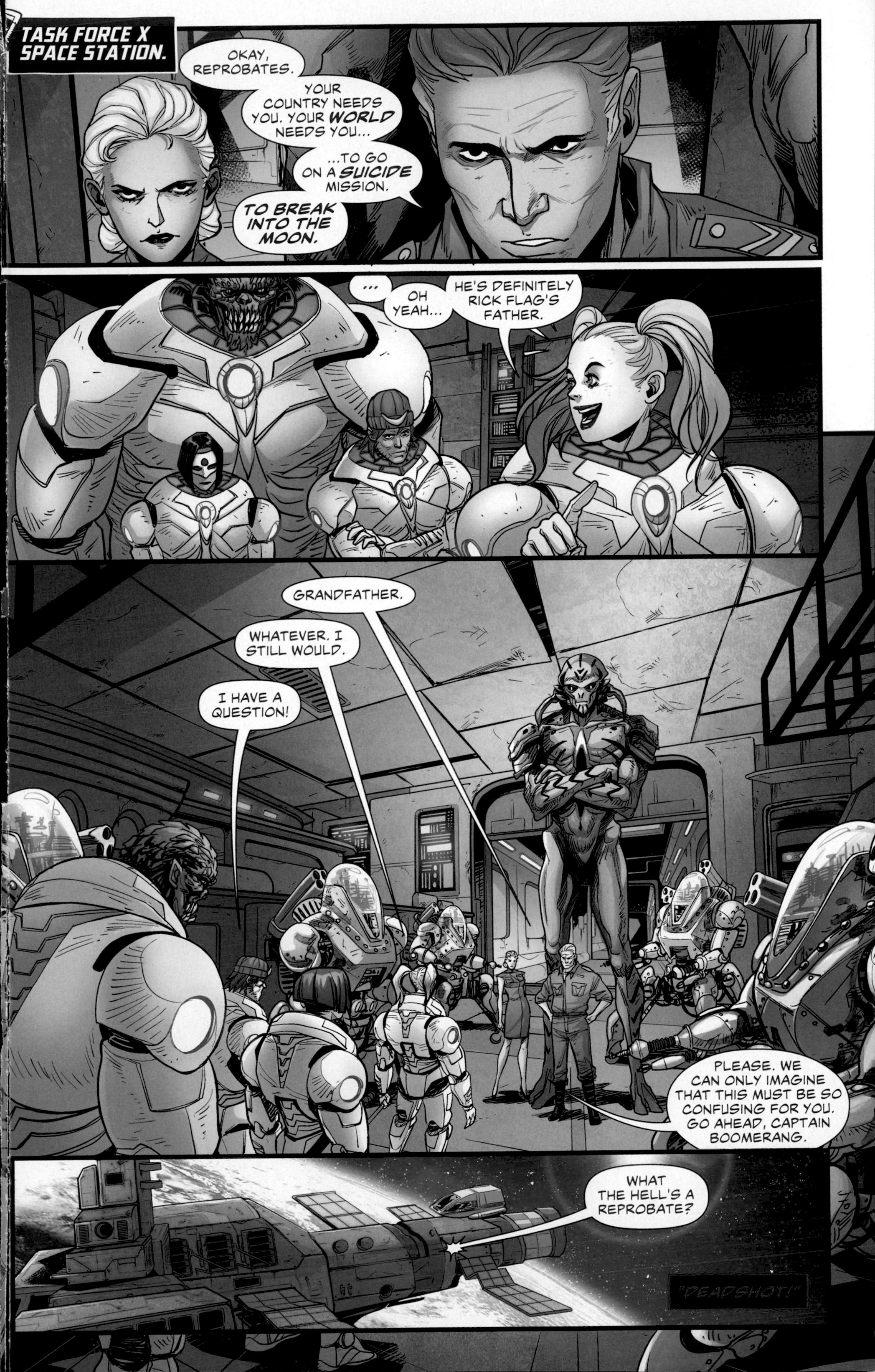
TASK FORCE X SPACE STATION.
OKAY, REPROBATES.
YOUR COUNTRY NEEDS YOU. YOUR WORLD NEEDS YOU...
...TO GO ON A SUICIDE MISSION.
TO BREAK INTO THE MOON.
...
OH YEAH...
HE'S DEFINITELY RICK FLAG'S FATHER.
GRANDFATHER.
WHATEVER. I STILL WOULD.
I HAVE A QUESTION!
PLEASE. WE CAN ONLY IMAGINE THAT THIS MUST BE SO CONFUSING FOR YOU. GO AHEAD, CAPTAIN BOOMERANG.
WHAT THE HELL'S A REPROBATE?
"DEADSHOT!"

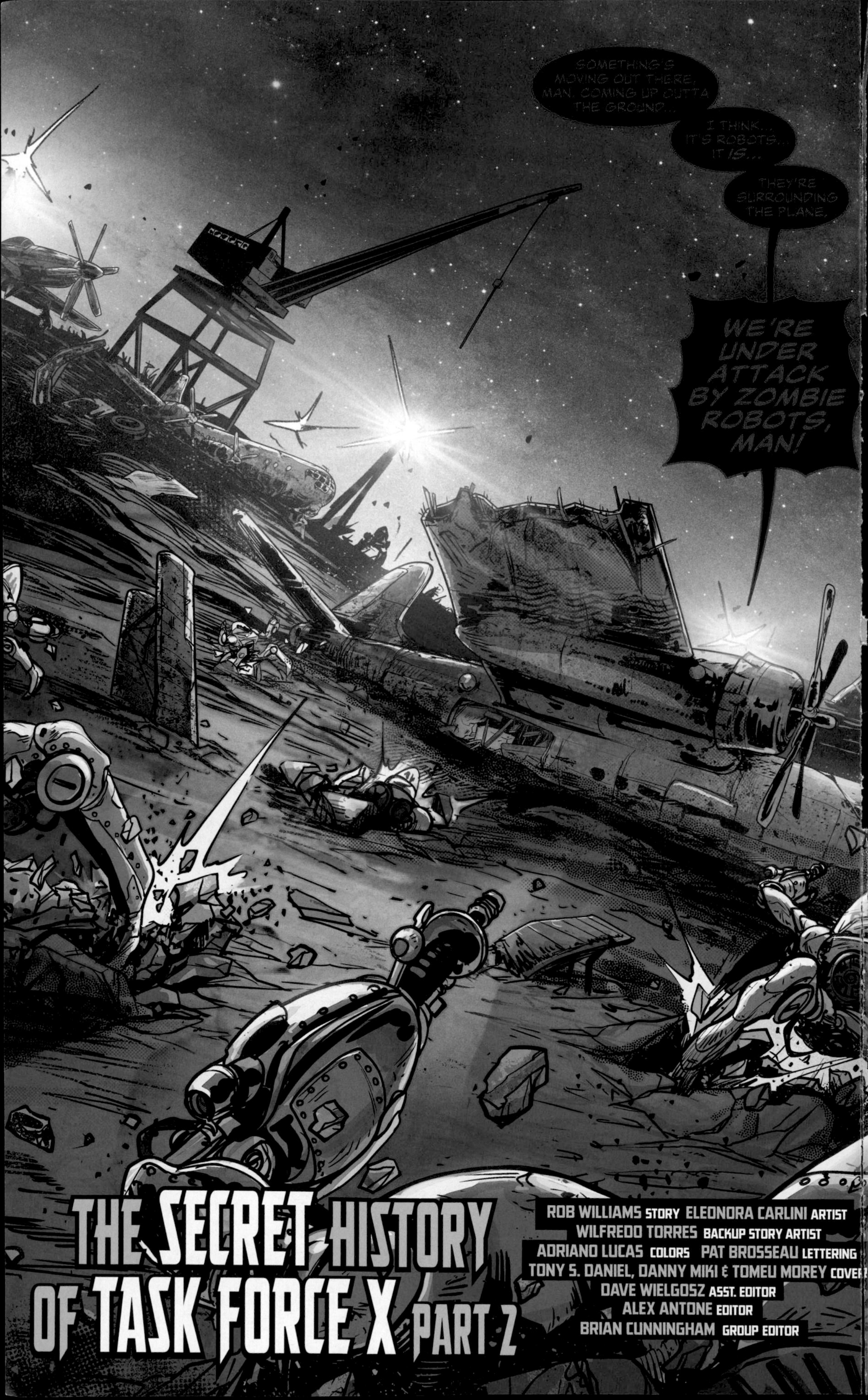
SOMETHING'S MOVING OUT THERE, MAN. COMING UP OUTTA THE GROUND...
I THINK... IT'S ROBOTS... IT IS...
THEY'RE SURROUNDING THE PLANE.
WE'RE UNDER ATTACK BY ZOMBIE ROBOTS, MAN!
THE SECRET HISTORY OF TASK FORCE X PART 2
ROB WILLIAMS STORY ELEONORA CARLINI ARTIST
WILFREDO TORRES BACKUP STORY ARTIST
ADRIANO LUCAS COLORS PAT BROSSEAU LETTERING
TONY S. DANIEL, DANNY MIKI & TOMEU MOREY COVER
DAVE WIELGOSZ ASST. EDITOR
ALEX ANTONE EDITOR
BRIAN CUNNINGHAM GROUP EDITOR

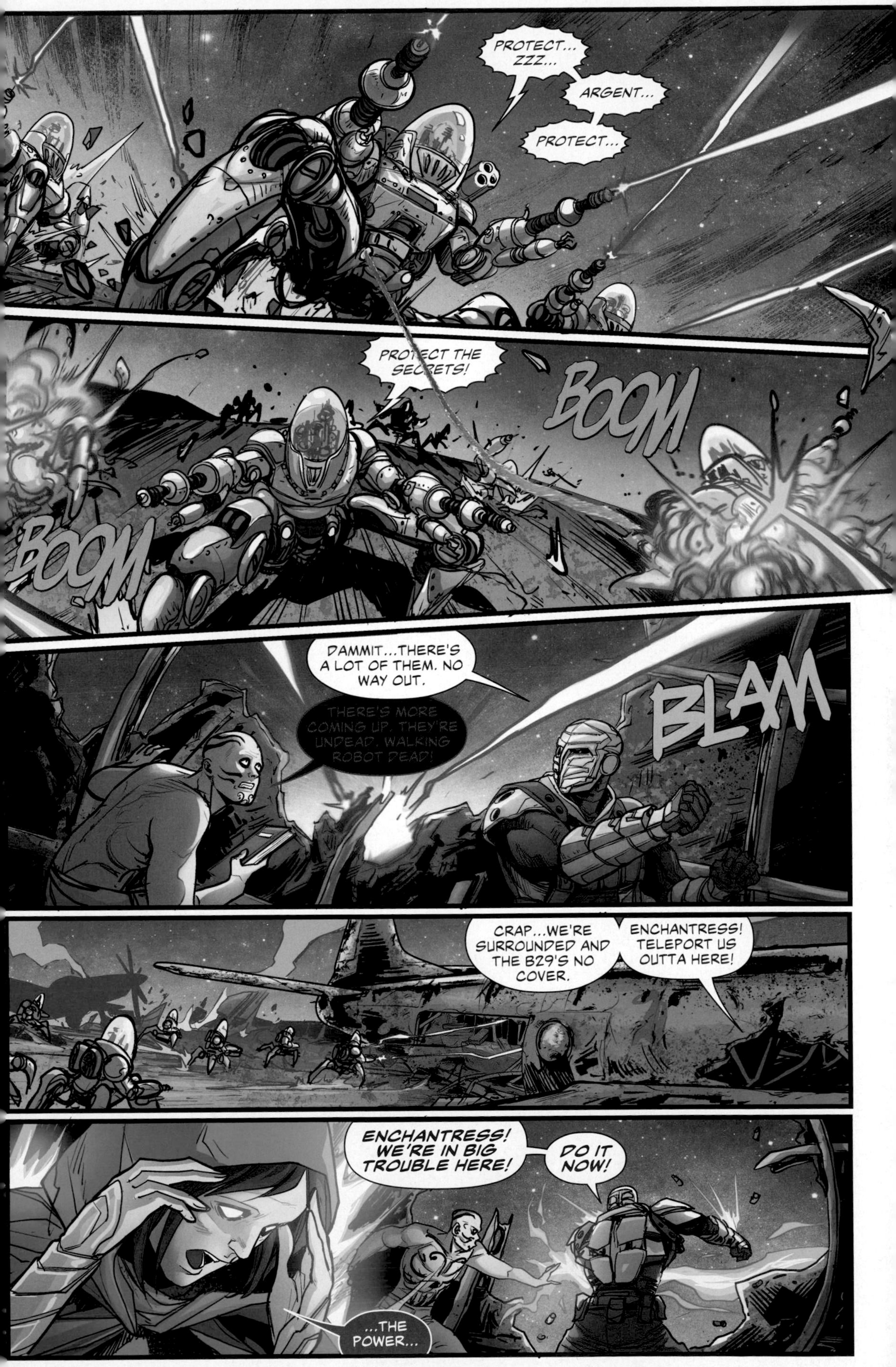
PROTECT... ZZZ...
ARGENT...
PROTECT...
PROTECT THE SECRETS!
BOOM
BOOM
DAMMIT...THERE'S A LOT OF THEM. NO WAY OUT.
THERE'S MORE COMING UP. THEY'RE UNDEAD. WALKING ROBOT DEAD!
BLAM
CRAP...WE'RE SURROUNDED AND THE B29'S NO COVER.
ENCHANTRESS! TELEPORT US OUTTA HERE!
ENCHANTRESS! WE'RE IN BIG TROUBLE HERE!
DO IT NOW!
...THE POWER...

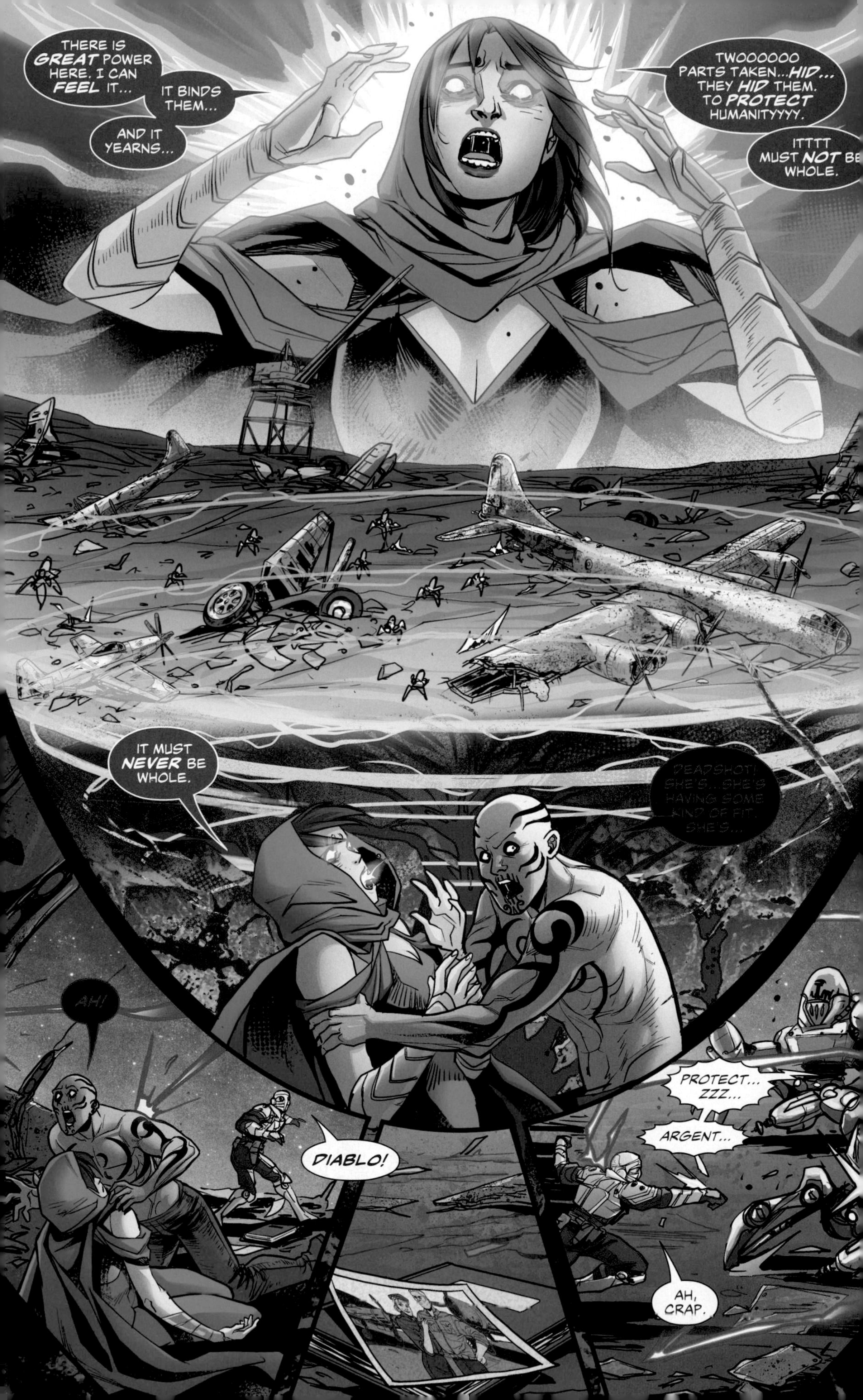
THERE IS GREAT POWER HERE. I CAN FEEL IT...
IT BINDS THEM...
AND IT YEARNS...
TWOOOOOO PARTS TAKEN...HID... THEY HID THEM. TO PROTECT HUMANITYYYY.
ITTTT MUST NOT BE WHOLE.
IT MUST NEVER BE WHOLE.
DEADSHOT! SHE'S...SHE'S HAVING SOME KIND OF FIT. SHE'S...
AH!
DIABLO!
PROTECT... ZZZ...
ARGENT...
AH, CRAP.

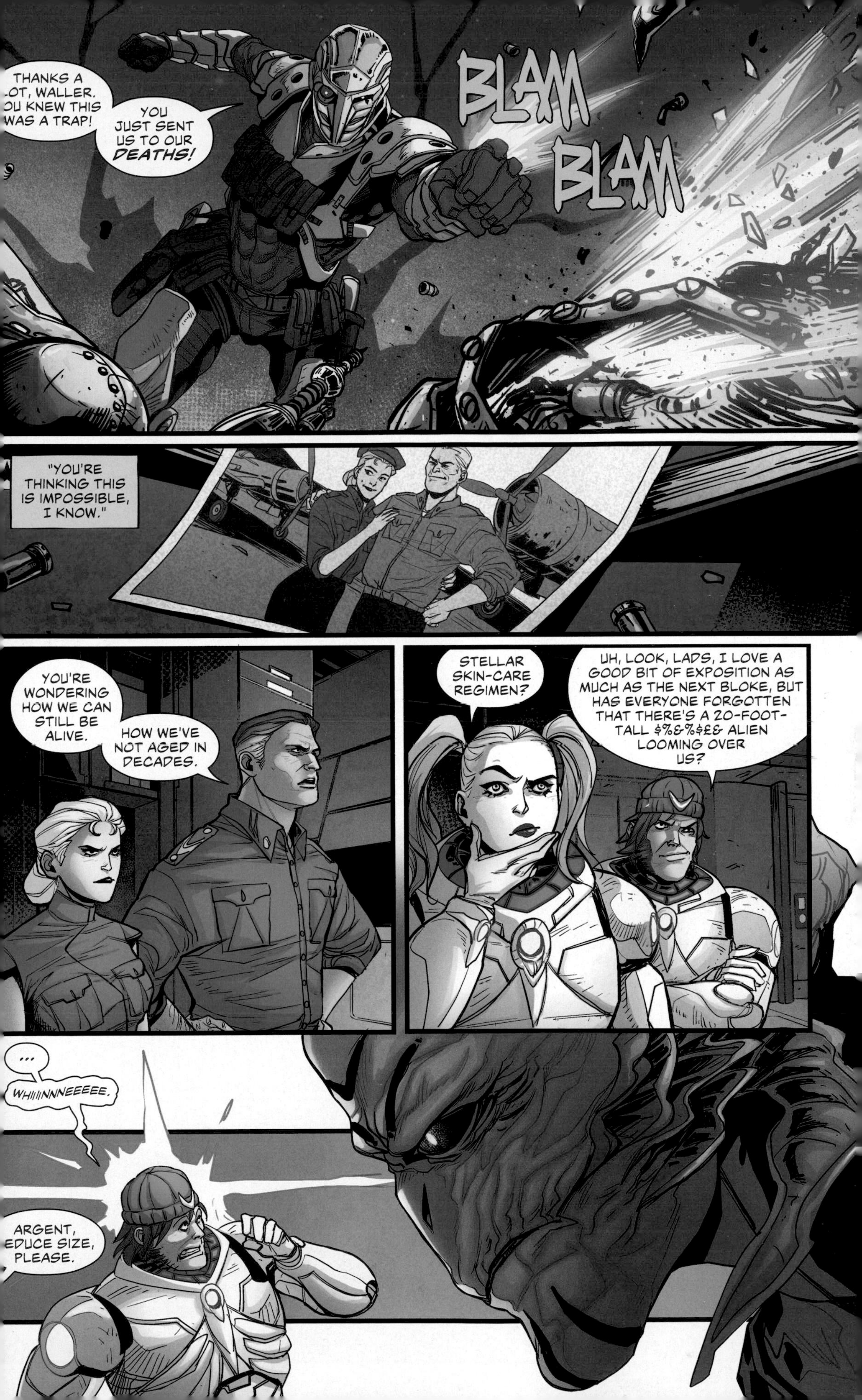
THANKS A
OT, WALLER.
OU KNEW THIS
WAS A TRAP!
YOU JUST SENT US TO OUR *DEATHS!*
BLAM
BLAM
"YOU'RE THINKING THIS IS IMPOSSIBLE, I KNOW."
YOU'RE WONDERING HOW WE CAN STILL BE ALIVE.
HOW WE'VE NOT AGED IN DECADES.
STELLAR SKIN-CARE REGIMEN?
UH, LOOK, LADS, I LOVE A GOOD BIT OF EXPOSITION AS MUCH AS THE NEXT BLOKE, BUT HAS EVERYONE FORGOTTEN THAT THERE'S A 20-FOOT-TALL $%&%$££ ALIEN LOOMING OVER US?
...
WHIIINNNEEEEE.
ARGENT,
EDUCE SIZE,
PLEASE.

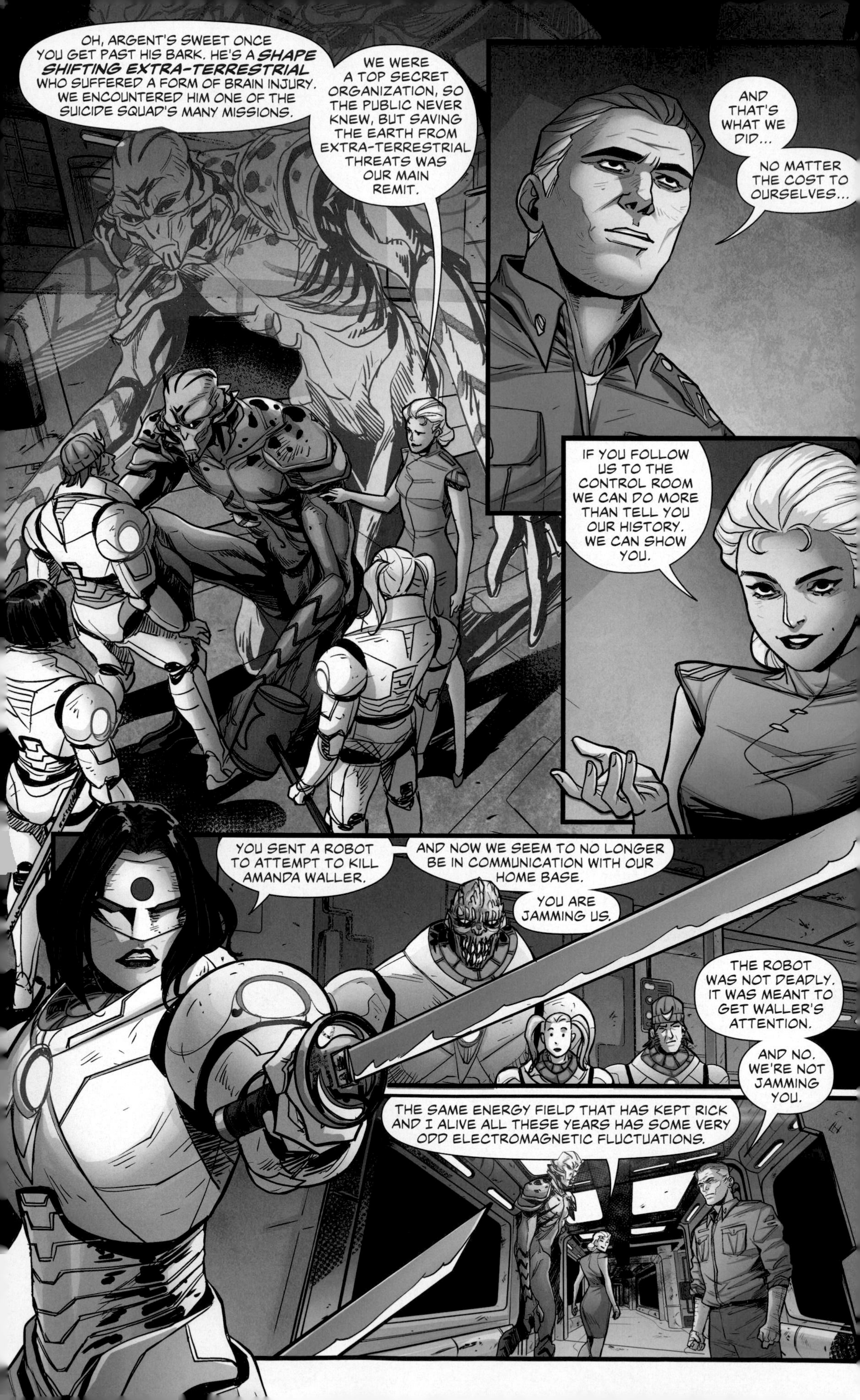

OH, ARGENT'S SWEET ONCE YOU GET PAST HIS BARK. HE'S A SHAPE SHIFTING EXTRA-TERRESTRIAL WHO SUFFERED A FORM OF BRAIN INJURY. WE ENCOUNTERED HIM ONE OF THE SUICIDE SQUAD'S MANY MISSIONS.
WE WERE A TOP SECRET ORGANIZATION, SO THE PUBLIC NEVER KNEW, BUT SAVING THE EARTH FROM EXTRA-TERRESTRIAL THREATS WAS OUR MAIN REMIT.
AND THAT'S WHAT WE DID...
NO MATTER THE COST TO OURSELVES...
IF YOU FOLLOW US TO THE CONTROL ROOM WE CAN DO MORE THAN TELL YOU OUR HISTORY. WE CAN SHOW YOU.
YOU SENT A ROBOT TO ATTEMPT TO KILL AMANDA WALLER.
AND NOW WE SEEM TO NO LONGER BE IN COMMUNICATION WITH OUR HOME BASE.
YOU ARE JAMMING US.
THE ROBOT WAS NOT DEADLY. IT WAS MEANT TO GET WALLER'S ATTENTION.
AND NO. WE'RE NOT JAMMING YOU.
THE SAME ENERGY FIELD THAT HAS KEPT RICK AND I ALIVE ALL THESE YEARS HAS SOME VERY ODD ELECTROMAGNETIC FLUCTUATIONS.

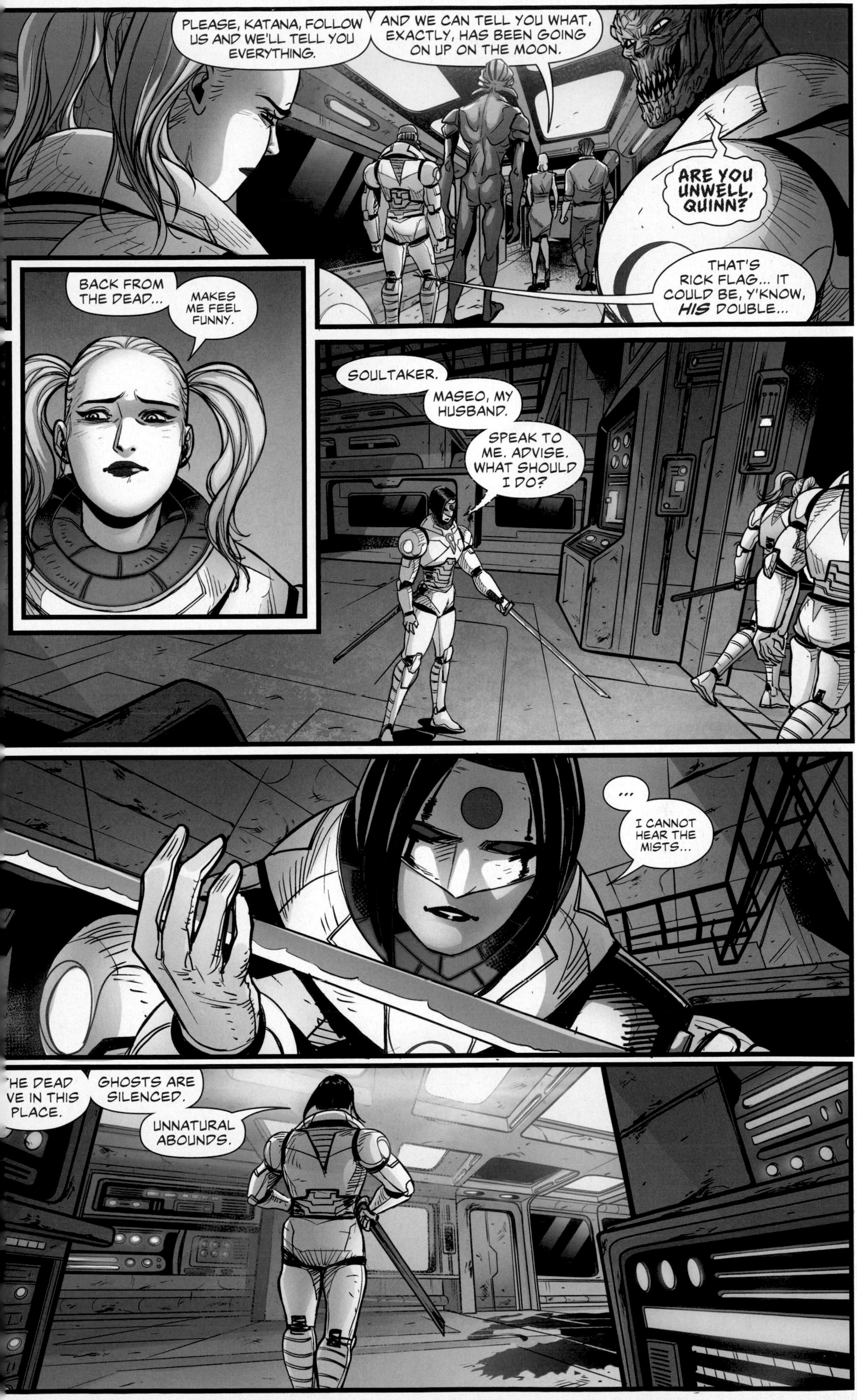
PLEASE, KATANA, FOLLOW US AND WE'LL TELL YOU EVERYTHING.
AND WE CAN TELL YOU WHAT, EXACTLY, HAS BEEN GOING ON UP ON THE MOON.
ARE YOU UNWELL, QUINN?
BACK FROM THE DEAD...
MAKES ME FEEL FUNNY.
THAT'S RICK FLAG... IT COULD BE, Y'KNOW, HIS DOUBLE...
SOULTAKER.
MASEO, MY HUSBAND.
SPEAK TO ME. ADVISE. WHAT SHOULD I DO?
...
I CANNOT HEAR THE MISTS...
HE DEAD VE IN THIS PLACE.
GHOSTS ARE SILENCED.
UNNATURAL ABOUNDS.

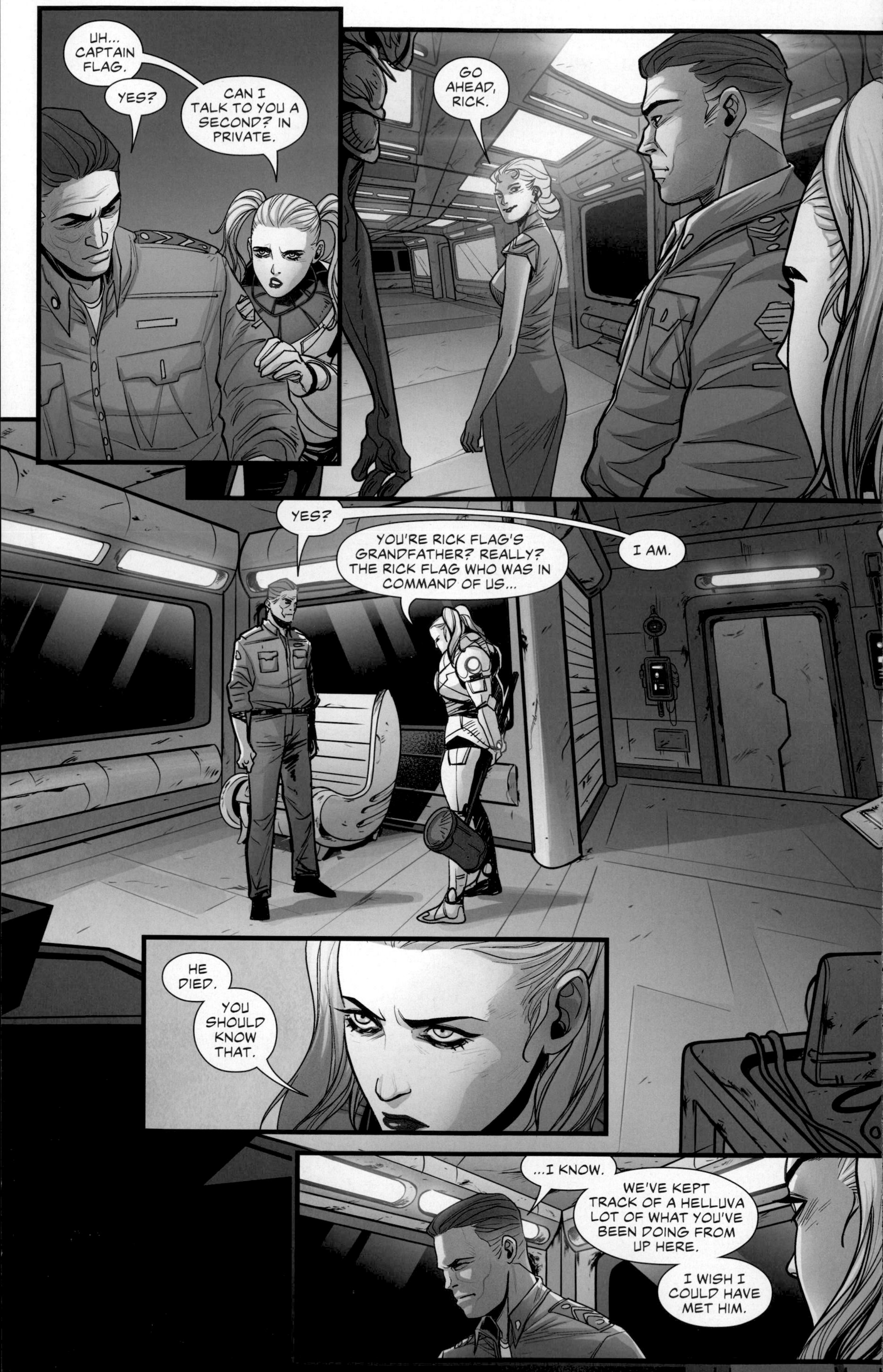
UH... CAPTAIN FLAG.
YES?
CAN I TALK TO YOU A SECOND? IN PRIVATE.
GO AHEAD, RICK.
YES?
YOU'RE RICK FLAG'S GRANDFATHER? REALLY? THE RICK FLAG WHO WAS IN COMMAND OF US...
I AM.
HE DIED.
YOU SHOULD KNOW THAT.
...I KNOW.
WE'VE KEPT TRACK OF A HELLUVA LOT OF WHAT YOU'VE BEEN DOING FROM UP HERE.
I WISH I COULD HAVE MET HIM.

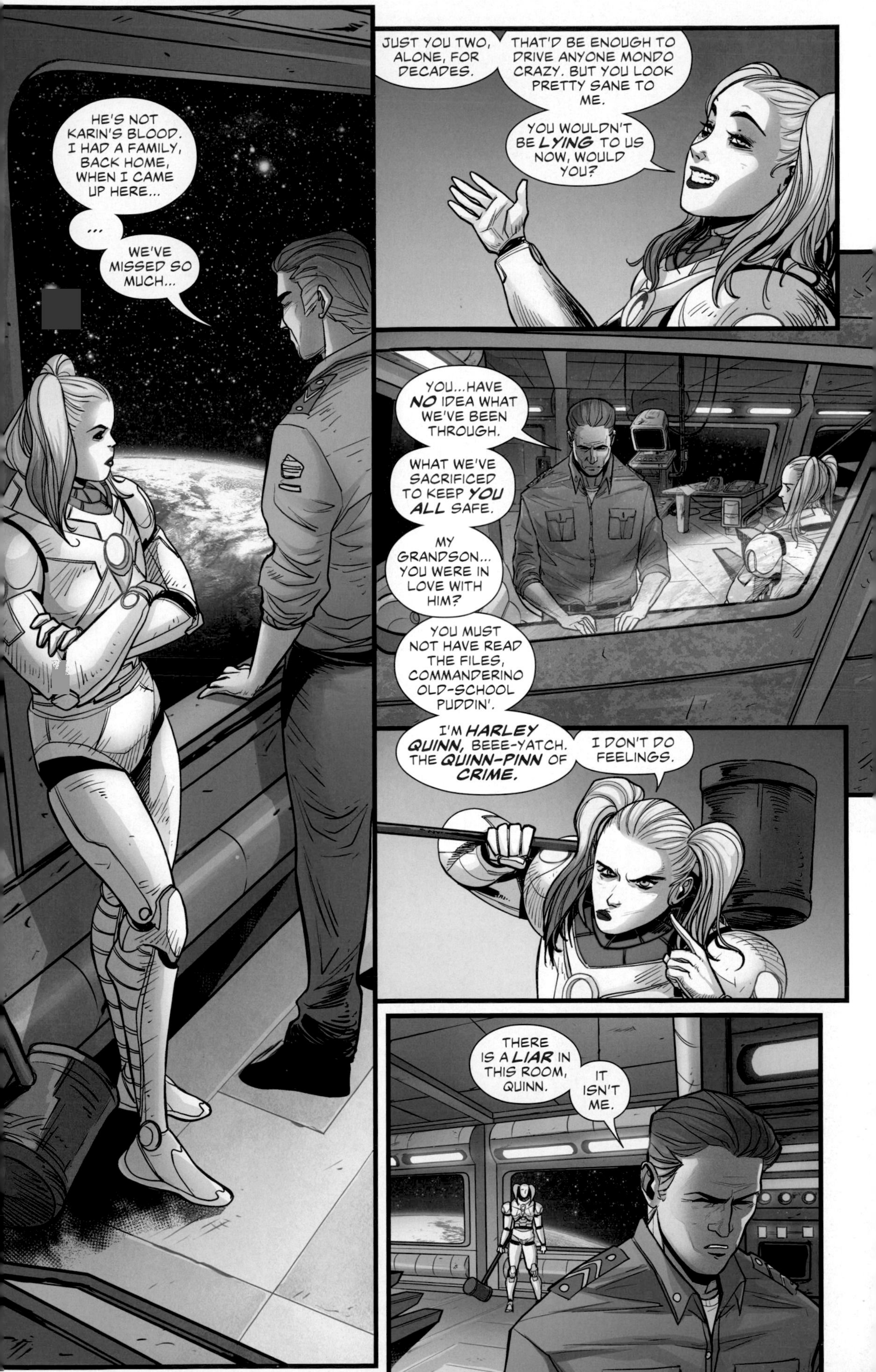
HE'S NOT KARIN'S BLOOD. I HAD A FAMILY, BACK HOME, WHEN I CAME UP HERE...
...
WE'VE MISSED SO MUCH...
JUST YOU TWO, ALONE, FOR DECADES.
THAT'D BE ENOUGH TO DRIVE ANYONE MONDO CRAZY. BUT YOU LOOK PRETTY SANE TO ME.
YOU WOULDN'T BE LYING TO US NOW, WOULD YOU?
YOU...HAVE NO IDEA WHAT WE'VE BEEN THROUGH.
WHAT WE'VE SACRIFICED TO KEEP YOU ALL SAFE.
MY GRANDSON... YOU WERE IN LOVE WITH HIM?
YOU MUST NOT HAVE READ THE FILES, COMMANDERINO OLD-SCHOOL PUDDIN'.
I'M HARLEY QUINN, BEEE-YATCH. THE QUINN-PINN OF CRIME.
I DON'T DO FEELINGS.
THERE IS A LIAR IN THIS ROOM, QUINN.
IT ISN'T ME.

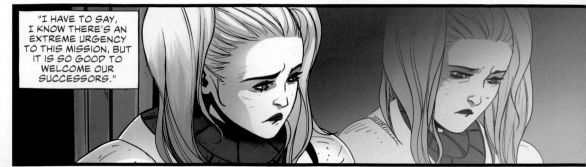

"I HAVE TO SAY, I KNOW THERE'S AN EXTREME URGENCY TO THIS MISSION, BUT IT IS SO GOOD TO WELCOME OUR SUCCESSORS."

HMPH.

WE'VE BEEN UP HERE SO LONG, KARIN'S HAPPY TO SEE ANY FACES THAT AREN'T MINE.

SHUSH YOU.

I NEVER GET TIRED OF SEEING YOUR FACE.

YOU WANT US TO GO TO THE MOON TO COMPLETE A MISSION THAT WILL SAVE THE LIVES OF THE PEOPLE OF THE EARTH BUT WHICH MAY COST OURS.

YOU'VE BEEN HERE DECADES. WHY NOW? AND WHY WOULD WE DO THIS?

BECAUSE OF THE *RED WAV MONSTER*.

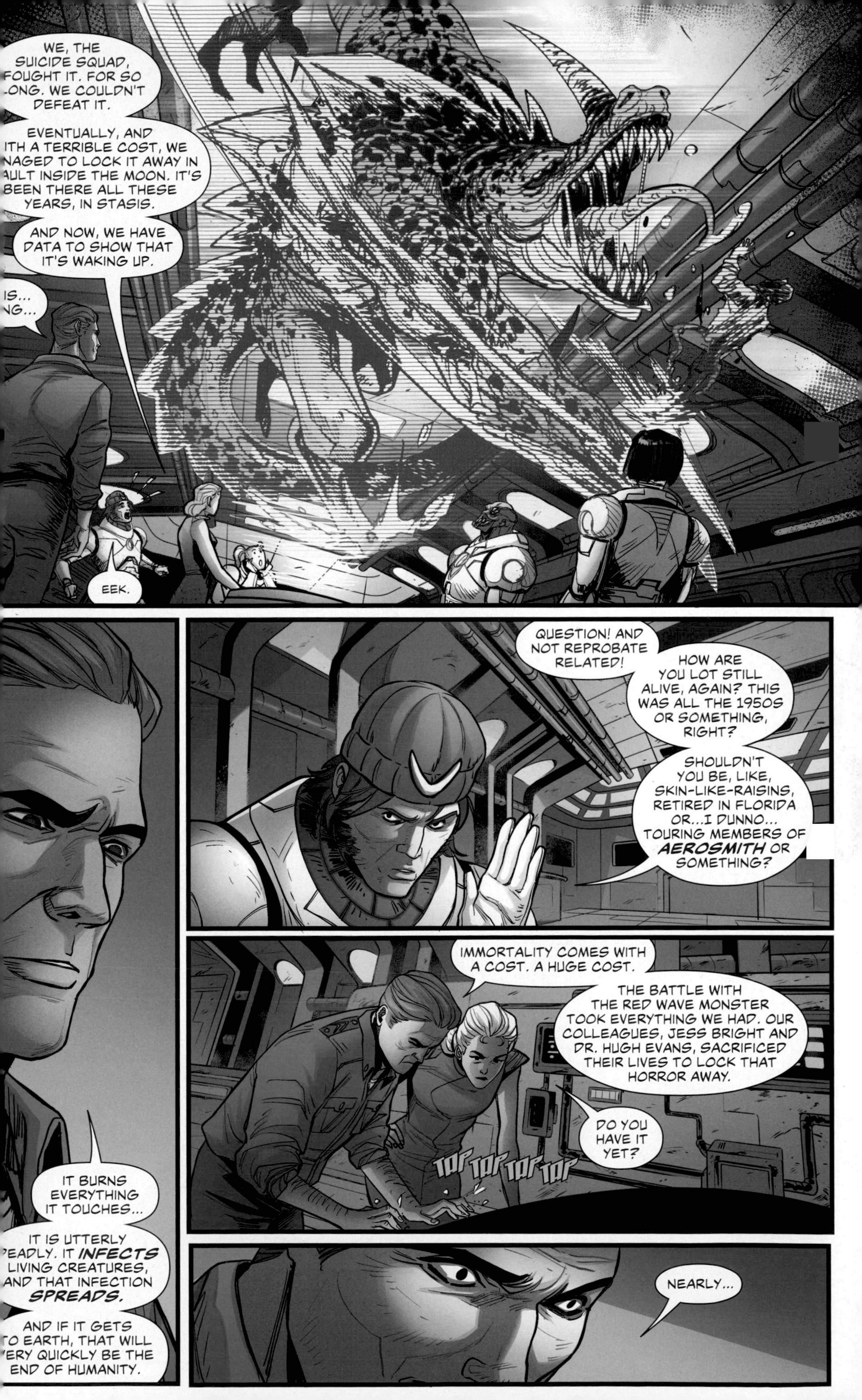
WE, THE SUICIDE SQUAD, FOUGHT IT. FOR SO -ONG. WE COULDN'T DEFEAT IT.
EVENTUALLY, AND ITH A TERRIBLE COST, WE NAGED TO LOCK IT AWAY IN AULT INSIDE THE MOON. IT'S BEEN THERE ALL THESE YEARS, IN STASIS.
AND NOW, WE HAVE DATA TO SHOW THAT IT'S WAKING UP.
IS... NG...
EEK.
IT BURNS EVERYTHING IT TOUCHES...
IT IS UTTERLY DEADLY. IT INFECTS LIVING CREATURES, AND THAT INFECTION SPREADS.
AND IF IT GETS TO EARTH, THAT WILL ERY QUICKLY BE THE END OF HUMANITY.
QUESTION! AND NOT REPROBATE RELATED!
HOW ARE YOU LOT STILL ALIVE, AGAIN? THIS WAS ALL THE 1950S OR SOMETHING, RIGHT?
SHOULDN'T YOU BE, LIKE, SKIN-LIKE-RAISINS, RETIRED IN FLORIDA OR...I DUNNO... TOURING MEMBERS OF AEROSMITH OR SOMETHING?
IMMORTALITY COMES WITH A COST. A HUGE COST.
THE BATTLE WITH THE RED WAVE MONSTER TOOK EVERYTHING WE HAD. OUR COLLEAGUES, JESS BRIGHT AND DR. HUGH EVANS, SACRIFICED THEIR LIVES TO LOCK THAT HORROR AWAY.
DO YOU HAVE IT YET?
TAP TAP TAP TAP
NEARLY...

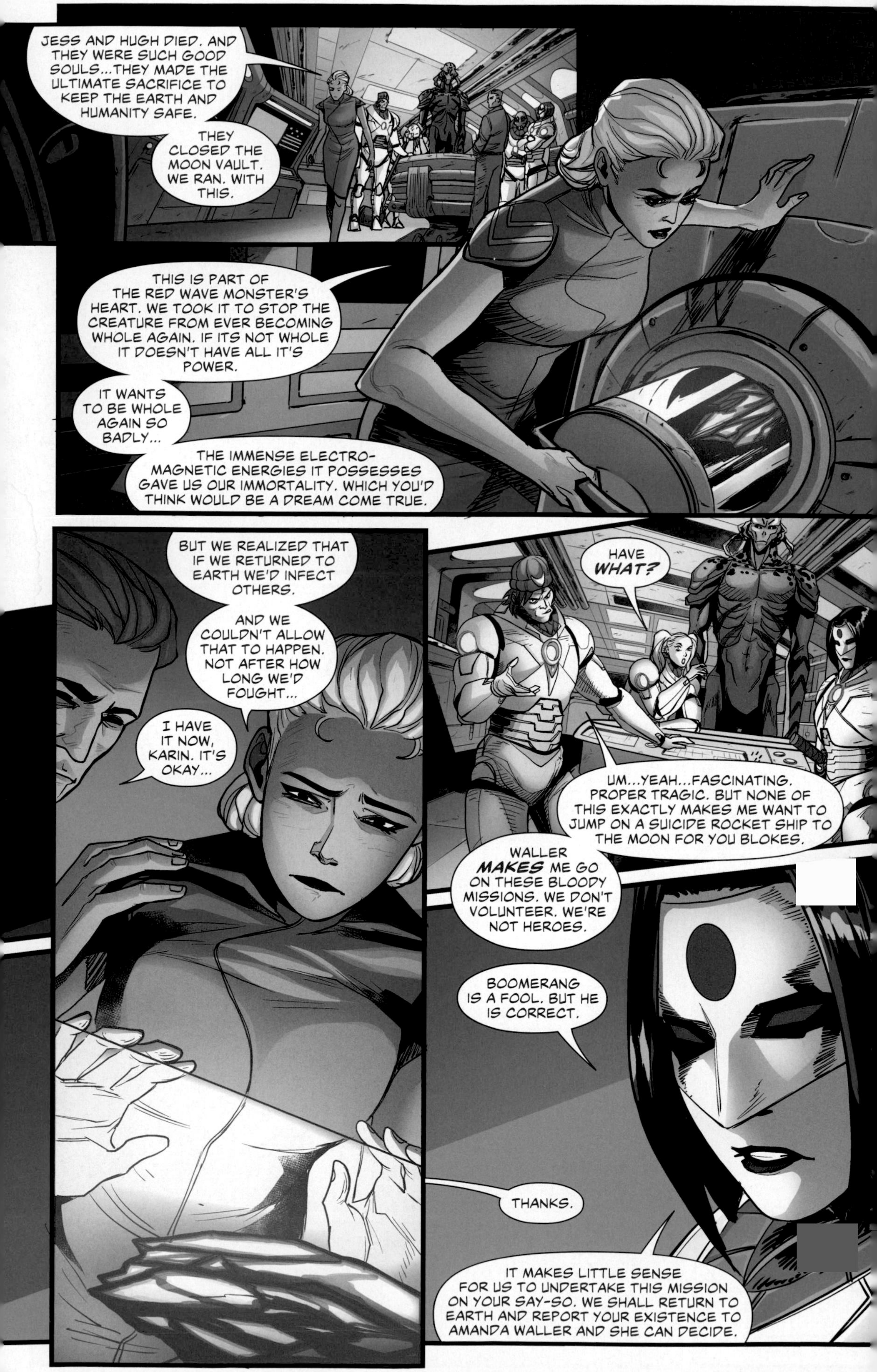
JESS AND HUGH DIED. AND THEY WERE SUCH GOOD SOULS...THEY MADE THE ULTIMATE SACRIFICE TO KEEP THE EARTH AND HUMANITY SAFE.
THEY CLOSED THE MOON VAULT. WE RAN. WITH THIS.
THIS IS PART OF THE RED WAVE MONSTER'S HEART. WE TOOK IT TO STOP THE CREATURE FROM EVER BECOMING WHOLE AGAIN. IF ITS NOT WHOLE IT DOESN'T HAVE ALL IT'S POWER.
IT WANTS TO BE WHOLE AGAIN SO BADLY...
THE IMMENSE ELECTRO-MAGNETIC ENERGIES IT POSSESSES GAVE US OUR IMMORTALITY. WHICH YOU'D THINK WOULD BE A DREAM COME TRUE.
BUT WE REALIZED THAT IF WE RETURNED TO EARTH WE'D INFECT OTHERS.
AND WE COULDN'T ALLOW THAT TO HAPPEN. NOT AFTER HOW LONG WE'D FOUGHT...
I HAVE IT NOW, KARIN. IT'S OKAY...
HAVE ***WHAT?***
UM...YEAH...FASCINATING. PROPER TRAGIC. BUT NONE OF THIS EXACTLY MAKES ME WANT TO JUMP ON A SUICIDE ROCKET SHIP TO THE MOON FOR YOU BLOKES.
WALLER ***MAKES*** ME GO ON THESE BLOODY MISSIONS. WE DON'T VOLUNTEER. WE'RE NOT HEROES.
BOOMERANG IS A FOOL. BUT HE IS CORRECT.
THANKS.
IT MAKES LITTLE SENSE FOR US TO UNDERTAKE THIS MISSION ON YOUR SAY-SO. WE SHALL RETURN TO EARTH AND REPORT YOUR EXISTENCE TO AMANDA WALLER AND SHE CAN DECIDE.

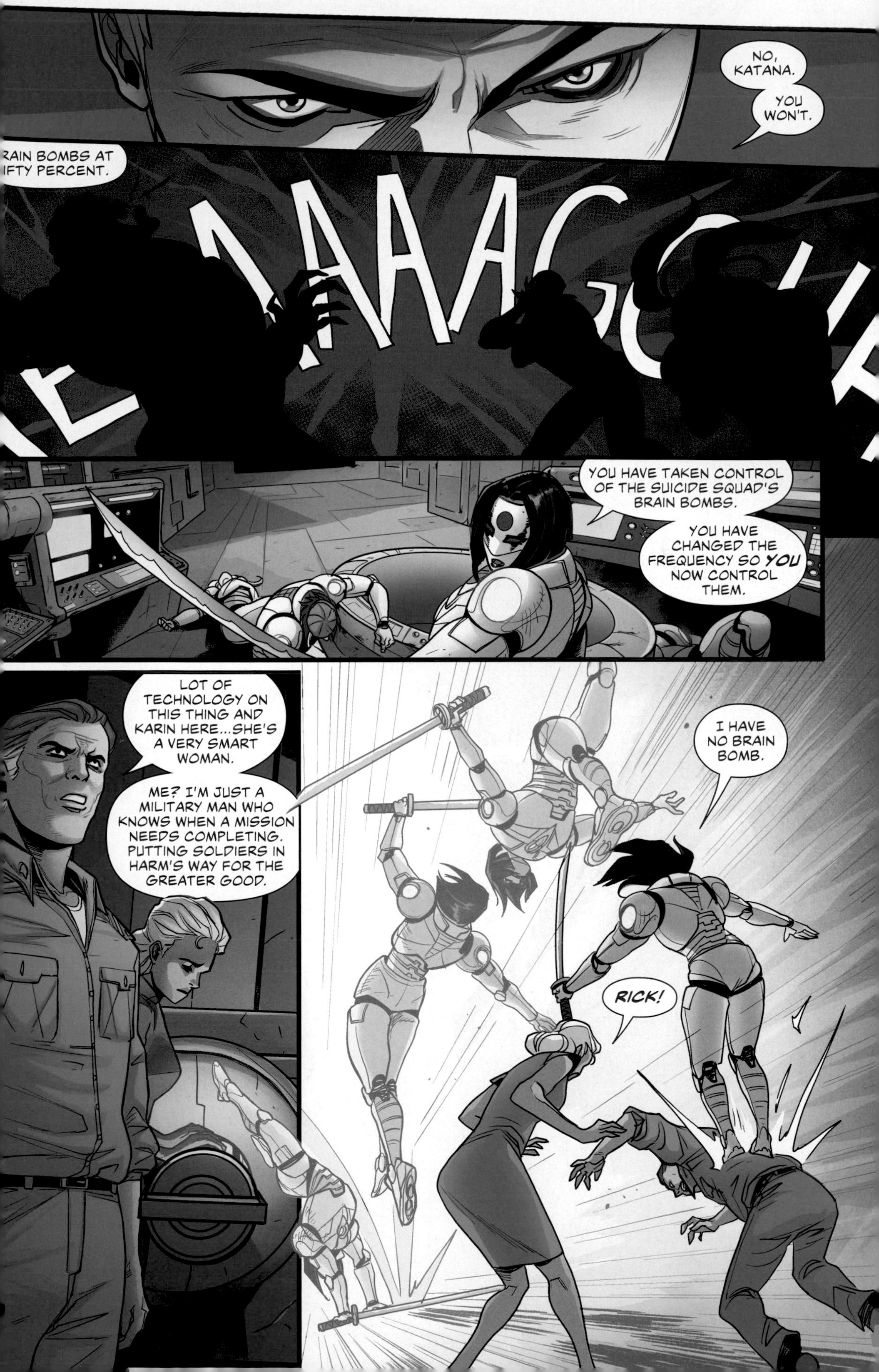

NO, KATANA.
YOU WON'T.
RAIN BOMBS AT IFTY PERCENT.
YOU HAVE TAKEN CONTROL OF THE SUICIDE SQUAD'S BRAIN BOMBS.
YOU HAVE CHANGED THE FREQUENCY SO *YOU* NOW CONTROL THEM.
LOT OF TECHNOLOGY ON THIS THING AND KARIN HERE...SHE'S A VERY SMART WOMAN.
ME? I'M JUST A MILITARY MAN WHO KNOWS WHEN A MISSION NEEDS COMPLETING. PUTTING SOLDIERS IN HARM'S WAY FOR THE GREATER GOOD.
I HAVE NO BRAIN BOMB.
RICK!

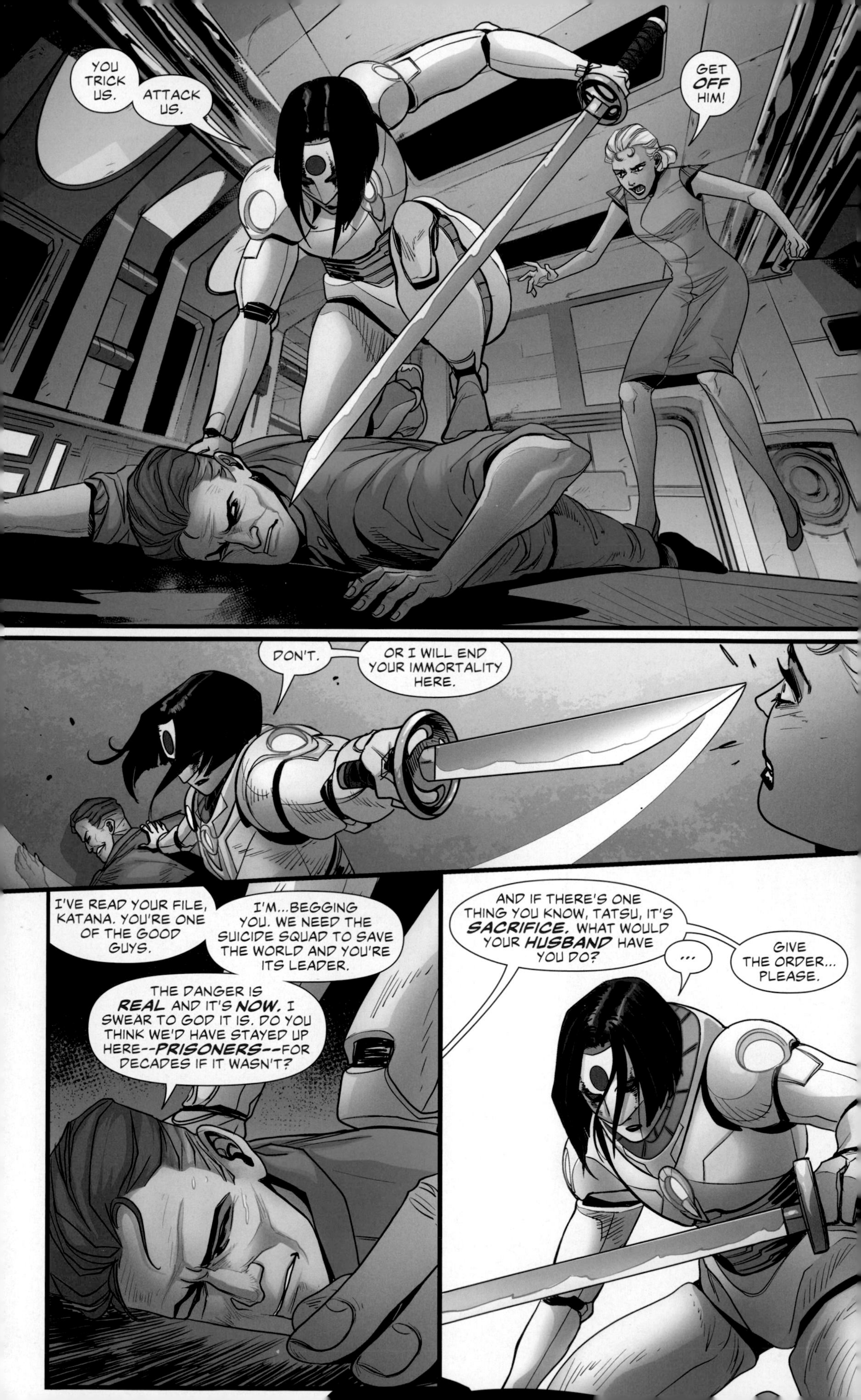
YOU TRICK US.
ATTACK US.
GET OFF HIM!
DON'T.
OR I WILL END YOUR IMMORTALITY HERE.
I'VE READ YOUR FILE, KATANA. YOU'RE ONE OF THE GOOD GUYS.
I'M...BEGGING YOU. WE NEED THE SUICIDE SQUAD TO SAVE THE WORLD AND YOU'RE ITS LEADER.
THE DANGER IS REAL AND IT'S NOW. I SWEAR TO GOD IT IS. DO YOU THINK WE'D HAVE STAYED UP HERE--PRISONERS--FOR DECADES IF IT WASN'T?
AND IF THERE'S ONE THING YOU KNOW, TATSU, IT'S SACRIFICE. WHAT WOULD YOUR HUSBAND HAVE YOU DO?
...
GIVE THE ORDER... PLEASE.

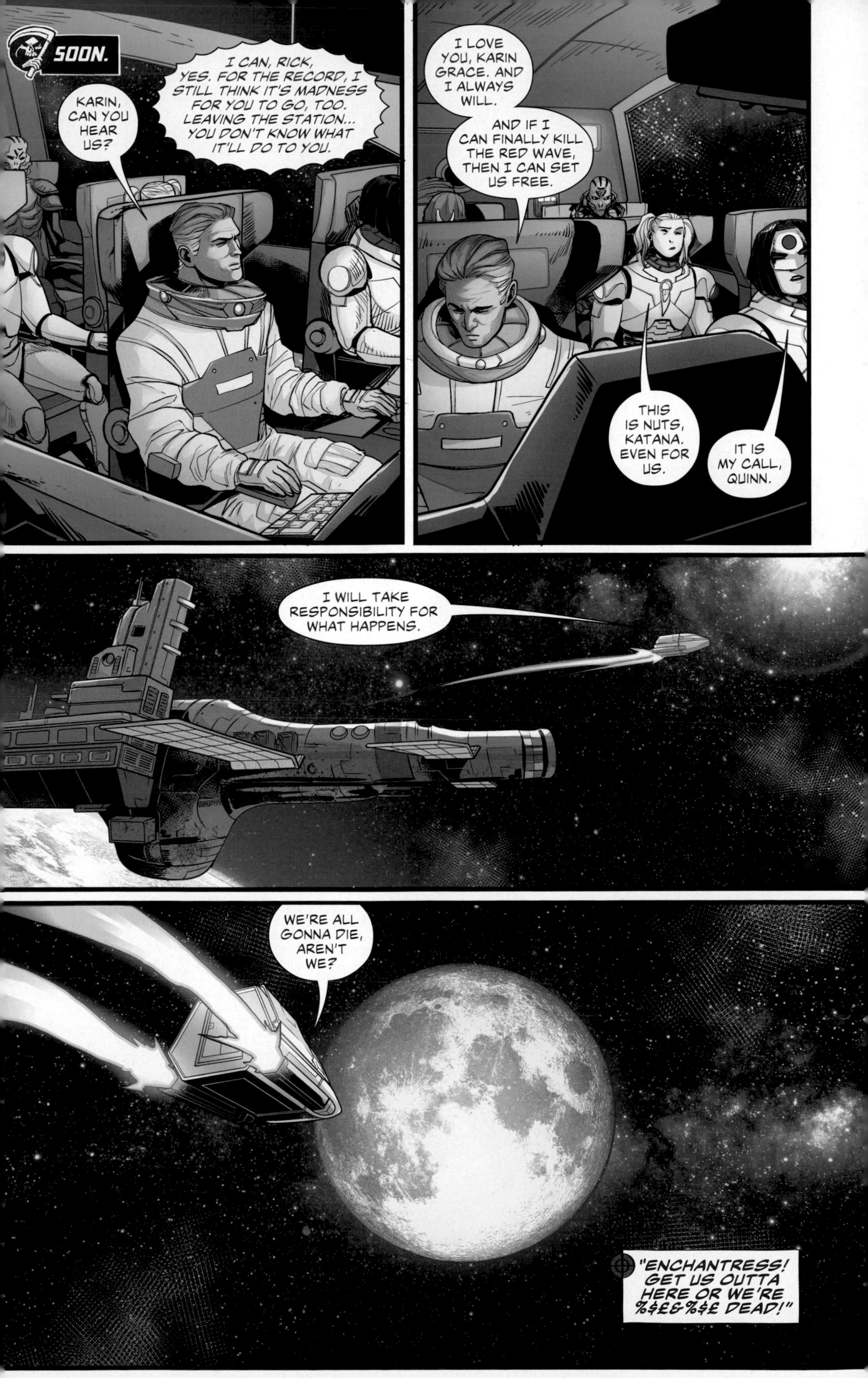
SOON.
KARIN, CAN YOU HEAR US?
I CAN, RICK, YES. FOR THE RECORD, I STILL THINK IT'S MADNESS FOR YOU TO GO, TOO. LEAVING THE STATION... YOU DON'T KNOW WHAT IT'LL DO TO YOU.
I LOVE YOU, KARIN GRACE. AND I ALWAYS WILL.
AND IF I CAN FINALLY KILL THE RED WAVE, THEN I CAN SET US FREE.
THIS IS NUTS, KATANA. EVEN FOR US.
IT IS MY CALL, QUINN.
I WILL TAKE RESPONSIBILITY FOR WHAT HAPPENS.
WE'RE ALL GONNA DIE, AREN'T WE?
"ENCHANTRESS! GET US OUTTA HERE OR WE'RE %$£&%$£ DEAD!"

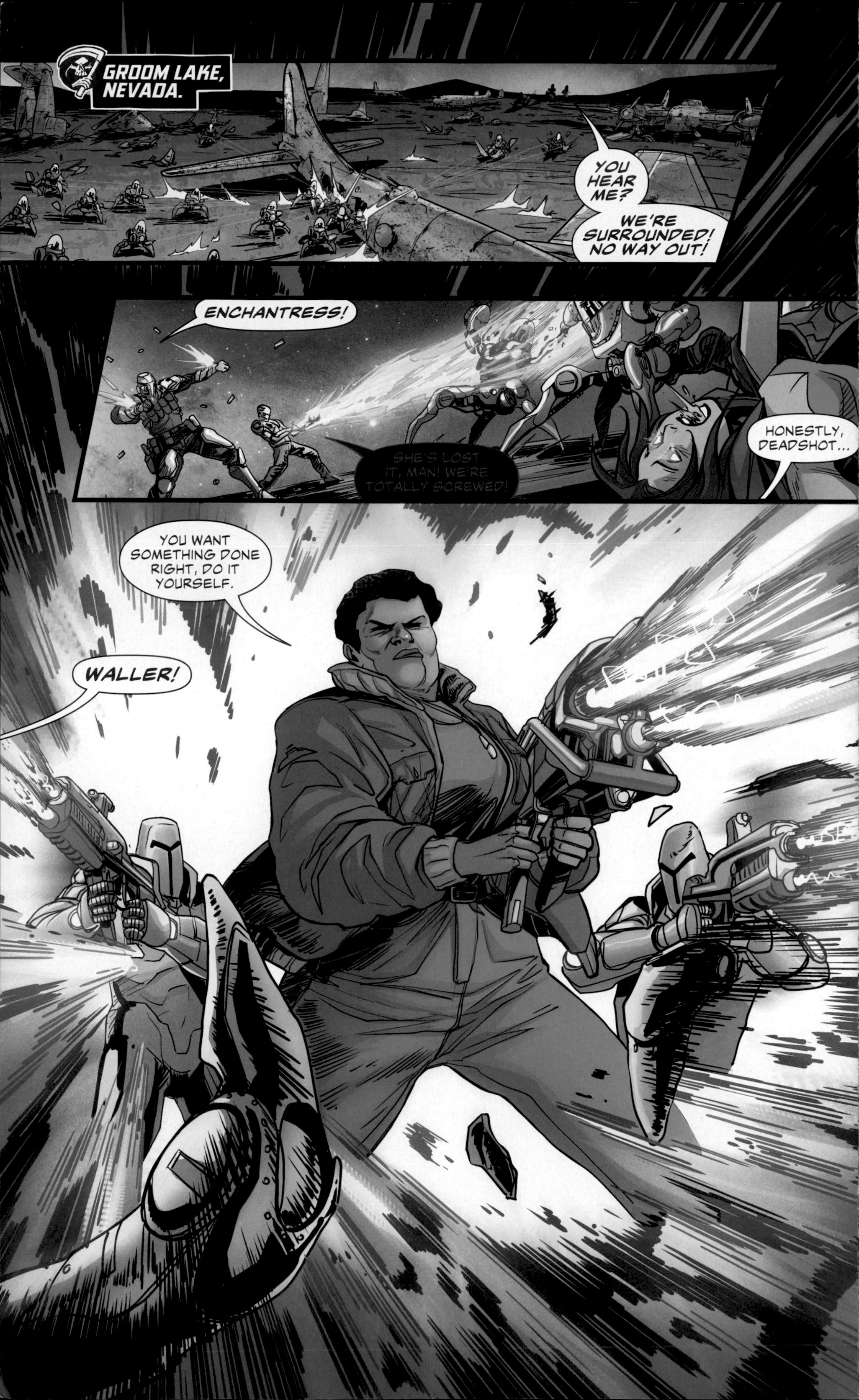
GROOM LAKE, NEVADA.
YOU HEAR ME?
WE'RE SURROUNDED! NO WAY OUT!
ENCHANTRESS!
SHE'S LOST IT, MAN! WE'RE TOTALLY SCREWED!
HONESTLY, DEADSHOT...
YOU WANT SOMETHING DONE RIGHT, DO IT YOURSELF.
WALLER!

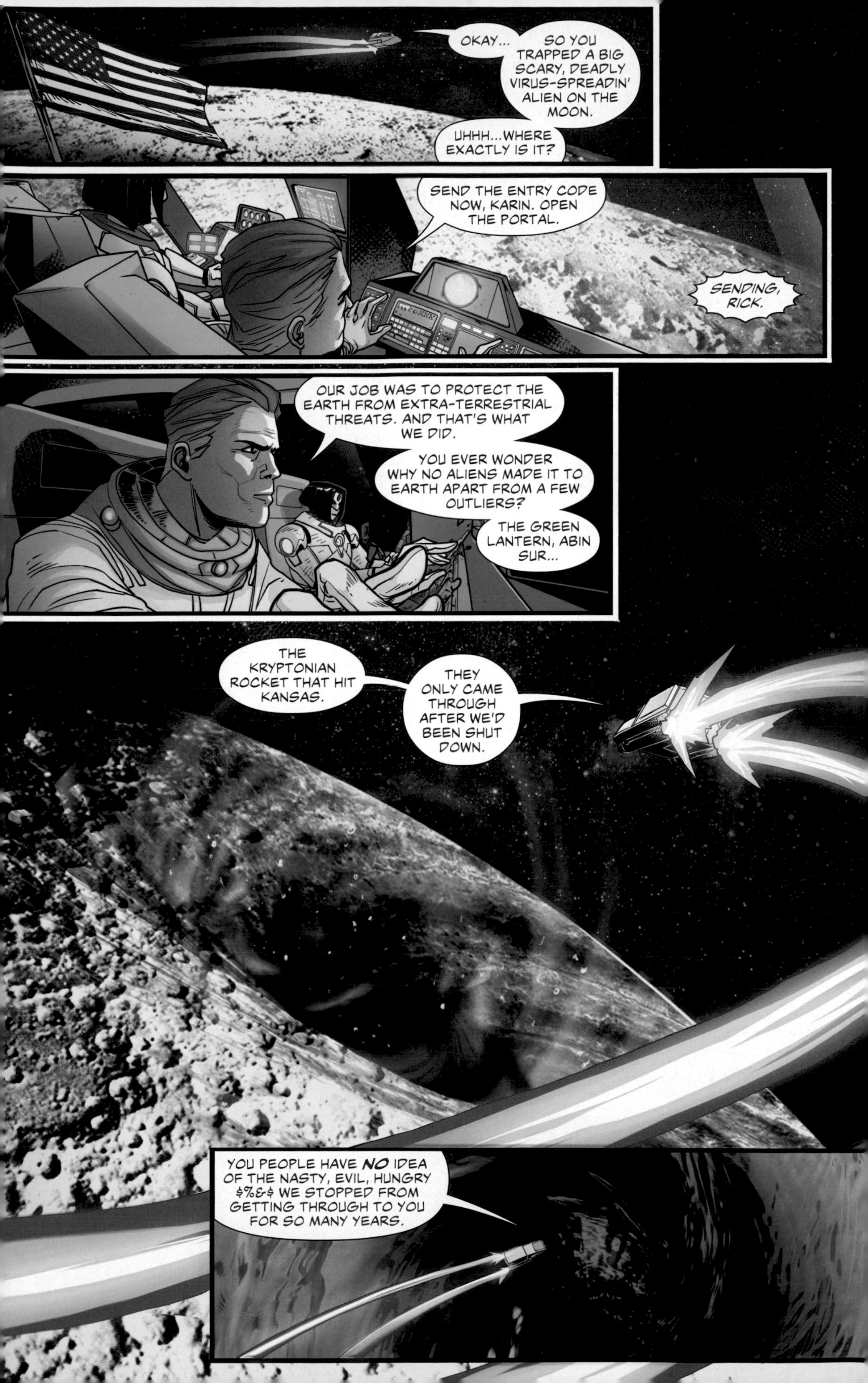
OKAY...
SO YOU TRAPPED A BIG SCARY, DEADLY VIRUS-SPREADIN' ALIEN ON THE MOON.
UHHH...WHERE EXACTLY IS IT?
SEND THE ENTRY CODE NOW, KARIN. OPEN THE PORTAL.
SENDING, RICK.
OUR JOB WAS TO PROTECT THE EARTH FROM EXTRA-TERRESTRIAL THREATS. AND THAT'S WHAT WE DID.
YOU EVER WONDER WHY NO ALIENS MADE IT TO EARTH APART FROM A FEW OUTLIERS?
THE GREEN LANTERN, ABIN SUR...
THE KRYPTONIAN ROCKET THAT HIT KANSAS.
THEY ONLY CAME THROUGH AFTER WE'D BEEN SHUT DOWN.
YOU PEOPLE HAVE ***NO*** IDEA OF THE NASTY, EVIL, HUNGRY $%&$ WE STOPPED FROM GETTING THROUGH TO YOU FOR SO MANY YEARS.

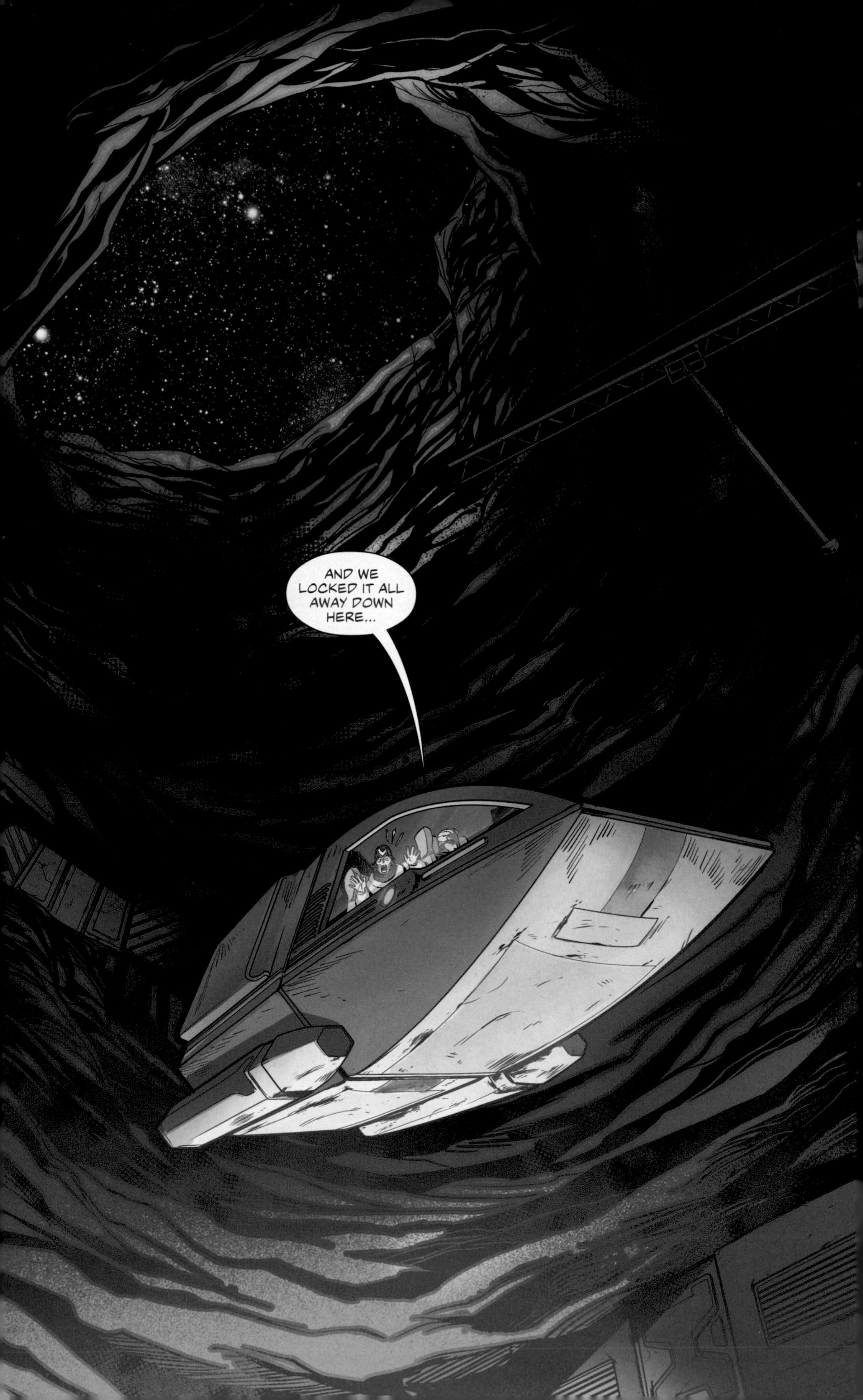
AND WE LOCKED IT ALL AWAY DOWN HERE...

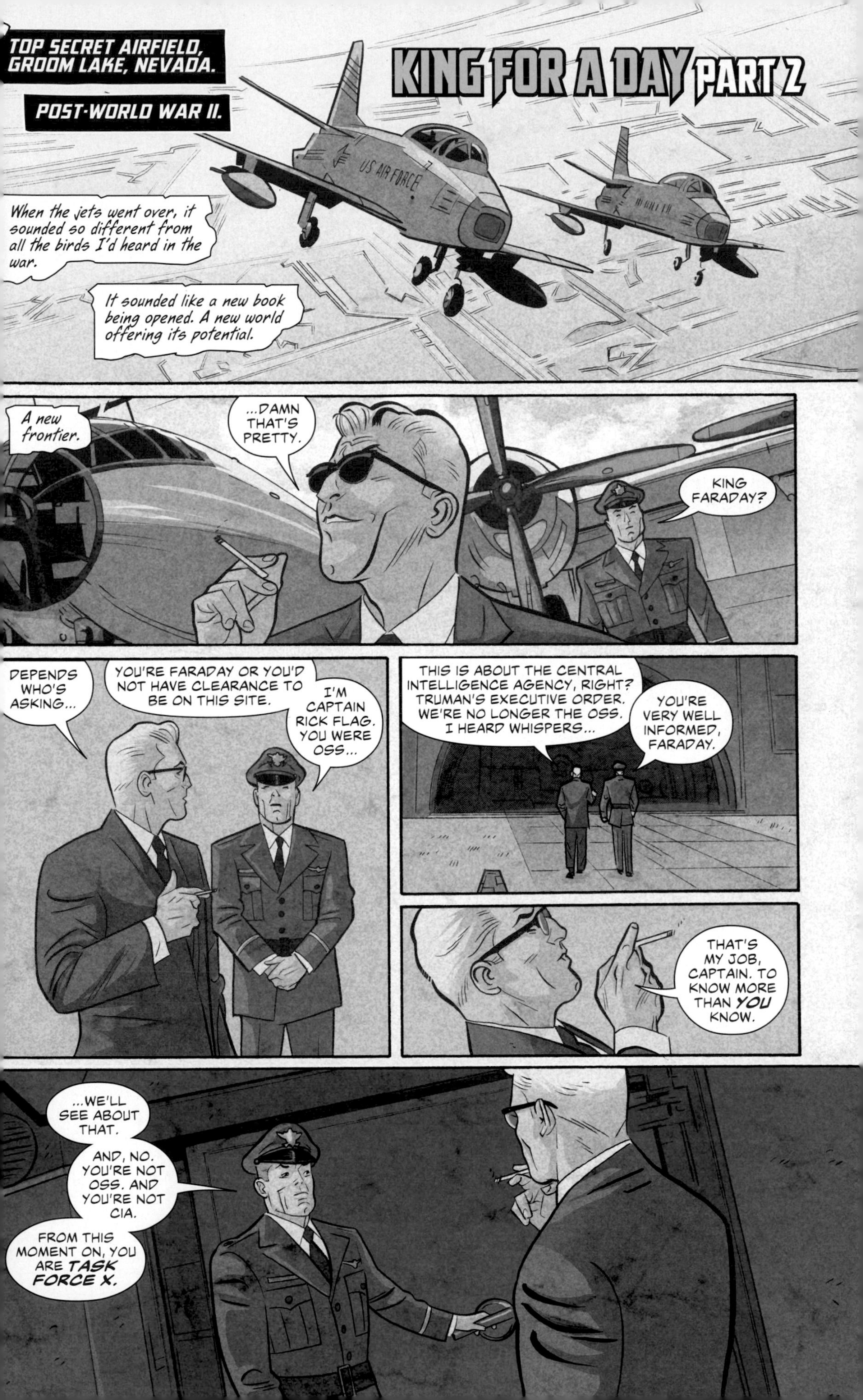
TOP SECRET AIRFIELD, GROOM LAKE, NEVADA.
POST-WORLD WAR II.
KING FOR A DAY PART 2
US AIR FORCE
When the jets went over, it sounded so different from all the birds I'd heard in the war.
It sounded like a new book being opened. A new world offering its potential.
A new frontier.
...DAMN THAT'S PRETTY.
KING FARADAY?
DEPENDS WHO'S ASKING...
YOU'RE FARADAY OR YOU'D NOT HAVE CLEARANCE TO BE ON THIS SITE.
I'M CAPTAIN RICK FLAG. YOU WERE OSS...
THIS IS ABOUT THE CENTRAL INTELLIGENCE AGENCY, RIGHT? TRUMAN'S EXECUTIVE ORDER. WE'RE NO LONGER THE OSS. I HEARD WHISPERS...
YOU'RE VERY WELL INFORMED, FARADAY.
THAT'S MY JOB, CAPTAIN. TO KNOW MORE THAN YOU KNOW.
...WE'LL SEE ABOUT THAT.
AND, NO. YOU'RE NOT OSS. AND YOU'RE NOT CIA.
FROM THIS MOMENT ON, YOU ARE TASK FORCE X.

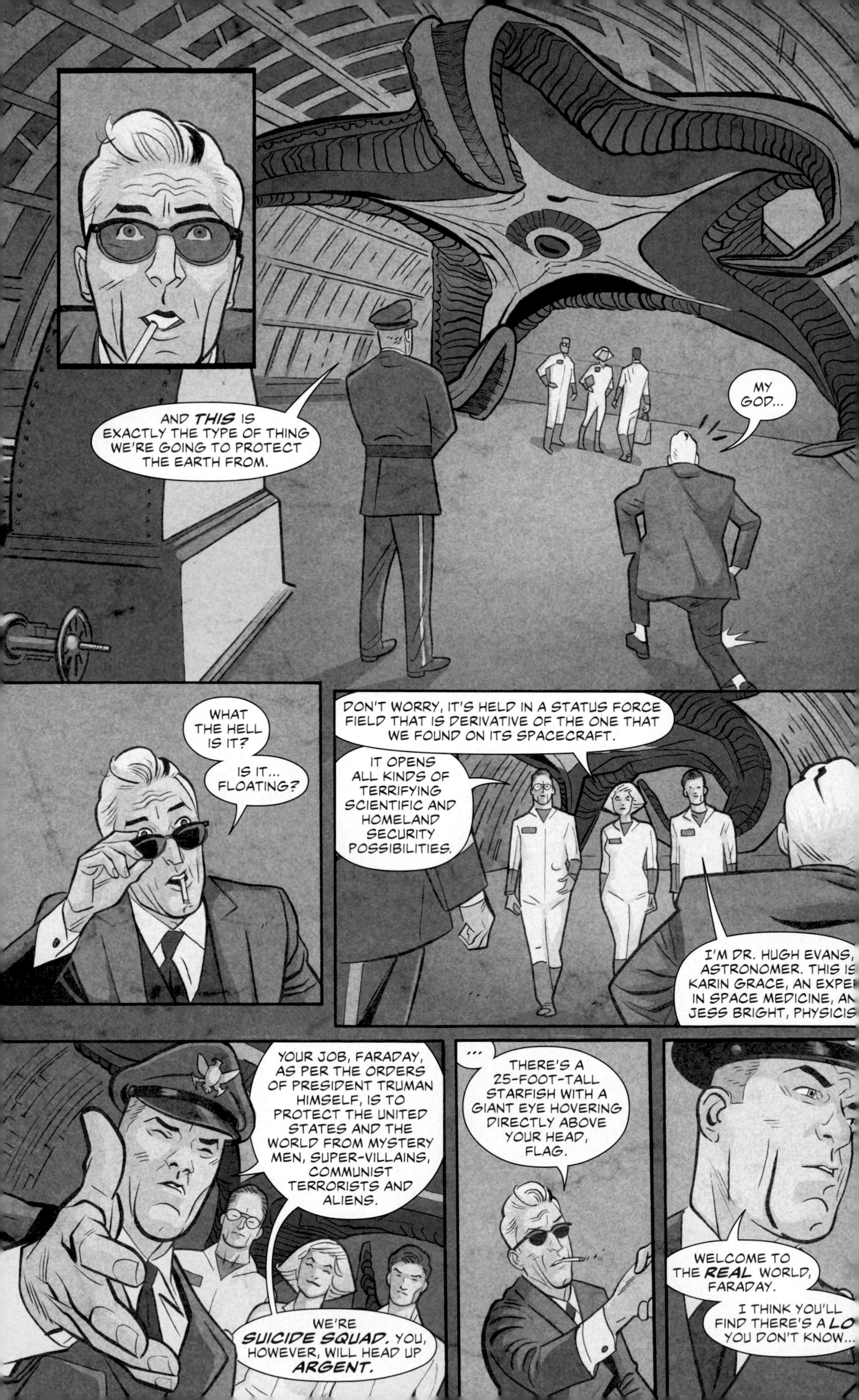

AND THIS IS EXACTLY THE TYPE OF THING WE'RE GOING TO PROTECT THE EARTH FROM.
MY GOD...
WHAT THE HELL IS IT?
IS IT... FLOATING?
DON'T WORRY, IT'S HELD IN A STATUS FORCE FIELD THAT IS DERIVATIVE OF THE ONE THAT WE FOUND ON ITS SPACECRAFT.
IT OPENS ALL KINDS OF TERRIFYING SCIENTIFIC AND HOMELAND SECURITY POSSIBILITIES.
I'M DR. HUGH EVANS, ASTRONOMER. THIS IS KARIN GRACE, AN EXPE IN SPACE MEDICINE, AN JESS BRIGHT, PHYSICIS
YOUR JOB, FARADAY, AS PER THE ORDERS OF PRESIDENT TRUMAN HIMSELF, IS TO PROTECT THE UNITED STATES AND THE WORLD FROM MYSTERY MEN, SUPER-VILLAINS, COMMUNIST TERRORISTS AND ALIENS.
WE'RE SUICIDE SQUAD. YOU, HOWEVER, WILL HEAD UP ARGENT.
...
THERE'S A 25-FOOT-TALL STARFISH WITH A GIANT EYE HOVERING DIRECTLY ABOVE YOUR HEAD, FLAG.
WELCOME TO THE REAL WORLD, FARADAY.
I THINK YOU'LL FIND THERE'S A LO YOU DON'T KNOW...

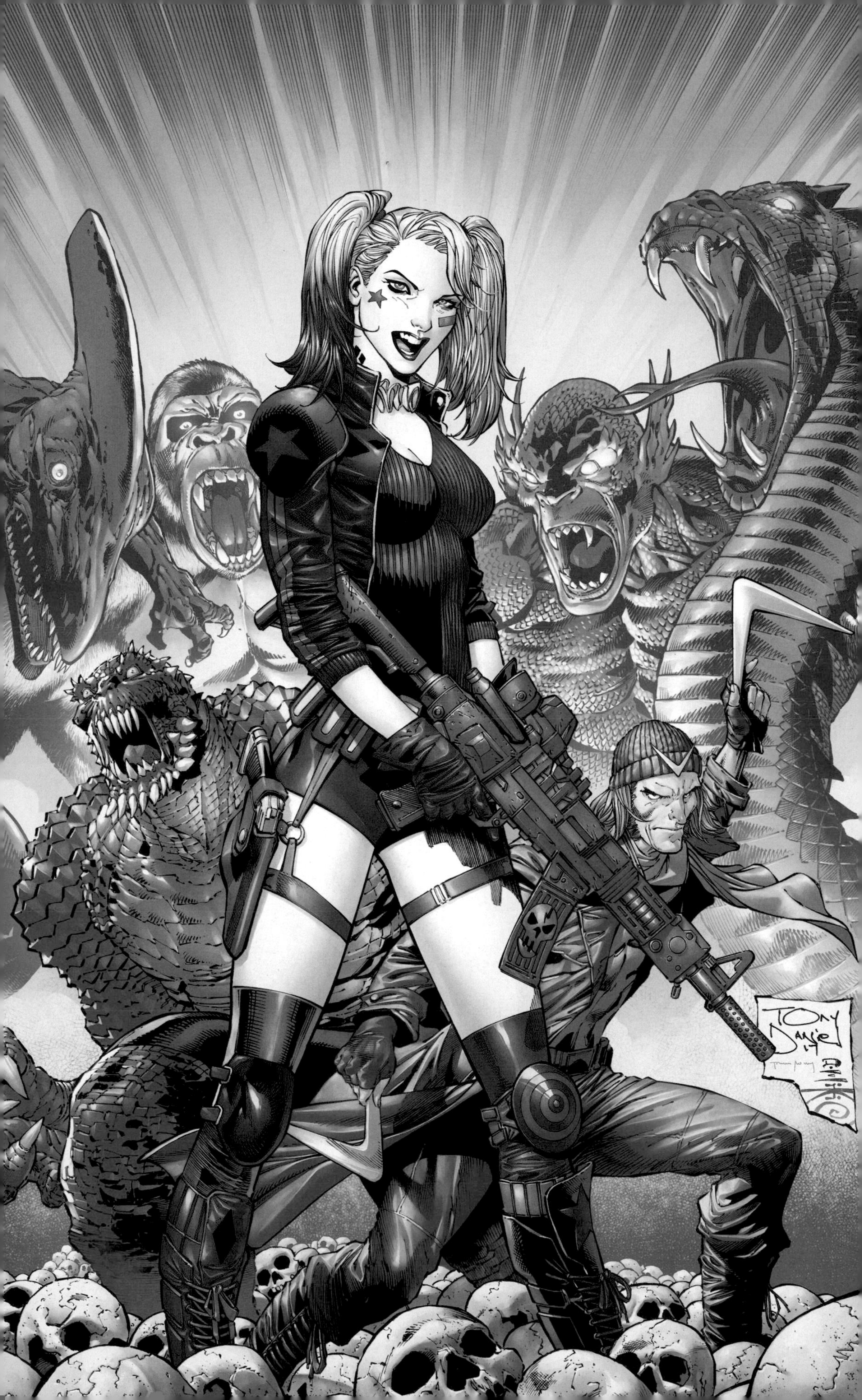

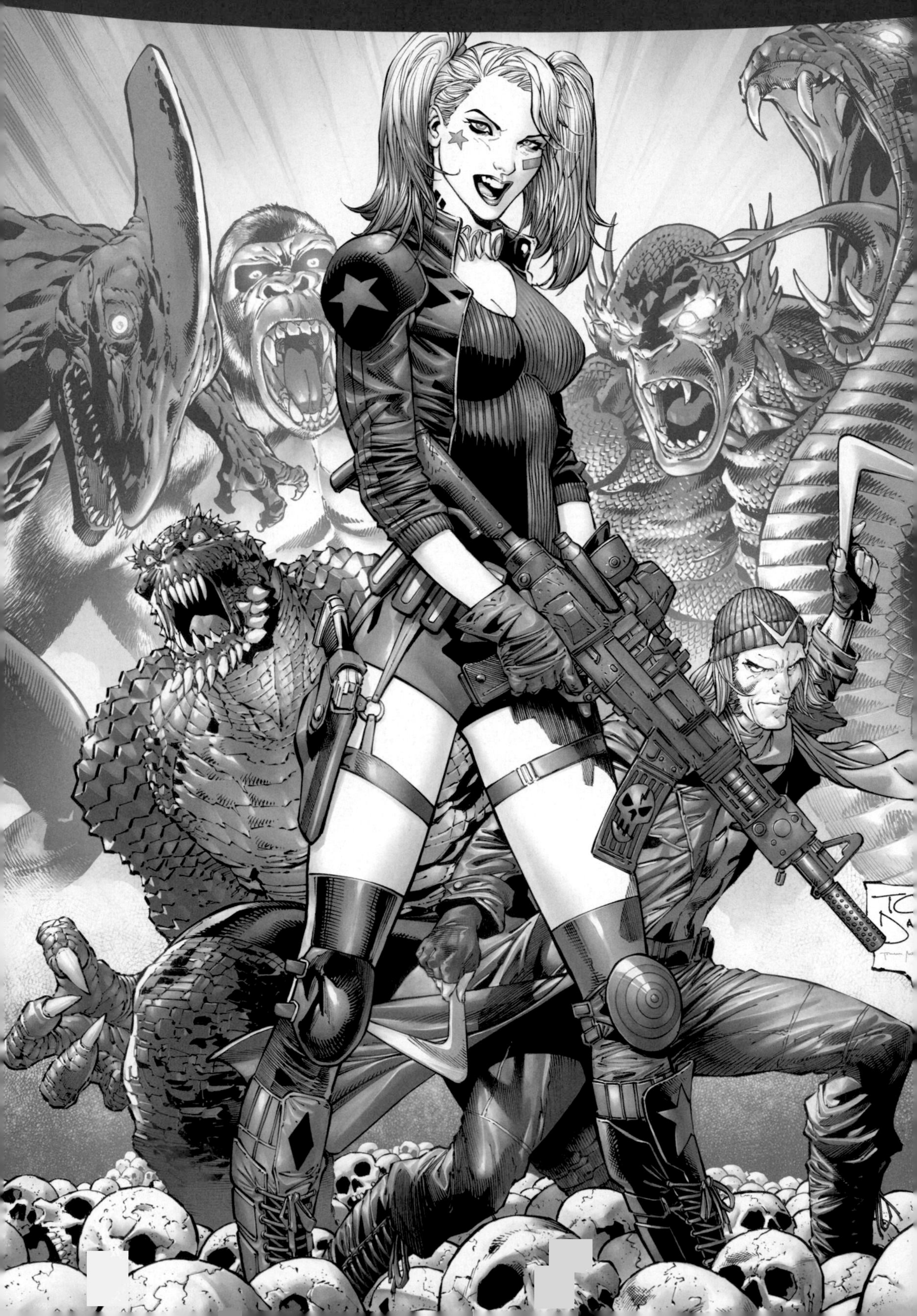

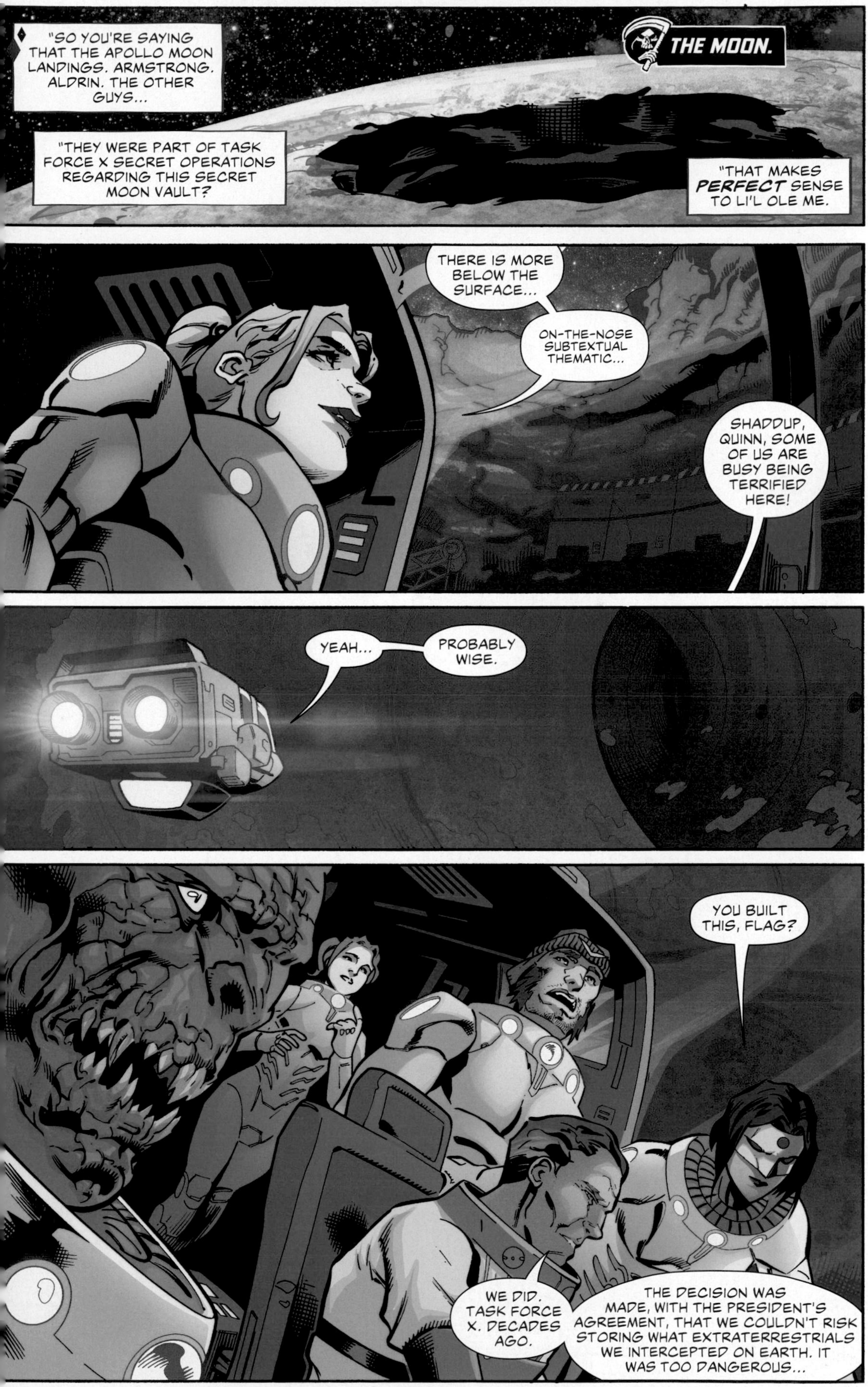
"SO YOU'RE SAYING THAT THE APOLLO MOON LANDINGS. ARMSTRONG. ALDRIN. THE OTHER GUYS...
THE MOON.
"THEY WERE PART OF TASK FORCE X SECRET OPERATIONS REGARDING THIS SECRET MOON VAULT?
"THAT MAKES PERFECT SENSE TO LI'L OLE ME.
THERE IS MORE BELOW THE SURFACE...
ON-THE-NOSE SUBTEXTUAL THEMATIC...
SHADDUP, QUINN, SOME OF US ARE BUSY BEING TERRIFIED HERE!
YEAH...
PROBABLY WISE.
YOU BUILT THIS, FLAG?
WE DID. TASK FORCE X. DECADES AGO.
THE DECISION WAS MADE, WITH THE PRESIDENT'S AGREEMENT, THAT WE COULDN'T RISK STORING WHAT EXTRATERRESTRIALS WE INTERCEPTED ON EARTH. IT WAS TOO DANGEROUS...

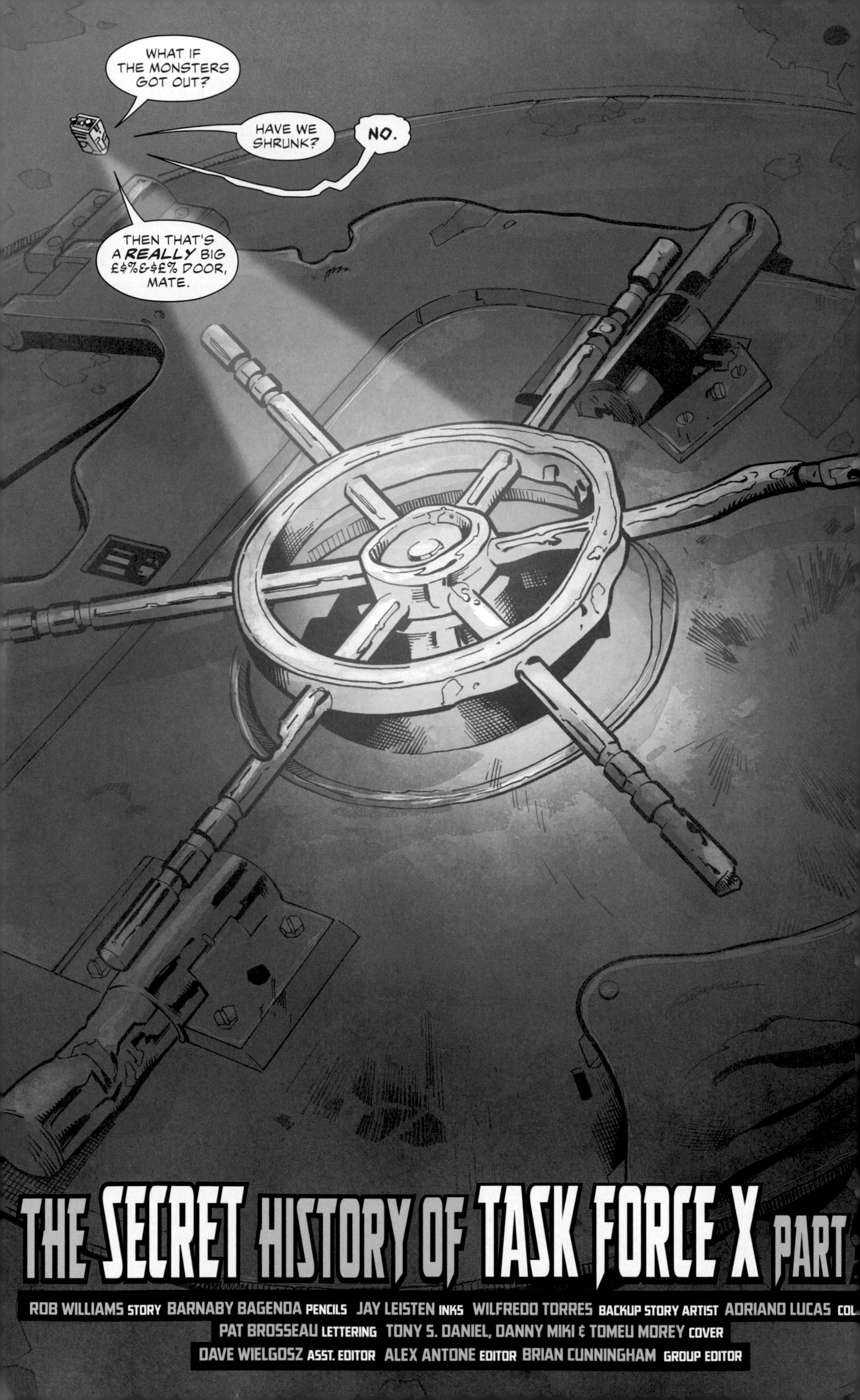
WHAT IF THE MONSTERS GOT OUT?
HAVE WE SHRUNK?
NO.
THEN THAT'S A *REALLY* BIG £$%&$£% DOOR, MATE.
THE SECRET HISTORY OF TASK FORCE X PART
ROB WILLIAMS STORY BARNABY BAGENDA PENCILS JAY LEISTEN INKS WILFREDO TORRES BACKUP STORY ARTIST ADRIANO LUCAS COL
PAT BROSSEAU LETTERING TONY S. DANIEL, DANNY MIKI & TOMEU MOREY COVER
DAVE WIELGOSZ ASST. EDITOR ALEX ANTONE EDITOR BRIAN CUNNINGHAM GROUP EDITOR

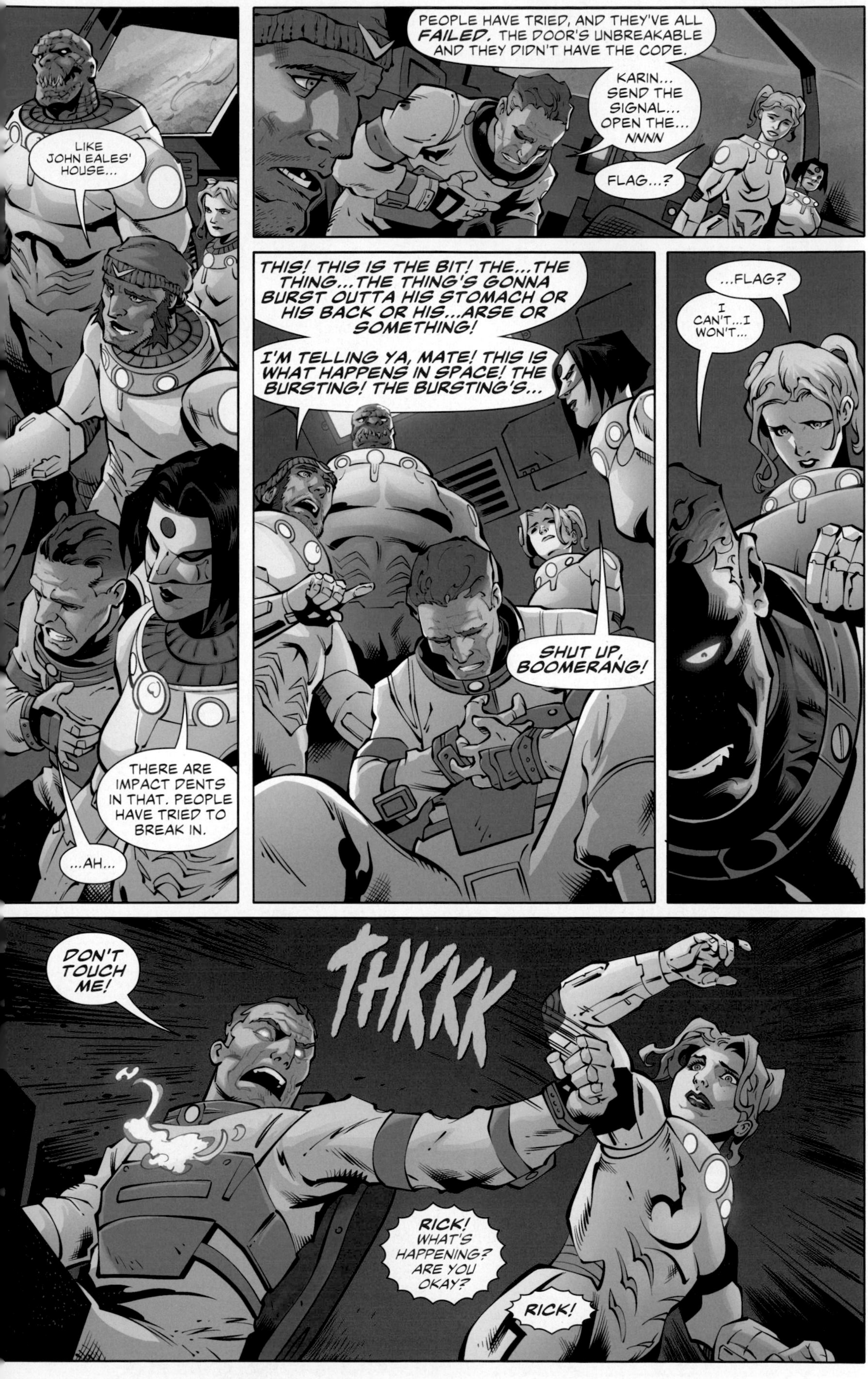

LIKE JOHN EALES' HOUSE...
THERE ARE IMPACT DENTS IN THAT. PEOPLE HAVE TRIED TO BREAK IN.
...AH...
PEOPLE HAVE TRIED, AND THEY'VE ALL FAILED. THE DOOR'S UNBREAKABLE AND THEY DIDN'T HAVE THE CODE.
KARIN... SEND THE SIGNAL... OPEN THE... NNNN
FLAG...?
THIS! THIS IS THE BIT! THE...THE THING...THE THING'S GONNA BURST OUTTA HIS STOMACH OR HIS BACK OR HIS...ARSE OR SOMETHING!
I'M TELLING YA, MATE! THIS IS WHAT HAPPENS IN SPACE! THE BURSTING! THE BURSTING'S...
SHUT UP, BOOMERANG!
...FLAG?
I CAN'T...I WON'T...
DON'T TOUCH ME!
THKKK
RICK! WHAT'S HAPPENING? ARE YOU OKAY?
RICK!

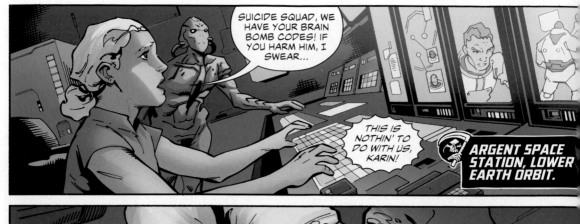

SUICIDE SQUAD, WE HAVE YOUR BRAIN BOMB CODES! IF YOU HARM HIM, I SWEAR...

THIS IS NOTHIN' TO DO WITH US, KARIN!

ARGENT SPACE STATION, LOWER EARTH ORBIT.

THE HEART...

...CANNOT...

...BE WHOLE.

I'M OPENING THE VAULT, RICK!

RICK, **GET INSIDE**, DO YOU HEAR ME! YOU'RE TOO FAR FROM THE SPACE STATION. WE KNEW THIS WOULD AFFECT YOU.

GET IN THE VAULT. THE NEARER YOU GET TO THE RED WAVE MONSTER'S RADIATION, THE STRONGER YOU'LL FEEL!

RICK...

PLEASE SPEAK TO ME...

WE CALCULATED YOU'D BE ABLE TO SURVIVE THE JOURNEY WITHOUT AGING.

OH GOD...

I CAN'T LOSE YOU, RICK, NOT NOW. WE'VE SUFFERED SO MUCH.

PLEASE...

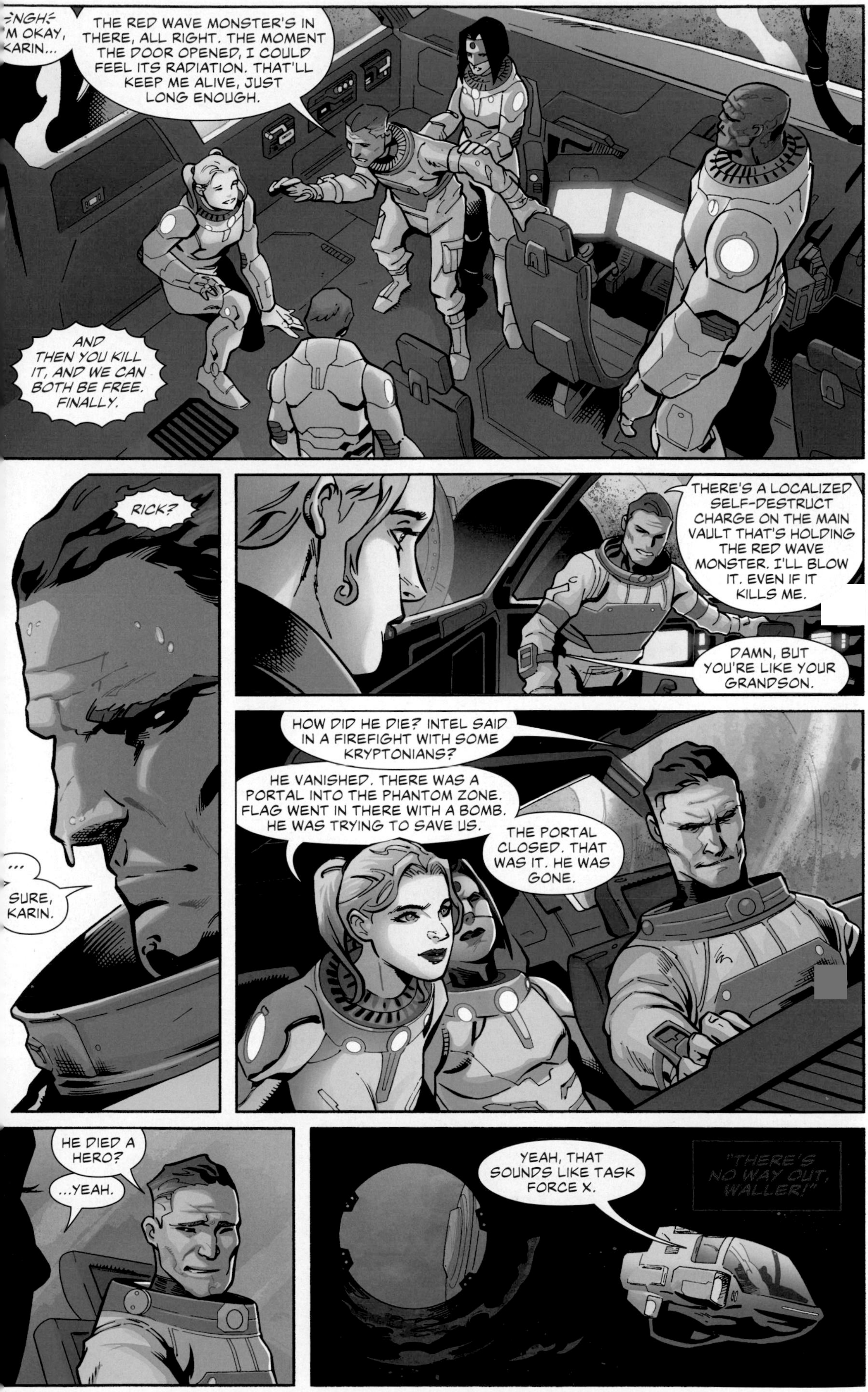
=NGH= 'M OKAY, KARIN...
THE RED WAVE MONSTER'S IN THERE, ALL RIGHT. THE MOMENT THE DOOR OPENED, I COULD FEEL ITS RADIATION. THAT'LL KEEP ME ALIVE, JUST LONG ENOUGH.
AND THEN YOU KILL IT, AND WE CAN BOTH BE FREE. FINALLY.
RICK?
...
SURE, KARIN.
THERE'S A LOCALIZED SELF-DESTRUCT CHARGE ON THE MAIN VAULT THAT'S HOLDING THE RED WAVE MONSTER. I'LL BLOW IT. EVEN IF IT KILLS ME.
DAMN, BUT YOU'RE LIKE YOUR GRANDSON.
HOW DID HE DIE? INTEL SAID IN A FIREFIGHT WITH SOME KRYPTONIANS?
HE VANISHED. THERE WAS A PORTAL INTO THE PHANTOM ZONE. FLAG WENT IN THERE WITH A BOMB. HE WAS TRYING TO SAVE US.
THE PORTAL CLOSED. THAT WAS IT. HE WAS GONE.
HE DIED A HERO?
...YEAH.
YEAH, THAT SOUNDS LIKE TASK FORCE X.
"THERE'S NO WAY OUT, WALLER!"

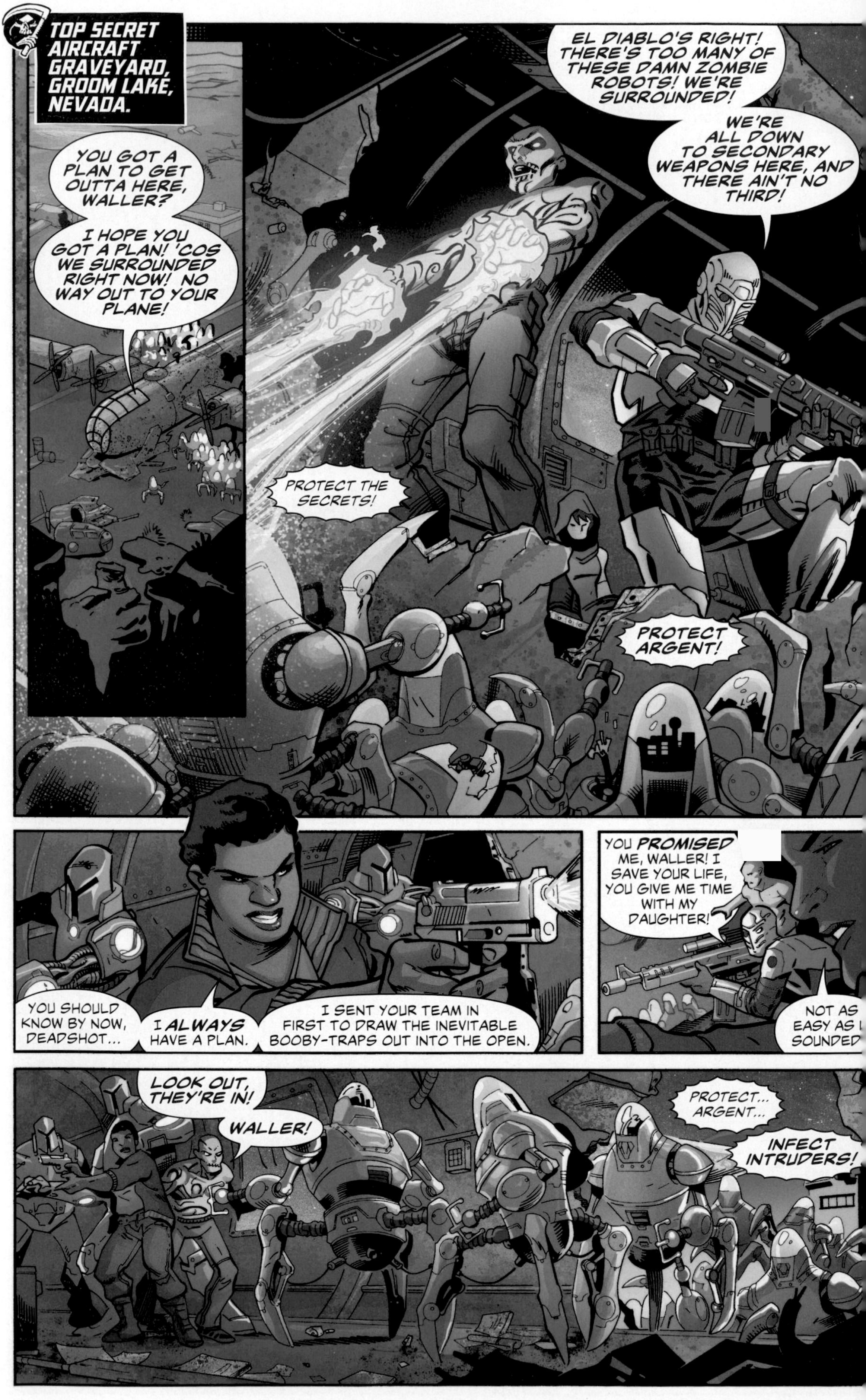
TOP SECRET AIRCRAFT GRAVEYARD, GROOM LAKE, NEVADA.
EL DIABLO'S RIGHT! THERE'S TOO MANY OF THESE DAMN ZOMBIE ROBOTS! WE'RE SURROUNDED!
WE'RE ALL DOWN TO SECONDARY WEAPONS HERE, AND THERE AIN'T NO THIRD!
YOU GOT A PLAN TO GET OUTTA HERE, WALLER?
I HOPE YOU GOT A PLAN! 'COS WE SURROUNDED RIGHT NOW! NO WAY OUT TO YOUR PLANE!
PROTECT THE SECRETS!
PROTECT ARGENT!
YOU SHOULD KNOW BY NOW, DEADSHOT...
I ALWAYS HAVE A PLAN.
I SENT YOUR TEAM IN FIRST TO DRAW THE INEVITABLE BOOBY-TRAPS OUT INTO THE OPEN.
YOU PROMISED ME, WALLER! I SAVE YOUR LIFE, YOU GIVE ME TIME WITH MY DAUGHTER!
NOT AS EASY AS I SOUNDED
LOOK OUT, THEY'RE IN!
WALLER!
PROTECT... ARGENT...
INFECT INTRUDERS!

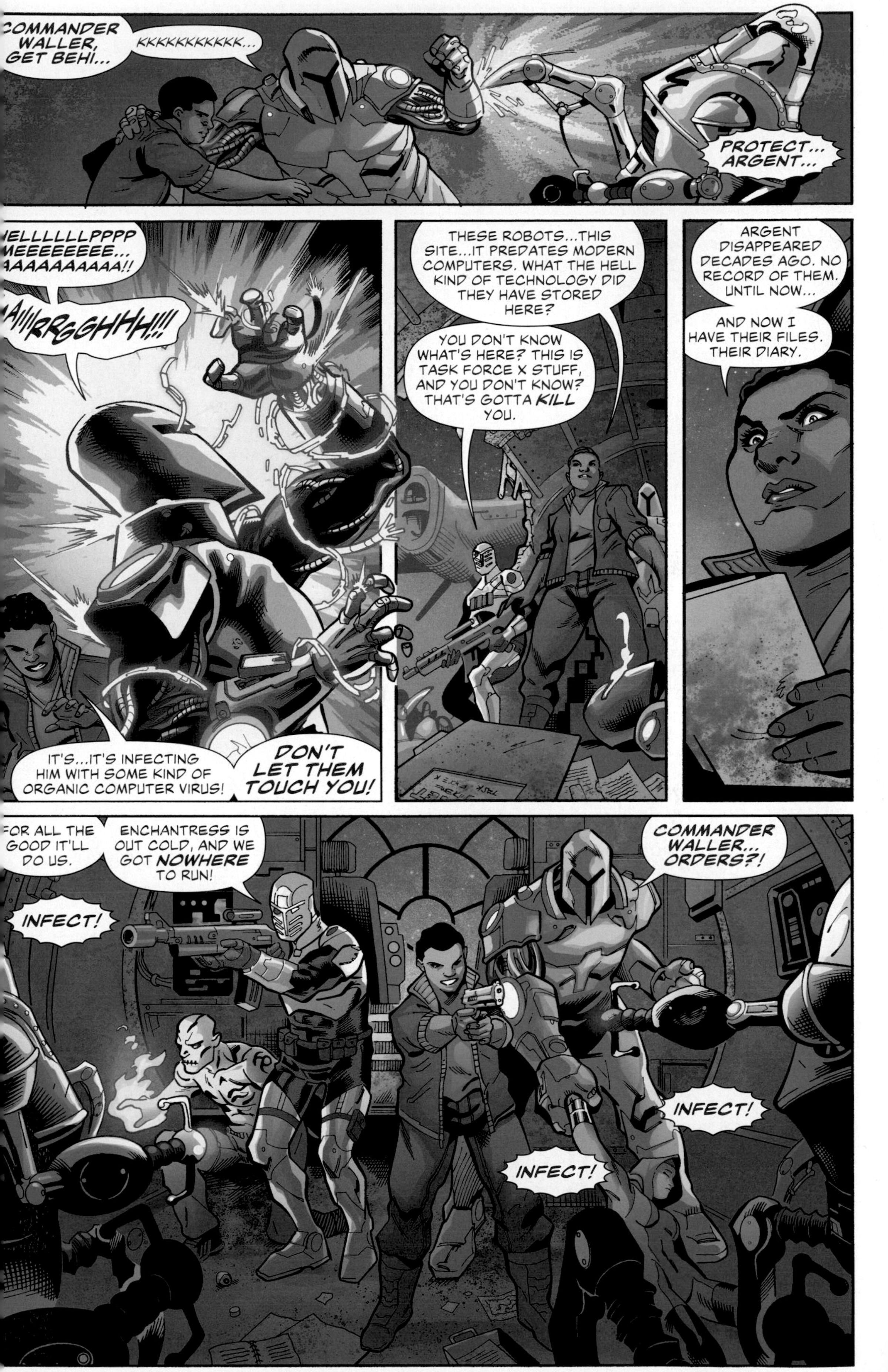

COMMANDER WALLER, GET BEHI...
KKKKKKKKKKK...
PROTECT... ARGENT...
HELLLLLLPPPP MEEEEEEEE... AAAAAAAAAA!!
AAIIIRRGGHHH!!!
IT'S...IT'S INFECTING HIM WITH SOME KIND OF ORGANIC COMPUTER VIRUS!
DON'T LET THEM TOUCH YOU!
THESE ROBOTS...THIS SITE...IT PREDATES MODERN COMPUTERS. WHAT THE HELL KIND OF TECHNOLOGY DID THEY HAVE STORED HERE?
YOU DON'T KNOW WHAT'S HERE? THIS IS TASK FORCE X STUFF, AND YOU DON'T KNOW? THAT'S GOTTA KILL YOU.
ARGENT DISAPPEARED DECADES AGO. NO RECORD OF THEM. UNTIL NOW...
AND NOW I HAVE THEIR FILES. THEIR DIARY.
FOR ALL THE GOOD IT'LL DO US.
ENCHANTRESS IS OUT COLD, AND WE GOT NOWHERE TO RUN!
COMMANDER WALLER... ORDERS?!
INFECT!
INFECT!
INFECT!

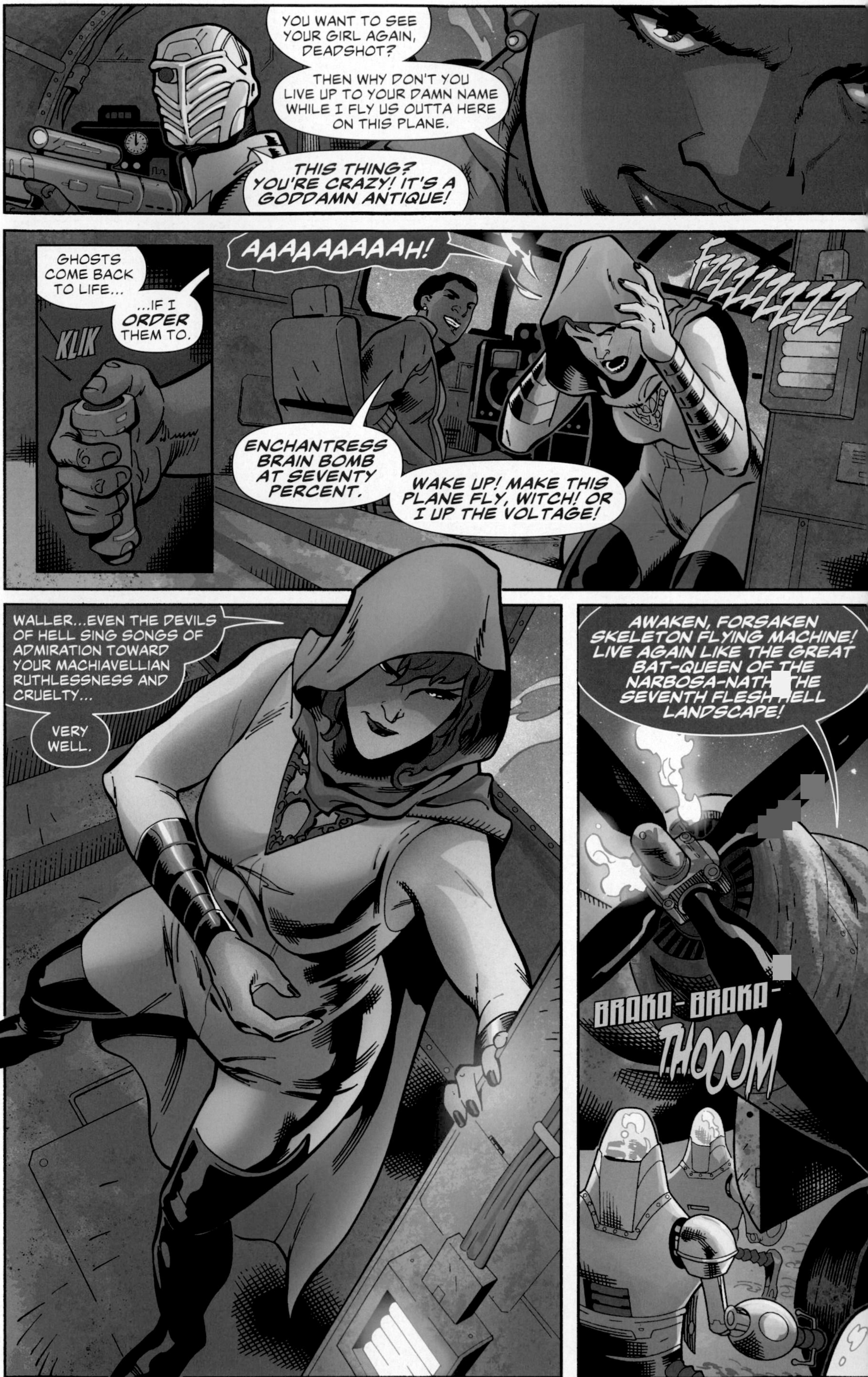
YOU WANT TO SEE YOUR GIRL AGAIN, DEADSHOT?
THEN WHY DON'T YOU LIVE UP TO YOUR DAMN NAME WHILE I FLY US OUTTA HERE ON THIS PLANE.
THIS THING? YOU'RE CRAZY! IT'S A GODDAMN ANTIQUE!
GHOSTS COME BACK TO LIFE...
...IF I ORDER THEM TO.
KLIK
AAAAAAAAAH!
FZZZZZZZZZ
ENCHANTRESS BRAIN BOMB AT SEVENTY PERCENT.
WAKE UP! MAKE THIS PLANE FLY, WITCH! OR I UP THE VOLTAGE!
WALLER...EVEN THE DEVILS OF HELL SING SONGS OF ADMIRATION TOWARD YOUR MACHIAVELLIAN RUTHLESSNESS AND CRUELTY...
VERY WELL.
AWAKEN, FORSAKEN SKELETON FLYING MACHINE! LIVE AGAIN LIKE THE GREAT BAT-QUEEN OF THE NARBOSA-NATH THE SEVENTH FLESH HELL LANDSCAPE!
BRAKA-BRAKA-
THOOOM

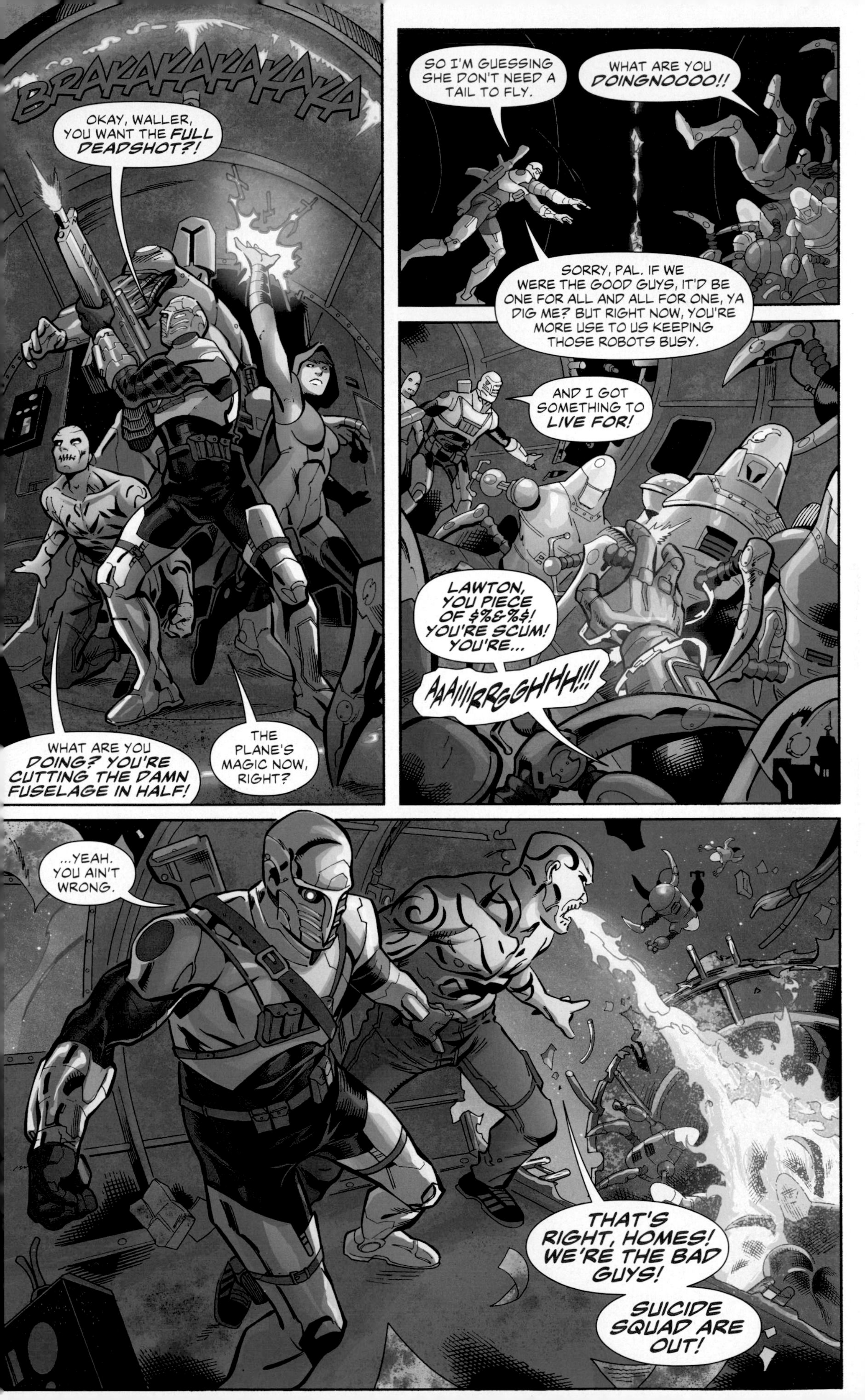
BRAKAKAKAKAKAKA
OKAY, WALLER, YOU WANT THE FULL DEADSHOT?!
WHAT ARE YOU DOING? YOU'RE CUTTING THE DAMN FUSELAGE IN HALF!
THE PLANE'S MAGIC NOW, RIGHT?
SO I'M GUESSING SHE DON'T NEED A TAIL TO FLY.
WHAT ARE YOU DOINGNOOOO!!
SORRY, PAL. IF WE WERE THE GOOD GUYS, IT'D BE ONE FOR ALL AND ALL FOR ONE, YA DIG ME? BUT RIGHT NOW, YOU'RE MORE USE TO US KEEPING THOSE ROBOTS BUSY.
AND I GOT SOMETHING TO LIVE FOR!
LAWTON, YOU PIECE OF $%&%$! YOU'RE SCUM! YOU'RE...
AAAIIIRRGGHHH!!!
...YEAH. YOU AIN'T WRONG.
THAT'S RIGHT, HOMES! WE'RE THE BAD GUYS!
SUICIDE SQUAD ARE OUT!

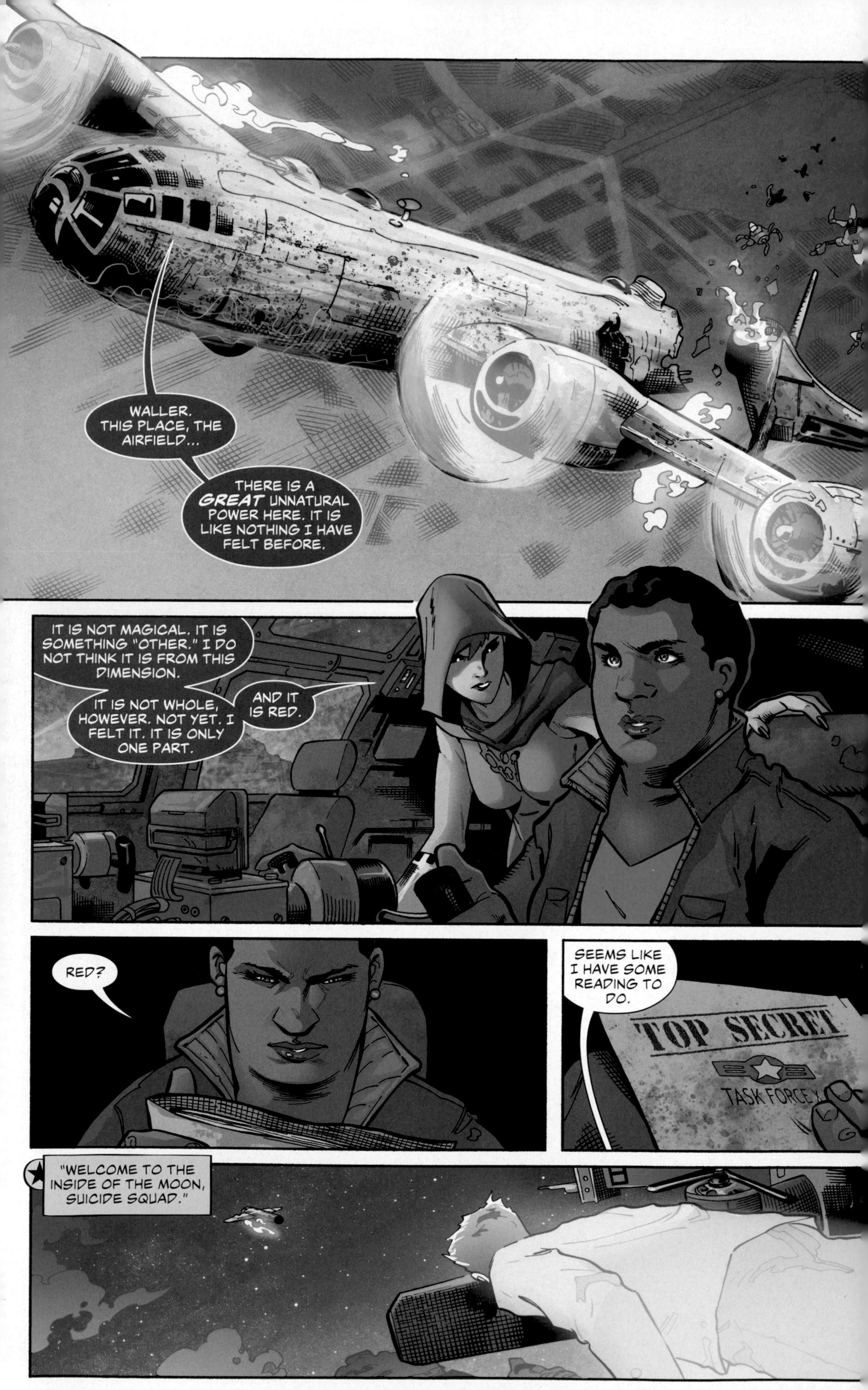
WALLER. THIS PLACE, THE AIRFIELD...
THERE IS A GREAT UNNATURAL POWER HERE. IT IS LIKE NOTHING I HAVE FELT BEFORE.
IT IS NOT MAGICAL. IT IS SOMETHING "OTHER." I DO NOT THINK IT IS FROM THIS DIMENSION.
IT IS NOT WHOLE, HOWEVER. NOT YET. I FELT IT. IT IS ONLY ONE PART.
AND IT IS RED.
RED?
SEEMS LIKE I HAVE SOME READING TO DO.
TOP SECRET
TASK FORCE X
"WELCOME TO THE INSIDE OF THE MOON, SUICIDE SQUAD."

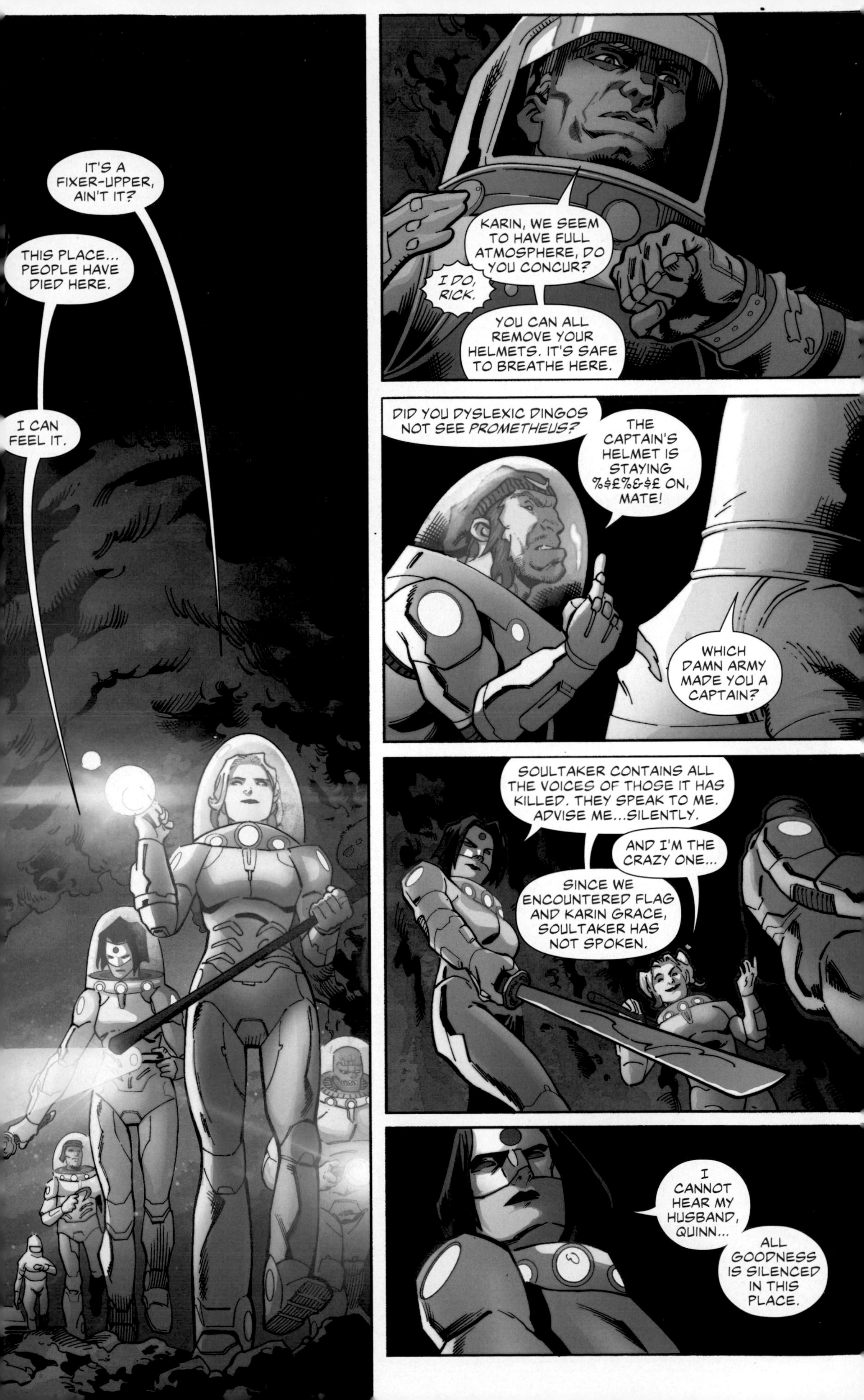
IT'S A FIXER-UPPER, AIN'T IT?
THIS PLACE... PEOPLE HAVE DIED HERE.
I CAN FEEL IT.
KARIN, WE SEEM TO HAVE FULL ATMOSPHERE, DO YOU CONCUR?
I DO, RICK.
YOU CAN ALL REMOVE YOUR HELMETS. IT'S SAFE TO BREATHE HERE.
DID YOU DYSLEXIC DINGOS NOT SEE *PROMETHEUS*?
THE CAPTAIN'S HELMET IS STAYING %$£%&$£ ON, MATE!
WHICH DAMN ARMY MADE YOU A CAPTAIN?
SOULTAKER CONTAINS ALL THE VOICES OF THOSE IT HAS KILLED. THEY SPEAK TO ME. ADVISE ME...SILENTLY.
AND I'M THE CRAZY ONE...
SINCE WE ENCOUNTERED FLAG AND KARIN GRACE, SOULTAKER HAS NOT SPOKEN.
I CANNOT HEAR MY HUSBAND, QUINN...
ALL GOODNESS IS SILENCED IN THIS PLACE.

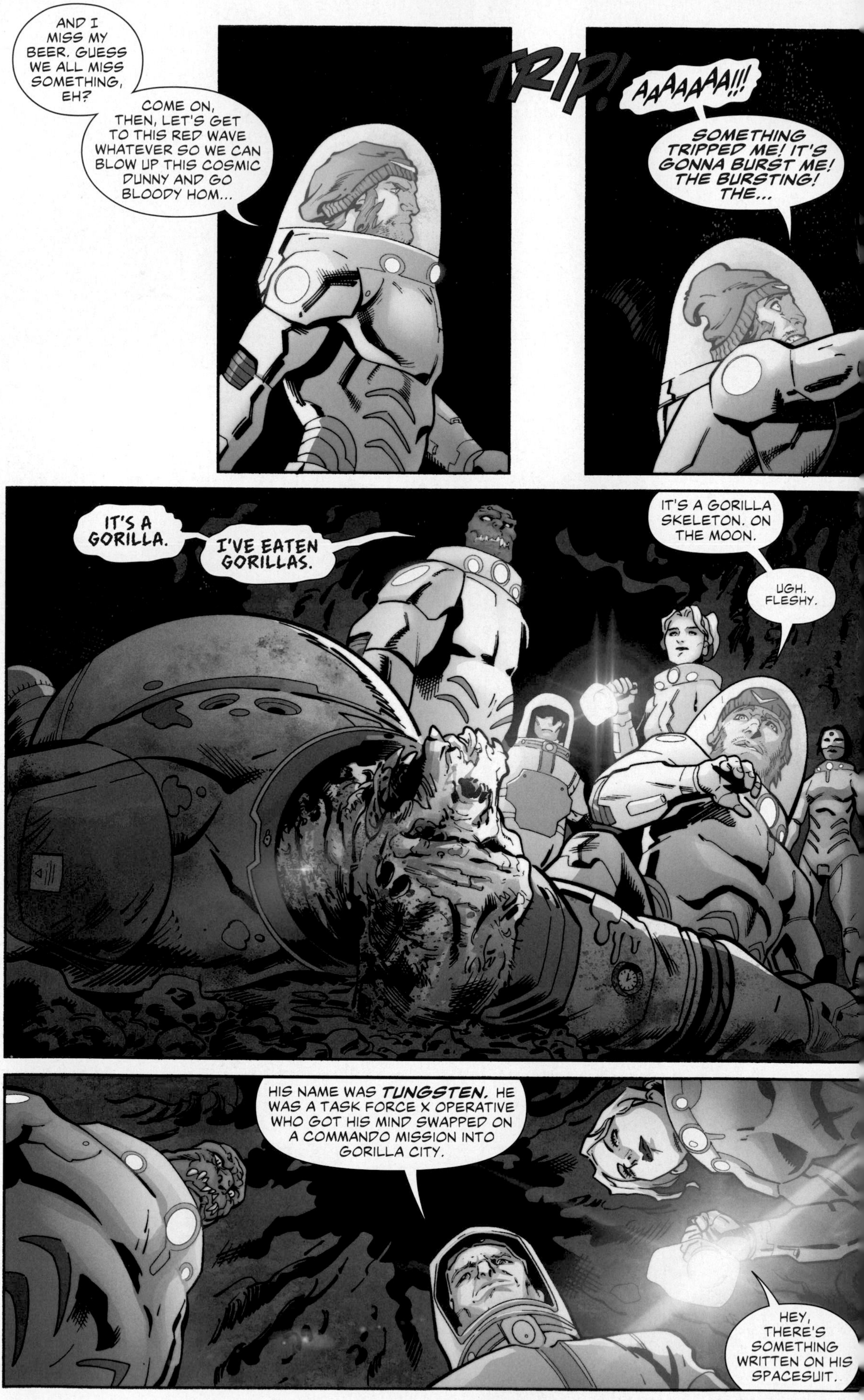
AND I MISS MY BEER. GUESS WE ALL MISS SOMETHING, EH?
COME ON, THEN, LET'S GET TO THIS RED WAVE WHATEVER SO WE CAN BLOW UP THIS COSMIC DUNNY AND GO BLOODY HOM...
TRIP!
AAAAAAA!!!
SOMETHING TRIPPED ME! IT'S GONNA BURST ME! THE BURSTING! THE...
IT'S A GORILLA.
I'VE EATEN GORILLAS.
IT'S A GORILLA SKELETON. ON THE MOON.
UGH. FLESHY.
HIS NAME WAS TUNGSTEN. HE WAS A TASK FORCE X OPERATIVE WHO GOT HIS MIND SWAPPED ON A COMMANDO MISSION INTO GORILLA CITY.
HEY, THERE'S SOMETHING WRITTEN ON HIS SPACESUIT.

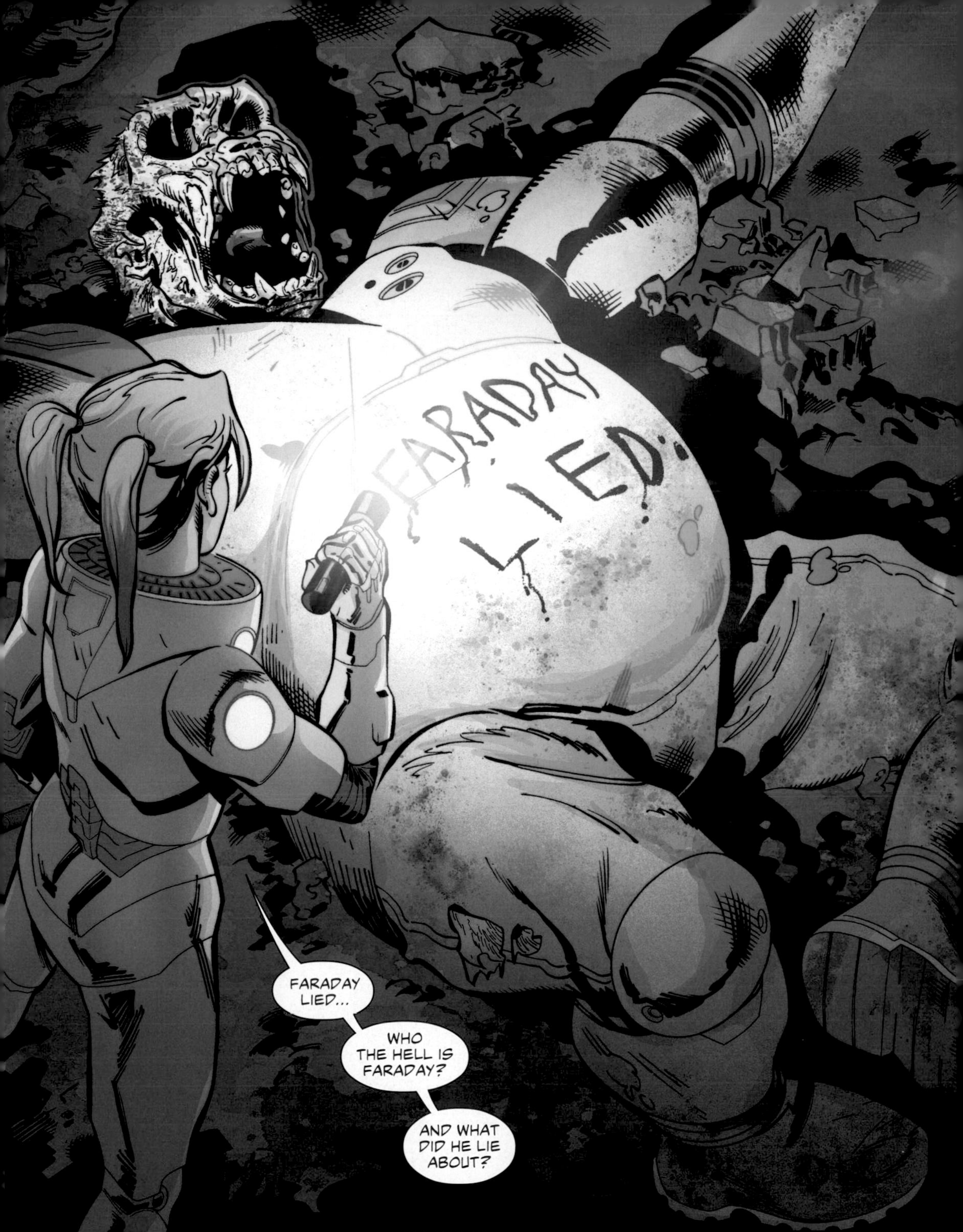
FARADAY LIED.
FARADAY LIED...
WHO THE HELL IS FARADAY?
AND WHAT DID HE LIE ABOUT?

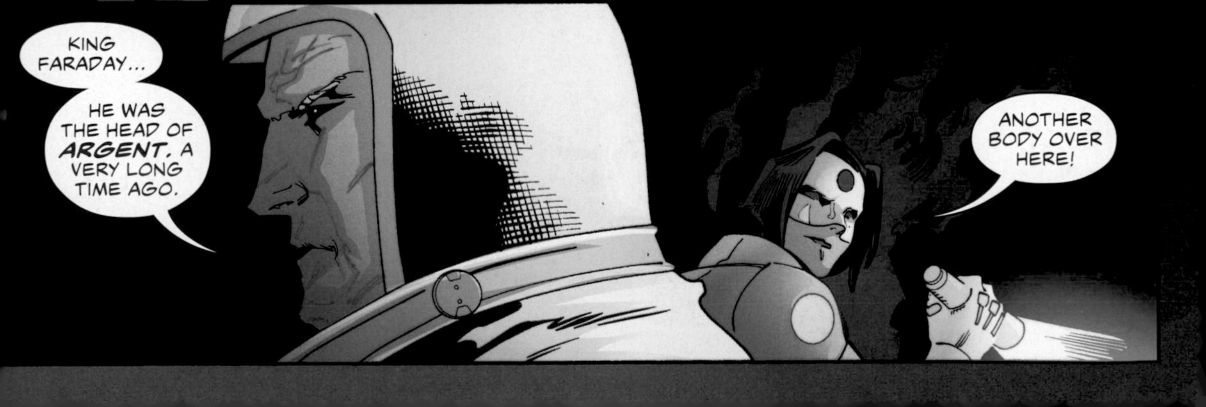
KING FARADAY...
HE WAS THE HEAD OF ARGENT. A VERY LONG TIME AGO.
ANOTHER BODY OVER HERE!

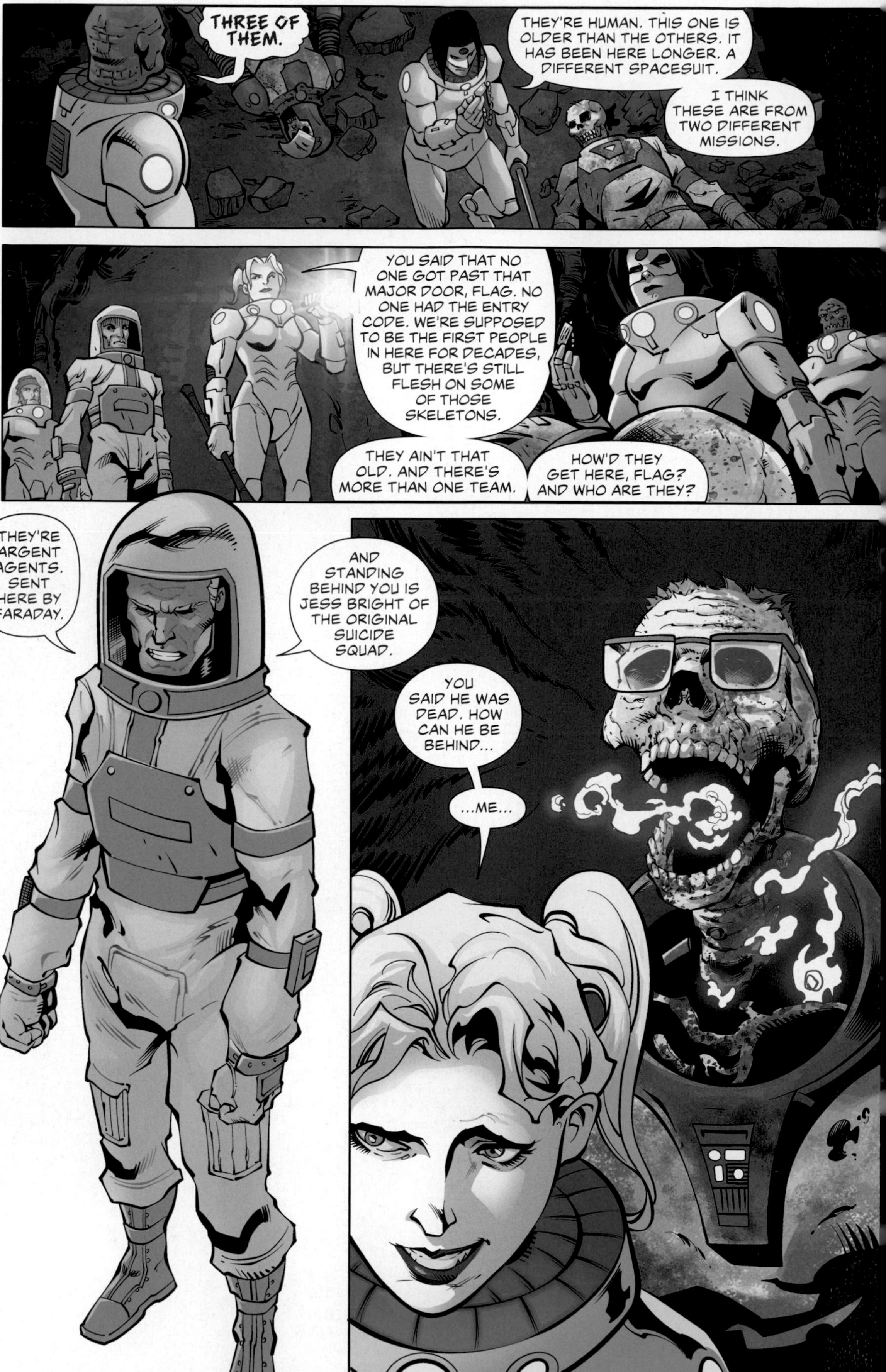
THREE OF THEM.
THEY'RE HUMAN. THIS ONE IS OLDER THAN THE OTHERS. IT HAS BEEN HERE LONGER. A DIFFERENT SPACESUIT.
I THINK THESE ARE FROM TWO DIFFERENT MISSIONS.
YOU SAID THAT NO ONE GOT PAST THAT MAJOR DOOR, FLAG. NO ONE HAD THE ENTRY CODE. WE'RE SUPPOSED TO BE THE FIRST PEOPLE IN HERE FOR DECADES, BUT THERE'S STILL FLESH ON SOME OF THOSE SKELETONS.
THEY AIN'T THAT OLD. AND THERE'S MORE THAN ONE TEAM.
HOW'D THEY GET HERE, FLAG? AND WHO ARE THEY?
THEY'RE ARGENT AGENTS. SENT HERE BY FARADAY.
AND STANDING BEHIND YOU IS JESS BRIGHT OF THE ORIGINAL SUICIDE SQUAD.
YOU SAID HE WAS DEAD. HOW CAN HE BE BEHIND...
...ME...

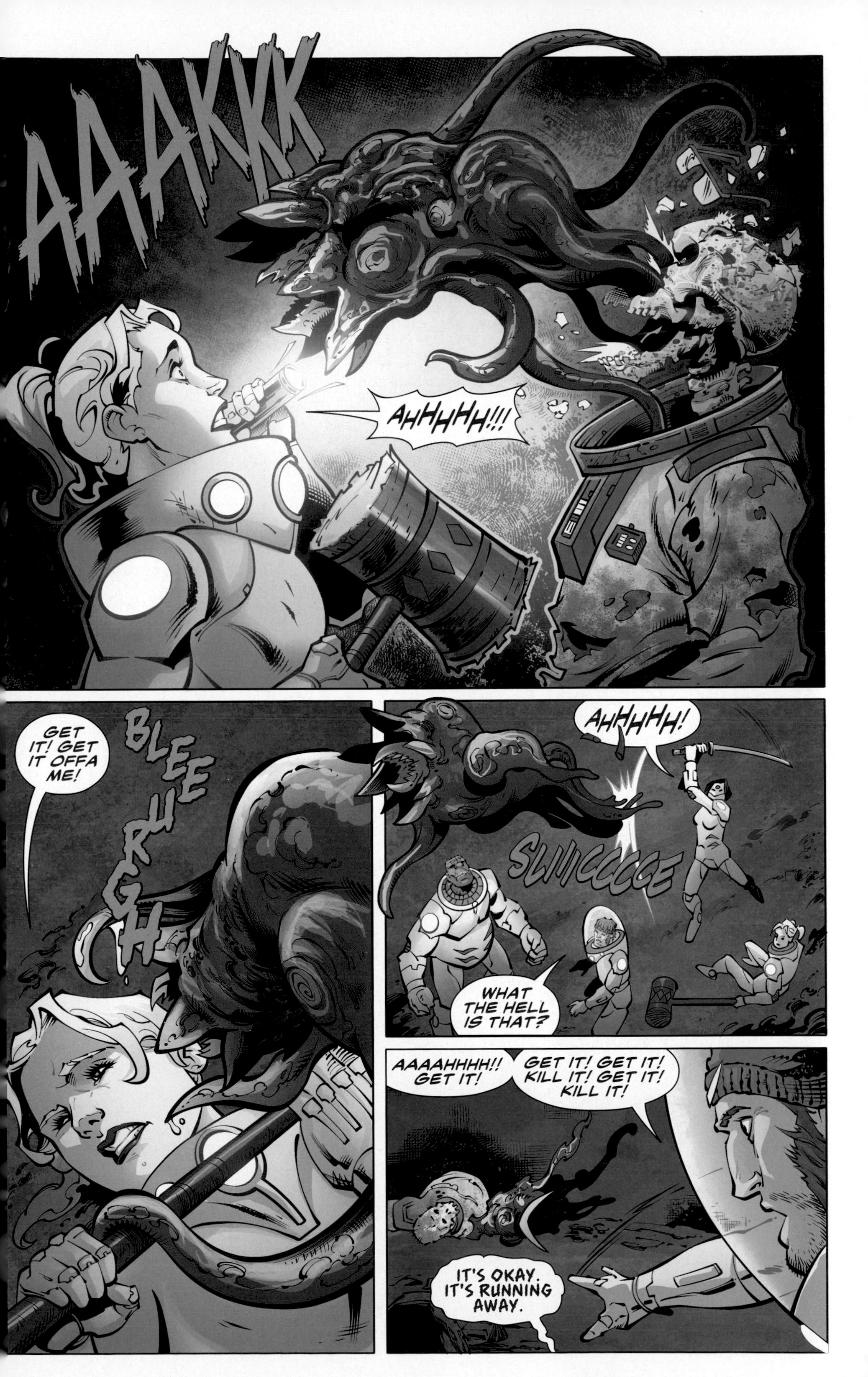
AAAKKK
AHHHHH!!!
GET IT! GET IT OFFA ME!
BLEEERRUGH
AHHHHH!
SLIICCCCCE
WHAT THE HELL IS THAT?
AAAAHHHH!! GET IT!
GET IT! GET IT! KILL IT! GET IT! KILL IT!
IT'S OKAY. IT'S RUNNING AWAY.

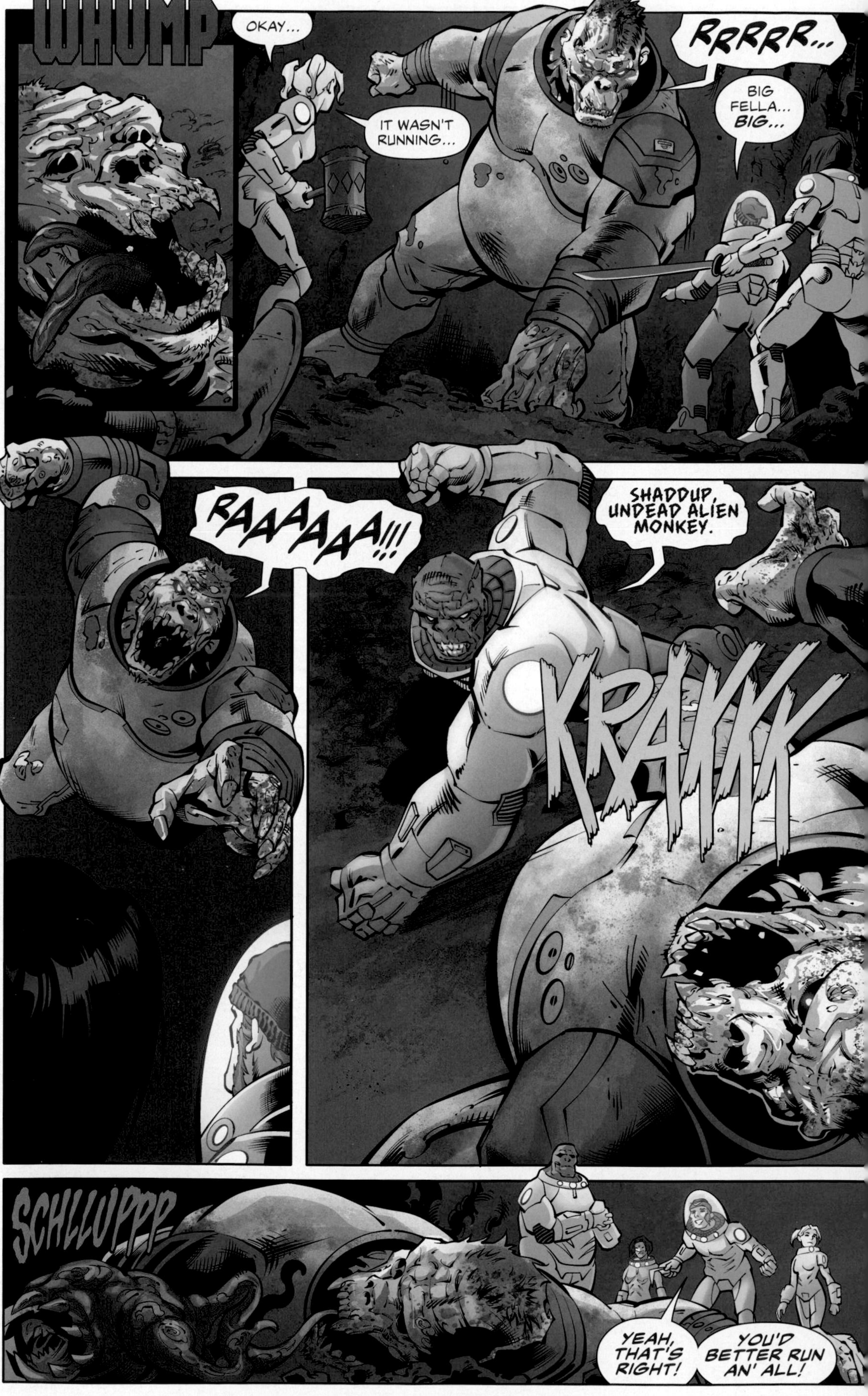
WHUMP
OKAY...
IT WASN'T RUNNING...
RRRRR...
BIG FELLA... BIG...
RAAAAAA!!!
SHADDUP, UNDEAD ALIEN MONKEY.
KRAKKK
SCHLLUPPP
YEAH, THAT'S RIGHT!
YOU'D BETTER RUN AN' ALL!

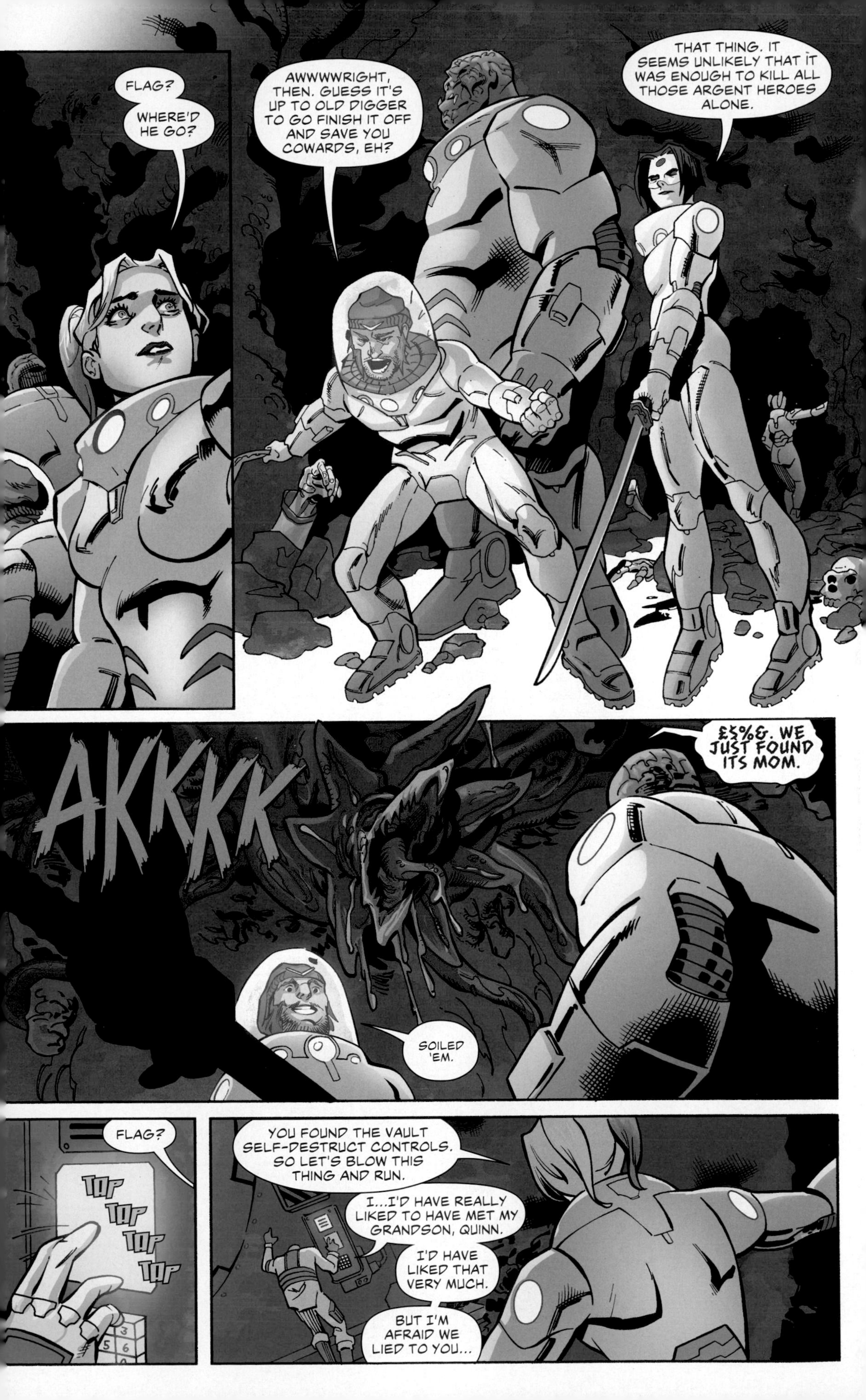
FLAG?
WHERE'D HE GO?
AWWWWRIGHT, THEN. GUESS IT'S UP TO OLD DIGGER TO GO FINISH IT OFF AND SAVE YOU COWARDS, EH?
THAT THING. IT SEEMS UNLIKELY THAT IT WAS ENOUGH TO KILL ALL THOSE ARGENT HEROES ALONE.
AKKKK
£$%&. WE JUST FOUND ITS MOM.
SOILED 'EM.
FLAG?
TAP TAP TAP TAP
YOU FOUND THE VAULT SELF-DESTRUCT CONTROLS. SO LET'S BLOW THIS THING AND RUN.
I...I'D HAVE REALLY LIKED TO HAVE MET MY GRANDSON, QUINN.
I'D HAVE LIKED THAT VERY MUCH.
BUT I'M AFRAID WE LIED TO YOU...

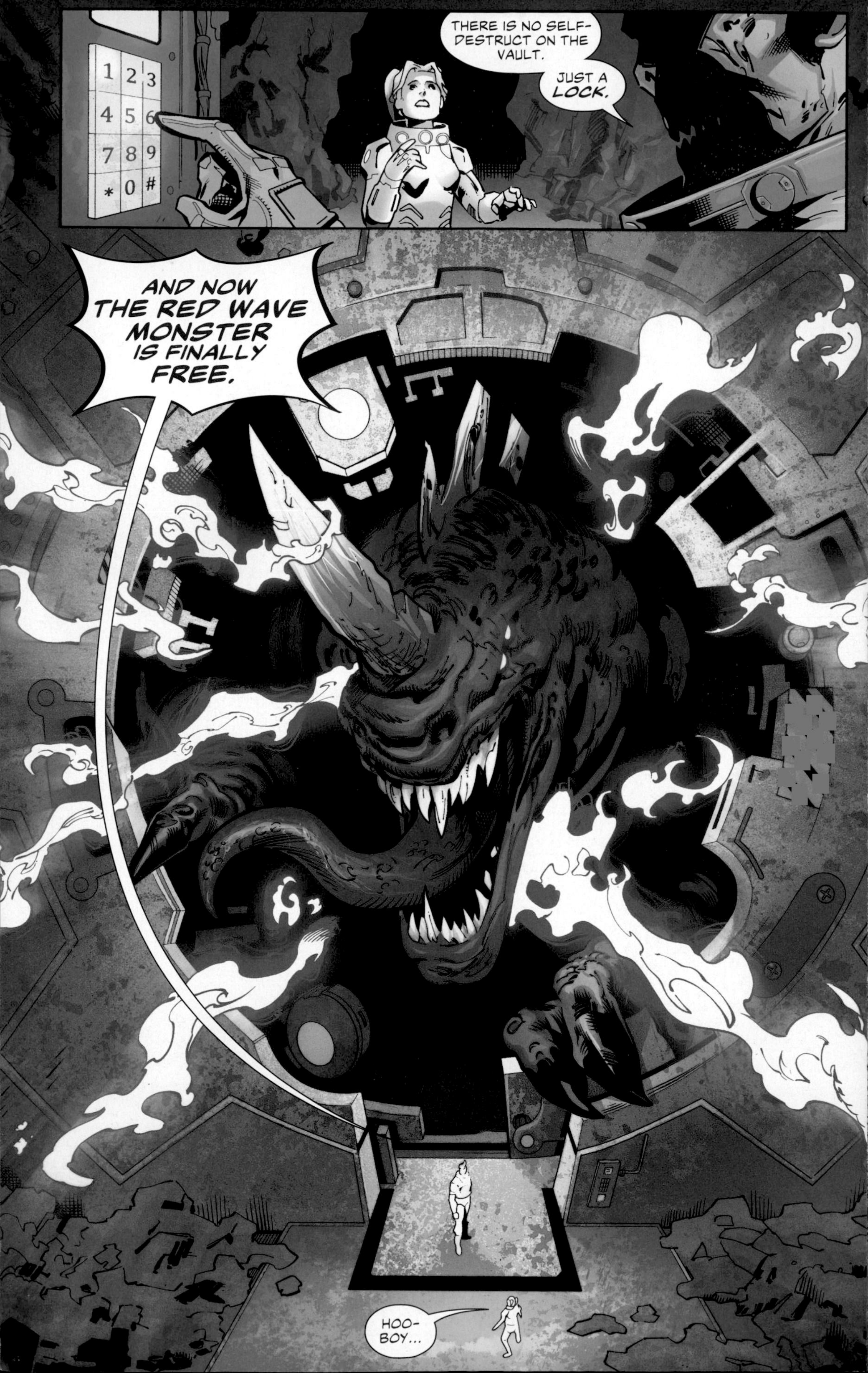
THERE IS NO SELF-DESTRUCT ON THE VAULT.
JUST A LOCK.
AND NOW THE RED WAVE MONSTER IS FINALLY FREE.
HOO-BOY...

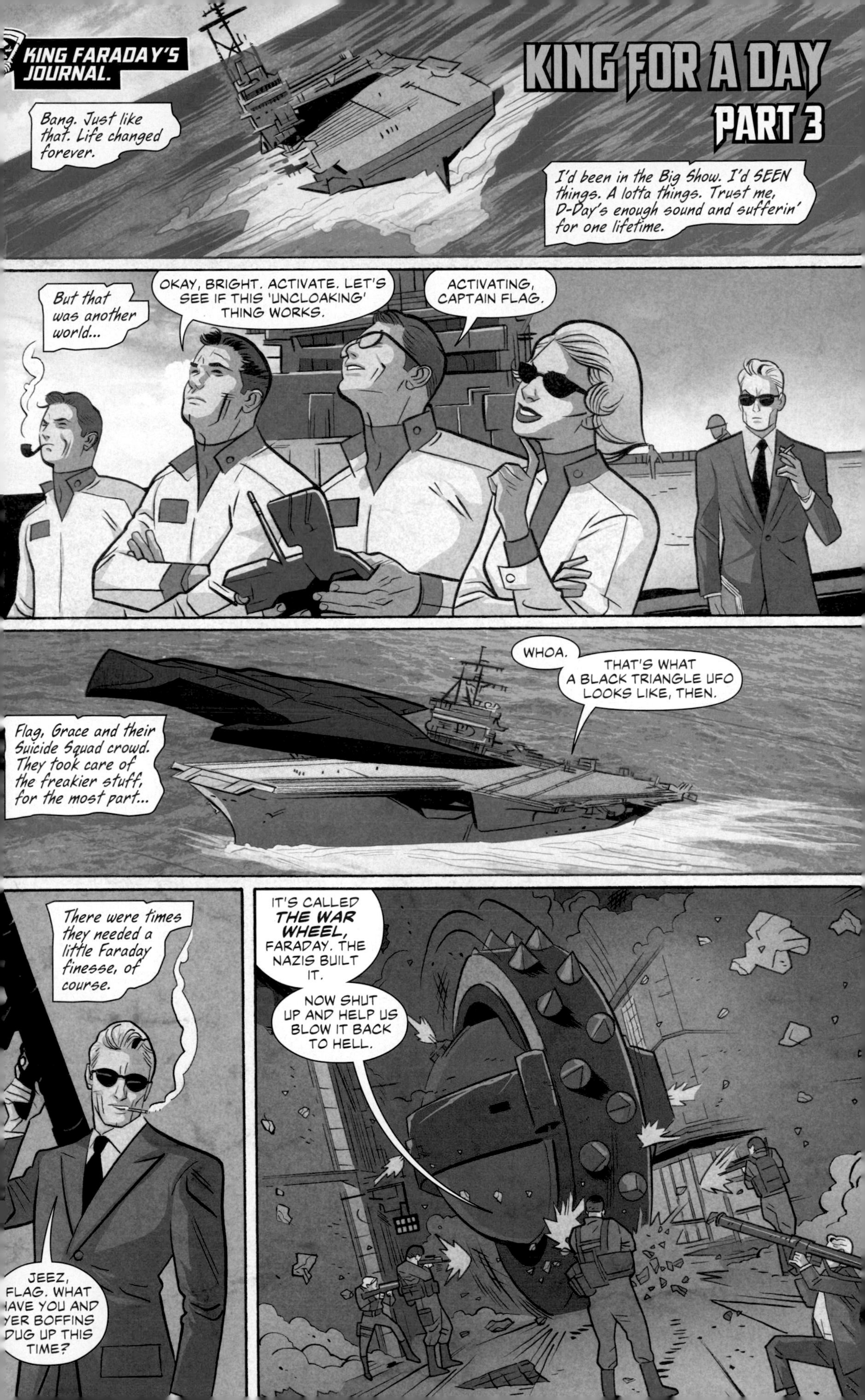
KING FARADAY'S JOURNAL.
KING FOR A DAY PART 3
Bang. Just like that. Life changed forever.
I'd been in the Big Show. I'd SEEN things. A lotta things. Trust me, D-Day's enough sound and sufferin' for one lifetime.
But that was another world...
OKAY, BRIGHT. ACTIVATE. LET'S SEE IF THIS 'UNCLOAKING' THING WORKS.
ACTIVATING, CAPTAIN FLAG.
Flag, Grace and their Suicide Squad crowd. They took care of the freakier stuff, for the most part...
WHOA.
THAT'S WHAT A BLACK TRIANGLE UFO LOOKS LIKE, THEN.
There were times they needed a little Faraday finesse, of course.
JEEZ, FLAG. WHAT HAVE YOU AND YER BOFFINS DUG UP THIS TIME?
IT'S CALLED THE WAR WHEEL, FARADAY. THE NAZIS BUILT IT.
NOW SHUT UP AND HELP US BLOW IT BACK TO HELL.

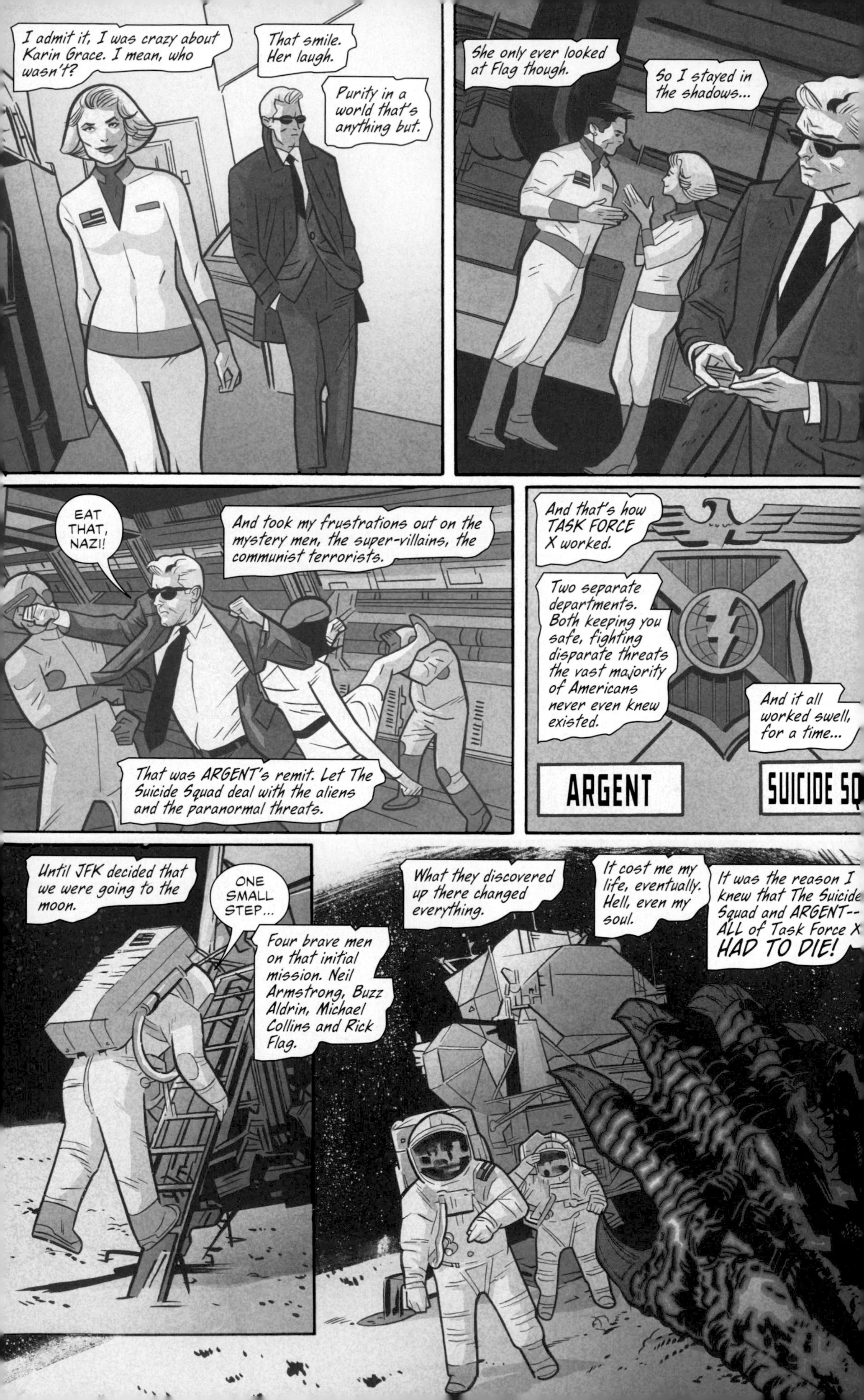
I admit it, I was crazy about Karin Grace. I mean, who wasn't?
That smile. Her laugh.
Purity in a world that's anything but.
She only ever looked at Flag though.
So I stayed in the shadows...
EAT THAT, NAZI!
And took my frustrations out on the mystery men, the super-villains, the communist terrorists.
That was ARGENT's remit. Let The Suicide Squad deal with the aliens and the paranormal threats.
And that's how TASK FORCE X worked.
Two separate departments. Both keeping you safe, fighting disparate threats the vast majority of Americans never even knew existed.
And it all worked swell, for a time...
ARGENT
SUICIDE SQ
Until JFK decided that we were going to the moon.
ONE SMALL STEP...
Four brave men on that initial mission. Neil Armstrong, Buzz Aldrin, Michael Collins and Rick Flag.
What they discovered up there changed everything.
It cost me my life, eventually. Hell, even my soul.
It was the reason I knew that The Suicide Squad and ARGENT-- ALL of Task Force X HAD TO DIE!

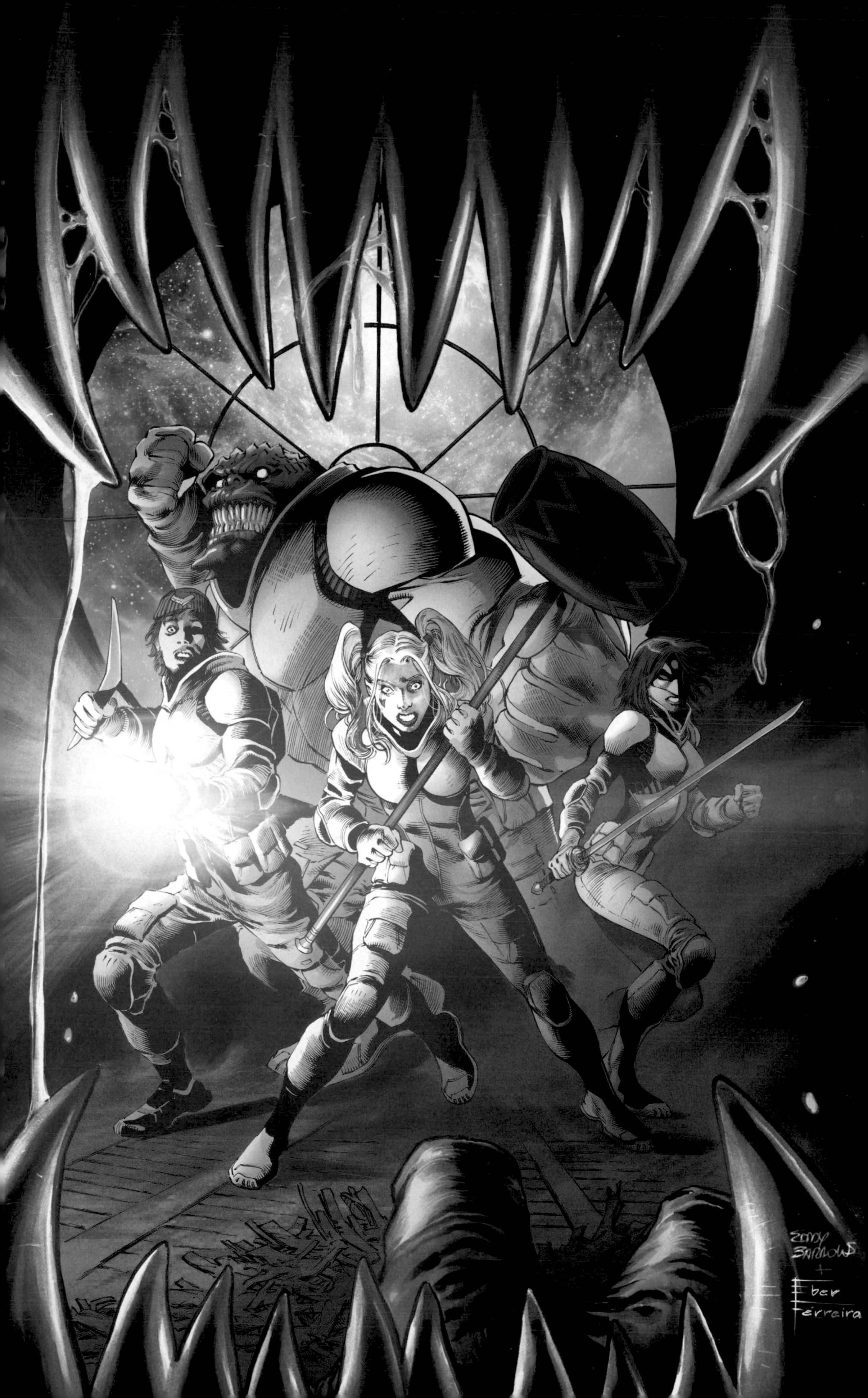
EDDY BARROWS
+
Eber
Ferreira

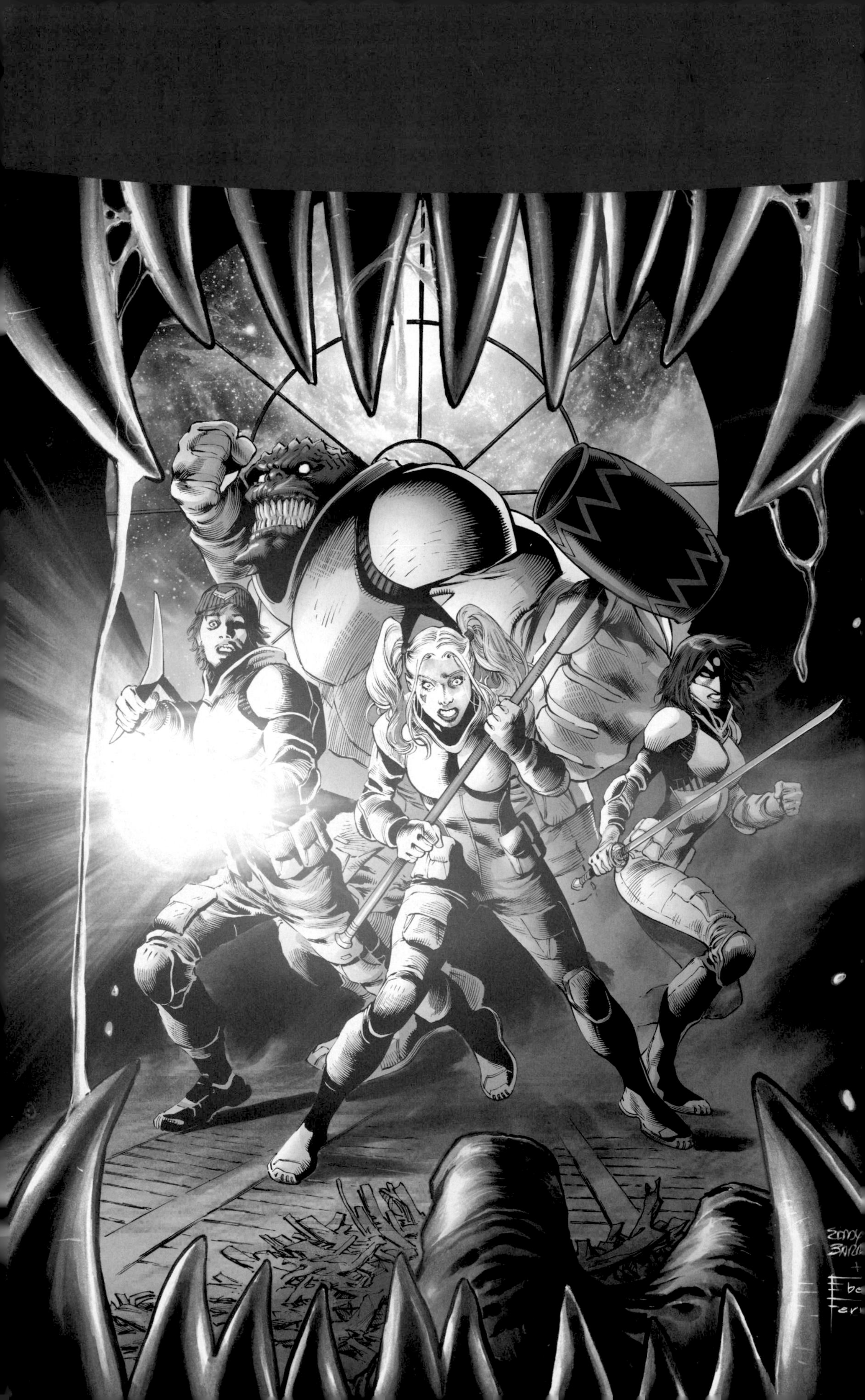

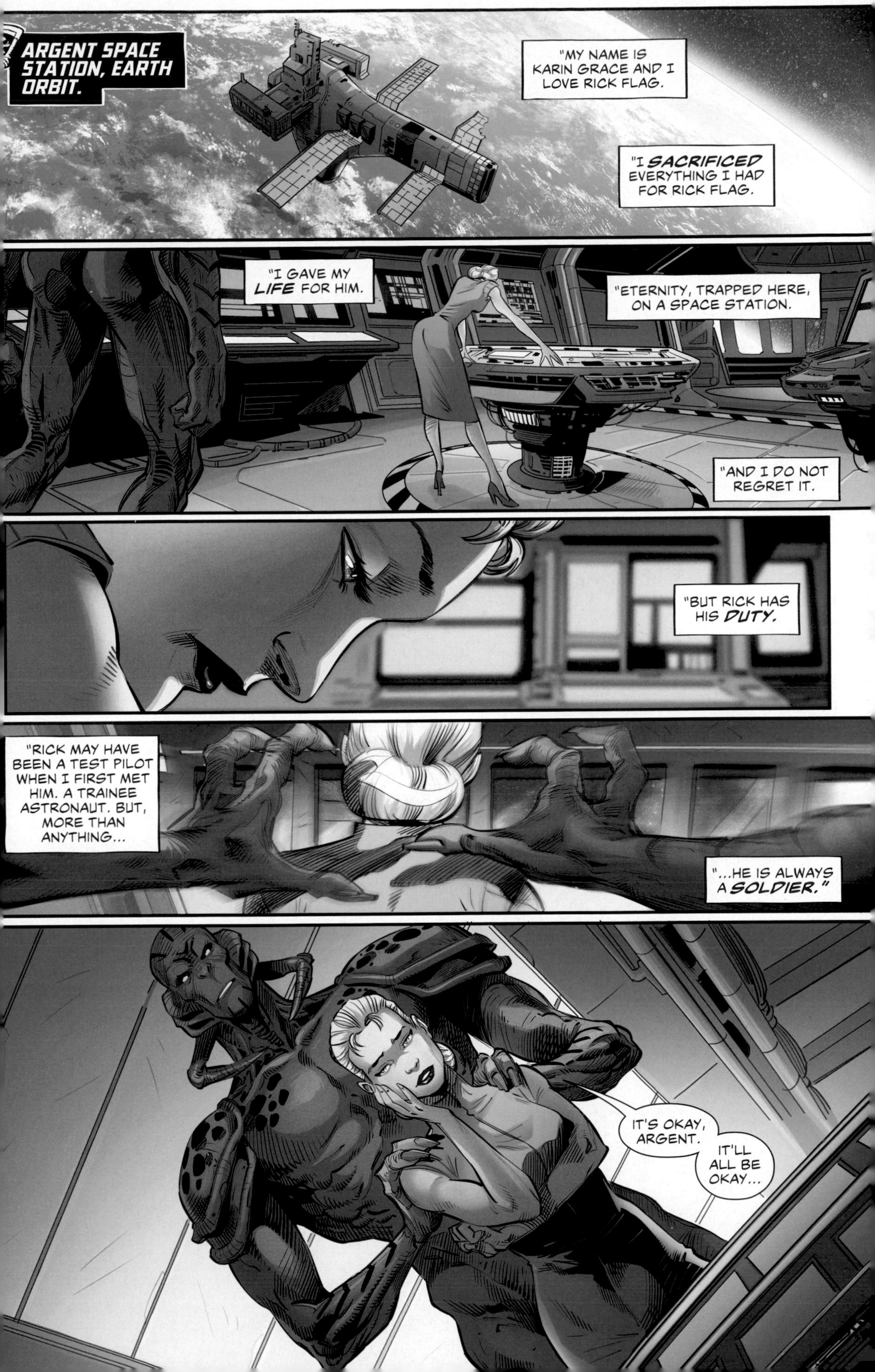
ARGENT SPACE STATION, EARTH ORBIT.
"MY NAME IS KARIN GRACE AND I LOVE RICK FLAG.
"I SACRIFICED EVERYTHING I HAD FOR RICK FLAG.
"I GAVE MY LIFE FOR HIM.
"ETERNITY, TRAPPED HERE, ON A SPACE STATION.
"AND I DO NOT REGRET IT.
"BUT RICK HAS HIS DUTY.
"RICK MAY HAVE BEEN A TEST PILOT WHEN I FIRST MET HIM. A TRAINEE ASTRONAUT. BUT, MORE THAN ANYTHING...
"...HE IS ALWAYS A SOLDIER."
IT'S OKAY, ARGENT.
IT'LL ALL BE OKAY...

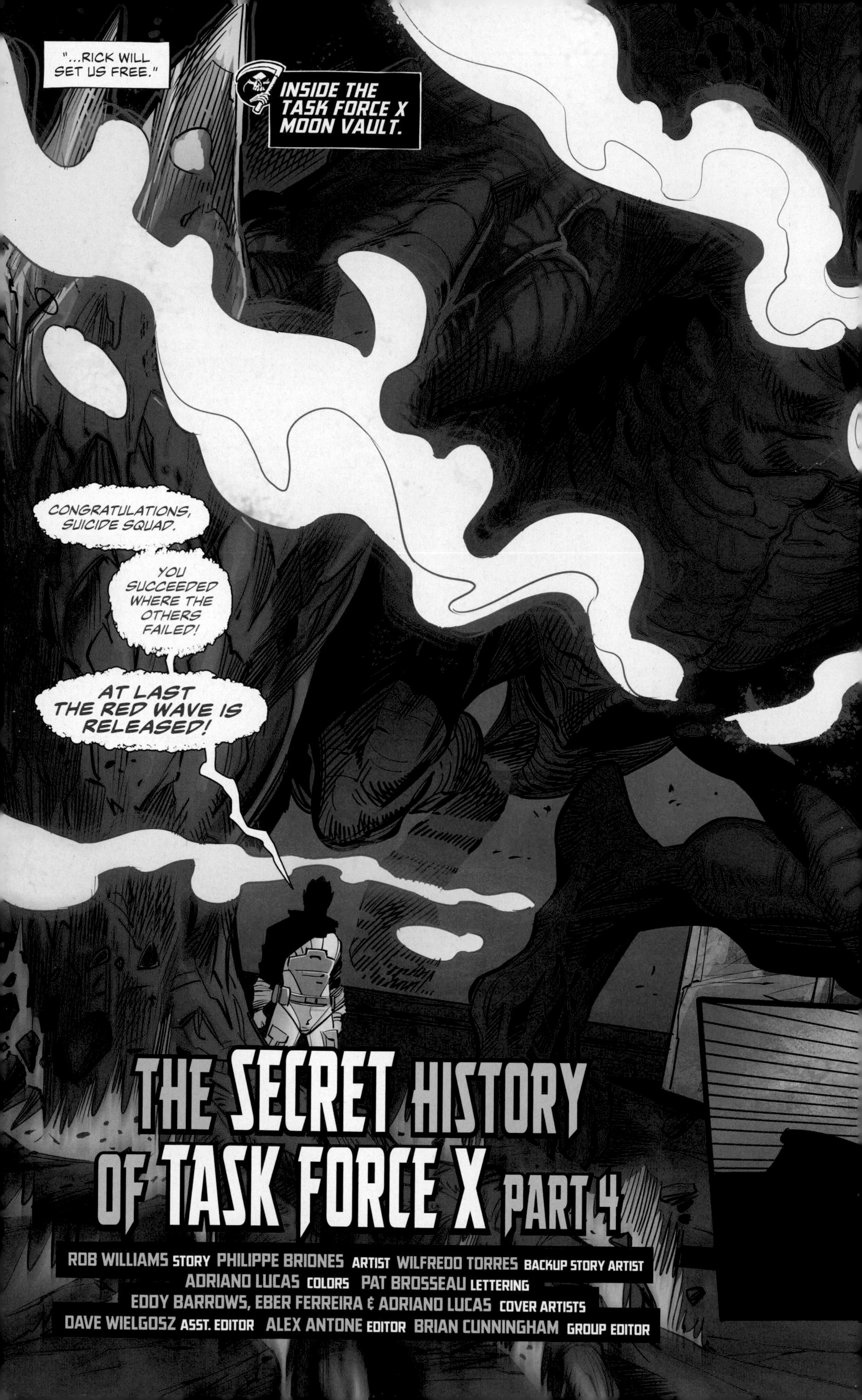
"...RICK WILL SET US FREE."
INSIDE THE TASK FORCE X MOON VAULT.
CONGRATULATIONS, SUICIDE SQUAD.
YOU SUCCEEDED WHERE THE OTHERS FAILED!
AT LAST THE RED WAVE IS RELEASED!
THE SECRET HISTORY OF TASK FORCE X PART 4
ROB WILLIAMS STORY PHILIPPE BRIONES ARTIST WILFREDO TORRES BACKUP STORY ARTIST
ADRIANO LUCAS COLORS PAT BROSSEAU LETTERING
EDDY BARROWS, EBER FERREIRA & ADRIANO LUCAS COVER ARTISTS
DAVE WIELGOSZ ASST. EDITOR ALEX ANTONE EDITOR BRIAN CUNNINGHAM GROUP EDITOR

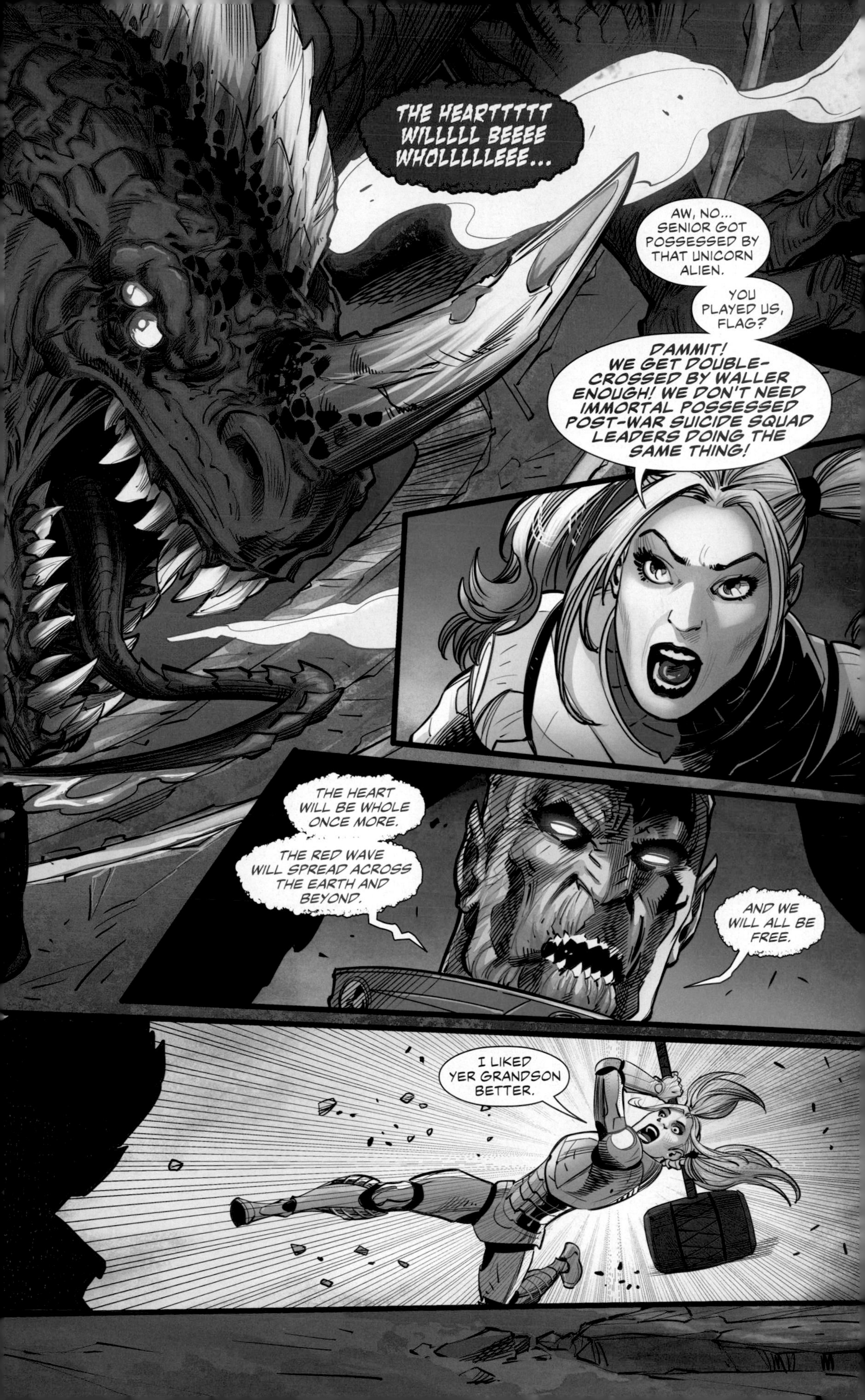
THE HEARTTTTT WILLLLL BEEEE WHOLLLLLEEE...
AW, NO... SENIOR GOT POSSESSED BY THAT UNICORN ALIEN.
YOU PLAYED US, FLAG?
DAMMIT! WE GET DOUBLE-CROSSED BY WALLER ENOUGH! WE DON'T NEED IMMORTAL POSSESSED POST-WAR SUICIDE SQUAD LEADERS DOING THE SAME THING!
THE HEART WILL BE WHOLE ONCE MORE.
THE RED WAVE WILL SPREAD ACROSS THE EARTH AND BEYOND.
AND WE WILL ALL BE FREE.
I LIKED YER GRANDSON BETTER.

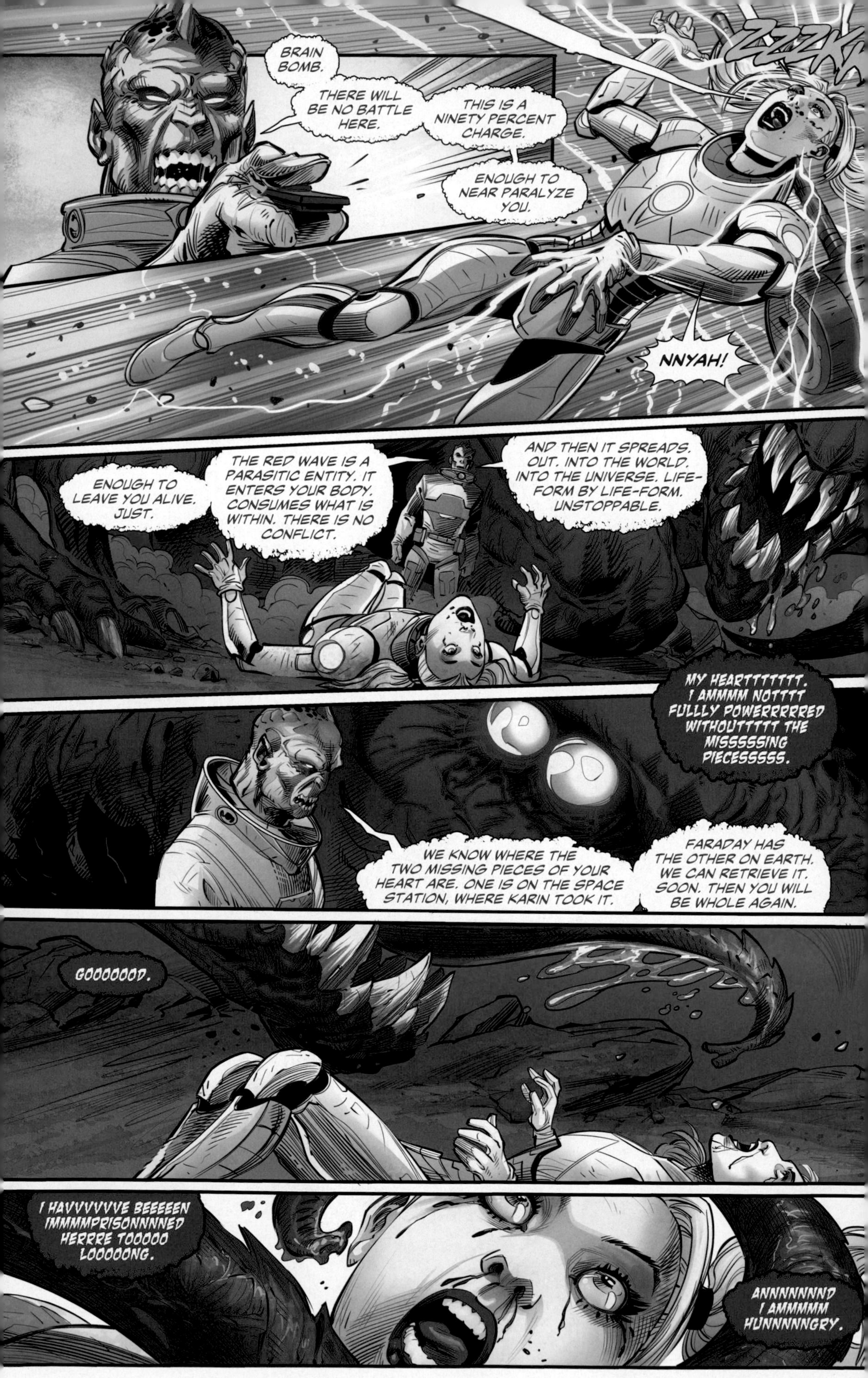
ZZZK!
BRAIN BOMB.
THERE WILL BE NO BATTLE HERE.
THIS IS A NINETY PERCENT CHARGE.
ENOUGH TO NEAR PARALYZE YOU.
NNYAH!
ENOUGH TO LEAVE YOU ALIVE. JUST.
THE RED WAVE IS A PARASITIC ENTITY. IT ENTERS YOUR BODY. CONSUMES WHAT IS WITHIN. THERE IS NO CONFLICT.
AND THEN IT SPREADS. OUT. INTO THE WORLD. INTO THE UNIVERSE. LIFE-FORM BY LIFE-FORM. UNSTOPPABLE.
MY HEARTTTTTTT. I AMMMM NOTTTT FULLLY POWERRRRRED WITHOUTTTTT THE MISSSSSING PIECESSSSS.
WE KNOW WHERE THE TWO MISSING PIECES OF YOUR HEART ARE. ONE IS ON THE SPACE STATION, WHERE KARIN TOOK IT.
FARADAY HAS THE OTHER ON EARTH. WE CAN RETRIEVE IT. SOON. THEN YOU WILL BE WHOLE AGAIN.
GOOOOOOD.
I HAVVVVVVE BEEEEEN IMMMMPRISONNNNED HERRRE TOOOOO LOOOOONG.
ANNNNNNND I AMMMMM HUNNNNNGRY.

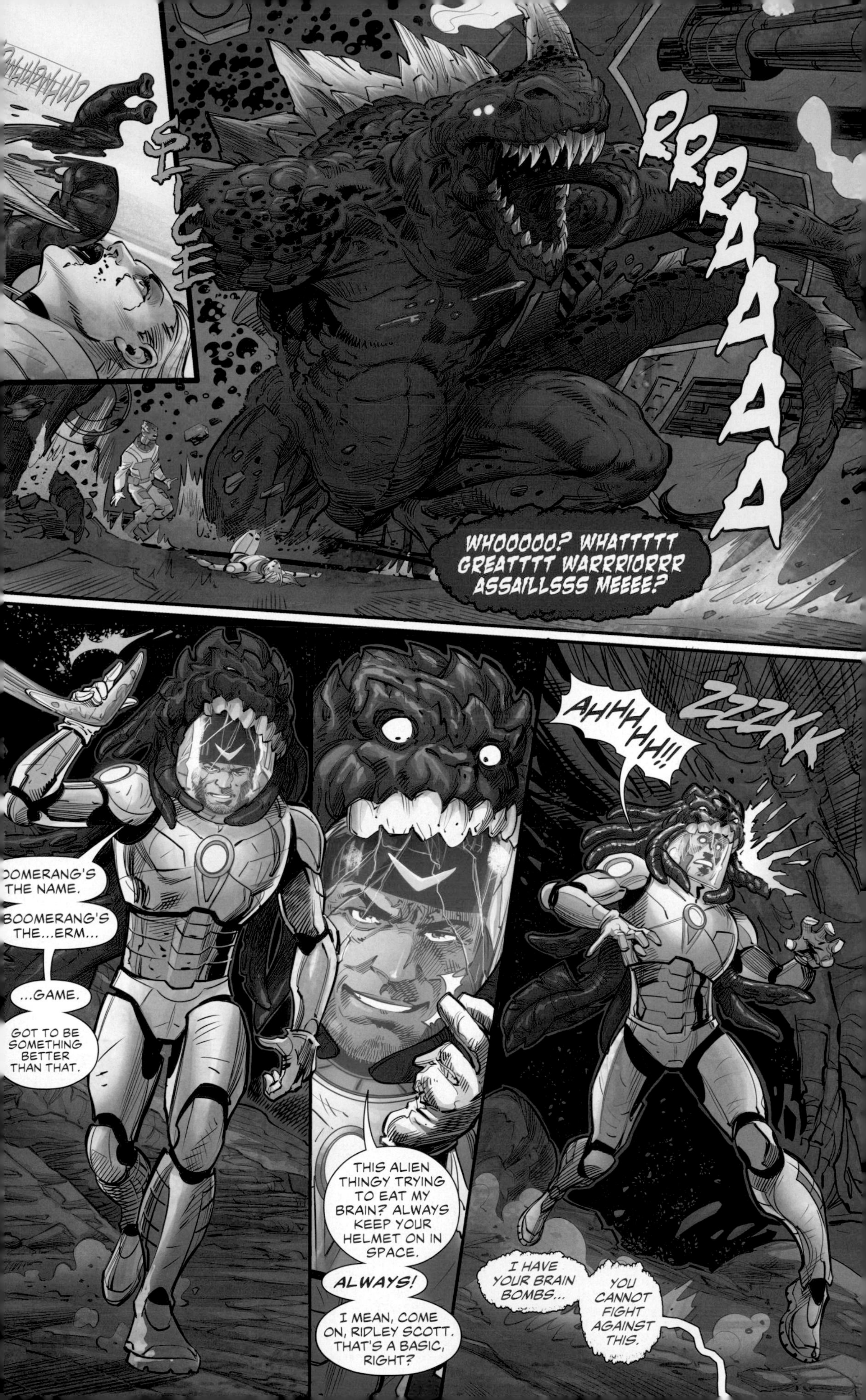
SHHUNHUNHUP
SLICE
RRRAAAAA
WHOOOOO? WHATTTTT GREATTTT WARRIORRR ASSAILLSSS MEEEE?
OOMERANG'S THE NAME.
BOOMERANG'S THE...ERM...
...GAME.
GOT TO BE SOMETHING BETTER THAN THAT.
THIS ALIEN THINGY TRYING TO EAT MY BRAIN? ALWAYS KEEP YOUR HELMET ON IN SPACE.
ALWAYS!
I MEAN, COME ON, RIDLEY SCOTT. THAT'S A BASIC, RIGHT?
ZZZKK
AHHHHH!!
I HAVE YOUR BRAIN BOMBS...
YOU CANNOT FIGHT AGAINST THIS.

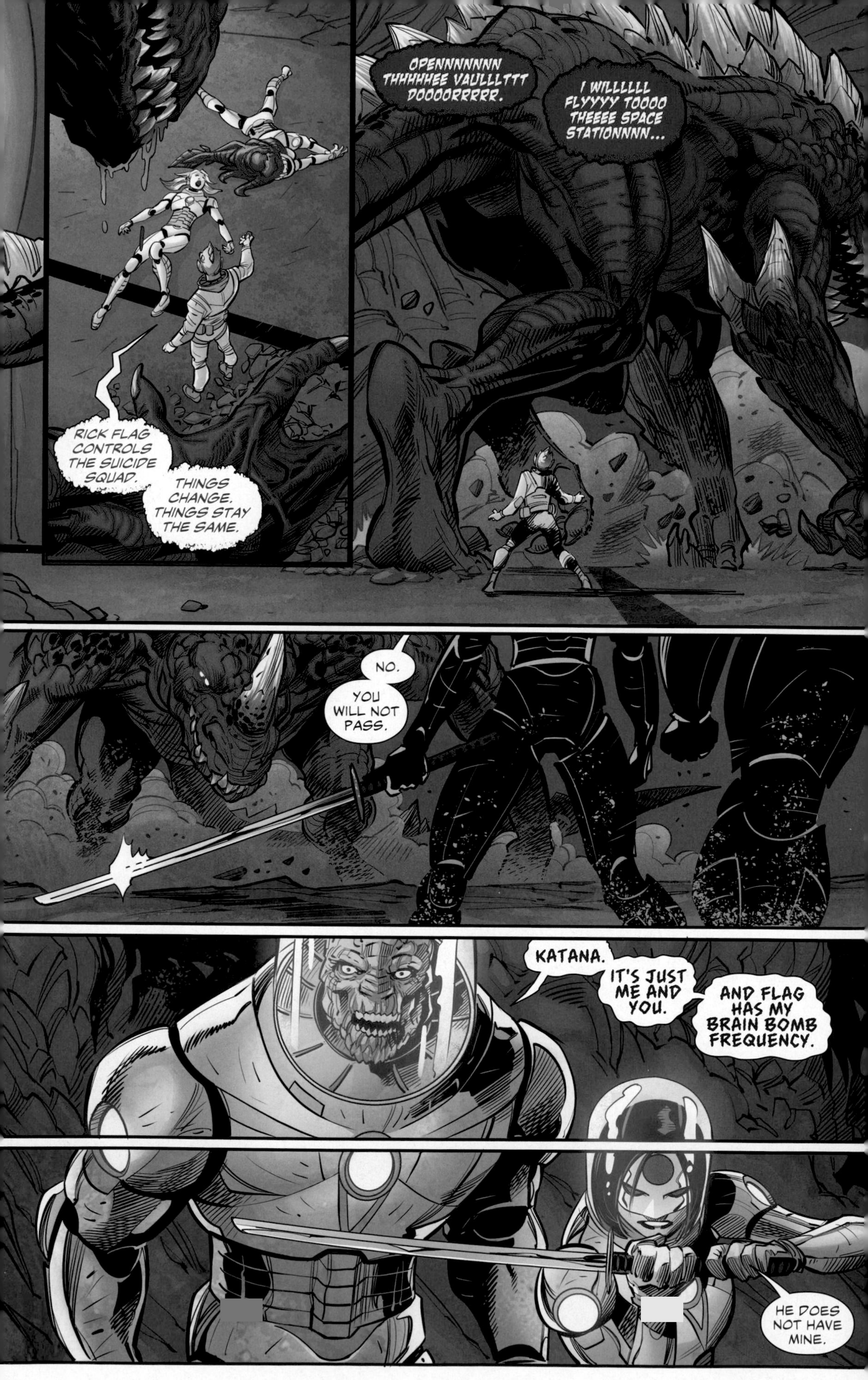
OPENNNNNNN THHHHHEE VAULLLTTT DOOOORRRRR.
I WILLLLLL FLYYYY TOOOO THEEEE SPACE STATIONNNN...
RICK FLAG CONTROLS THE SUICIDE SQUAD.
THINGS CHANGE. THINGS STAY THE SAME.
NO.
YOU WILL NOT PASS.
KATANA.
IT'S JUST ME AND YOU.
AND FLAG HAS MY BRAIN BOMB FREQUENCY.
HE DOES NOT HAVE MINE.

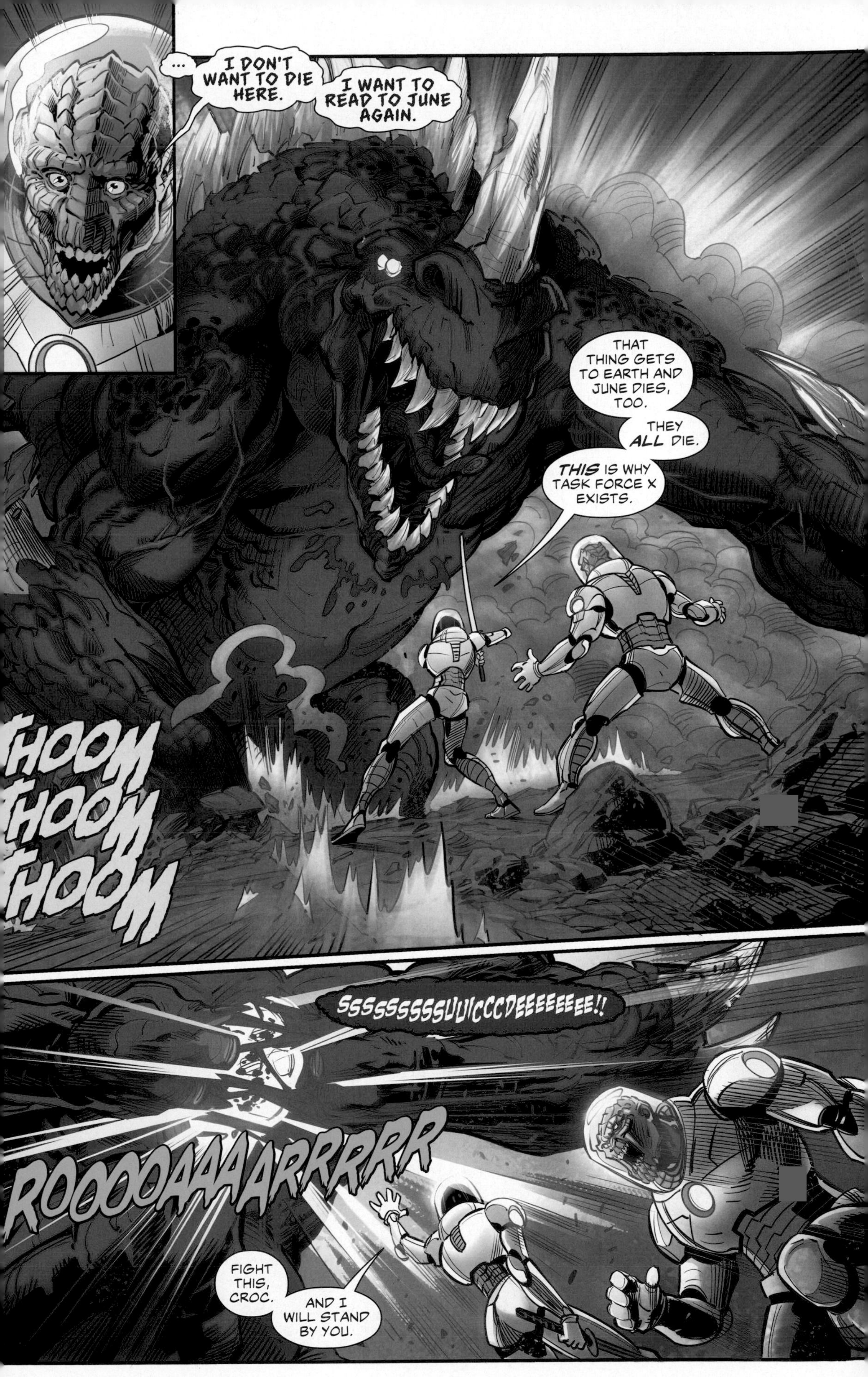
...
I DON'T WANT TO DIE HERE.
I WANT TO READ TO JUNE AGAIN.
THAT THING GETS TO EARTH AND JUNE DIES, TOO.
THEY ALL DIE.
THIS IS WHY TASK FORCE X EXISTS.
THOOM THOOM THOOM
SSSSSSSSSUUICCCDEEEEEEEE!!
ROOOOAAAARRRRR
FIGHT THIS, CROC.
AND I WILL STAND BY YOU.

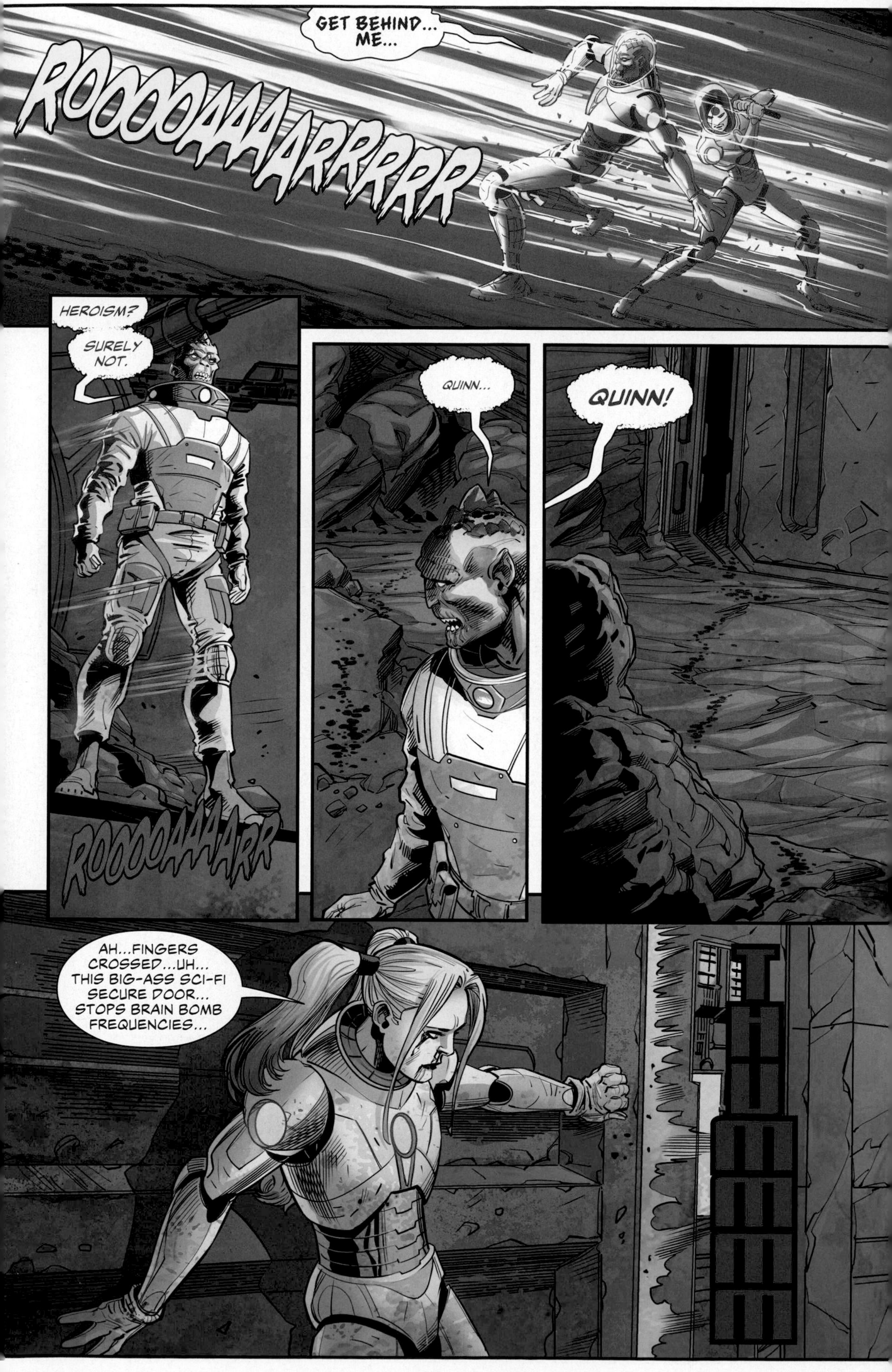
GET BEHIND... ME...
ROOOOAAAARRRRR
HEROISM?
SURELY NOT.
ROOOOAAAARR
QUINN...
QUINN!
AH...FINGERS CROSSED...UH... THIS BIG-ASS SCI-FI SECURE DOOR... STOPS BRAIN BOMB FREQUENCIES...
THUMMMM

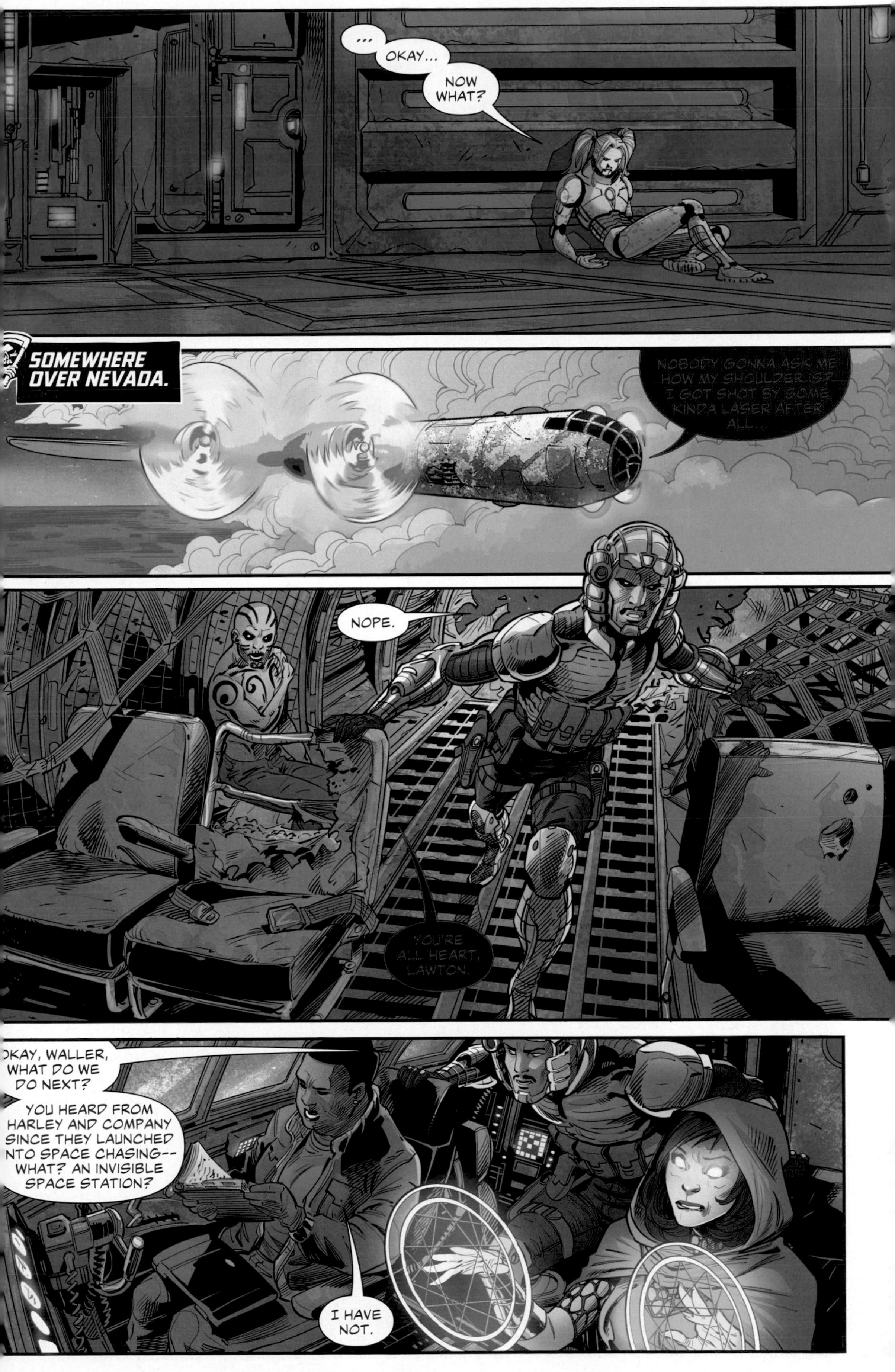
...
OKAY...
NOW WHAT?
SOMEWHERE OVER NEVADA.
NOBODY GONNA ASK ME HOW MY SHOULDER IS? I GOT SHOT BY SOME KINDA LASER AFTER ALL...
NOPE.
YOU'RE ALL HEART, LAWTON.
OKAY, WALLER, WHAT DO WE DO NEXT?
YOU HEARD FROM HARLEY AND COMPANY SINCE THEY LAUNCHED INTO SPACE CHASING-- WHAT? AN INVISIBLE SPACE STATION?
I HAVE NOT.

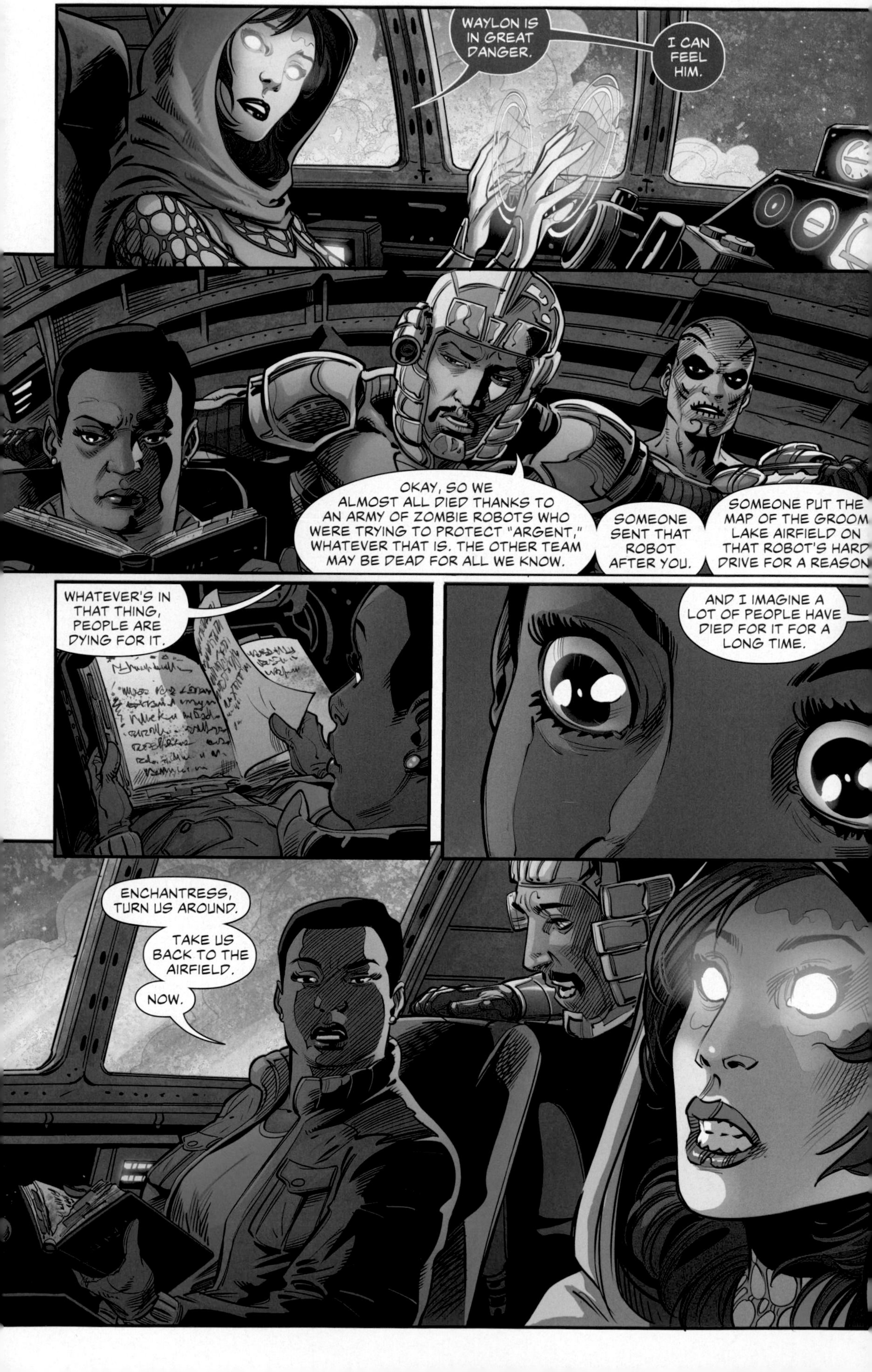
WAYLON IS IN GREAT DANGER.
I CAN FEEL HIM.
OKAY, SO WE ALMOST ALL DIED THANKS TO AN ARMY OF ZOMBIE ROBOTS WHO WERE TRYING TO PROTECT "ARGENT," WHATEVER THAT IS. THE OTHER TEAM MAY BE DEAD FOR ALL WE KNOW.
SOMEONE SENT THAT ROBOT AFTER YOU.
SOMEONE PUT THE MAP OF THE GROOM LAKE AIRFIELD ON THAT ROBOT'S HARD DRIVE FOR A REASON
WHATEVER'S IN THAT THING, PEOPLE ARE DYING FOR IT.
AND I IMAGINE A LOT OF PEOPLE HAVE DIED FOR IT FOR A LONG TIME.
ENCHANTRESS, TURN US AROUND.
TAKE US BACK TO THE AIRFIELD.
NOW.

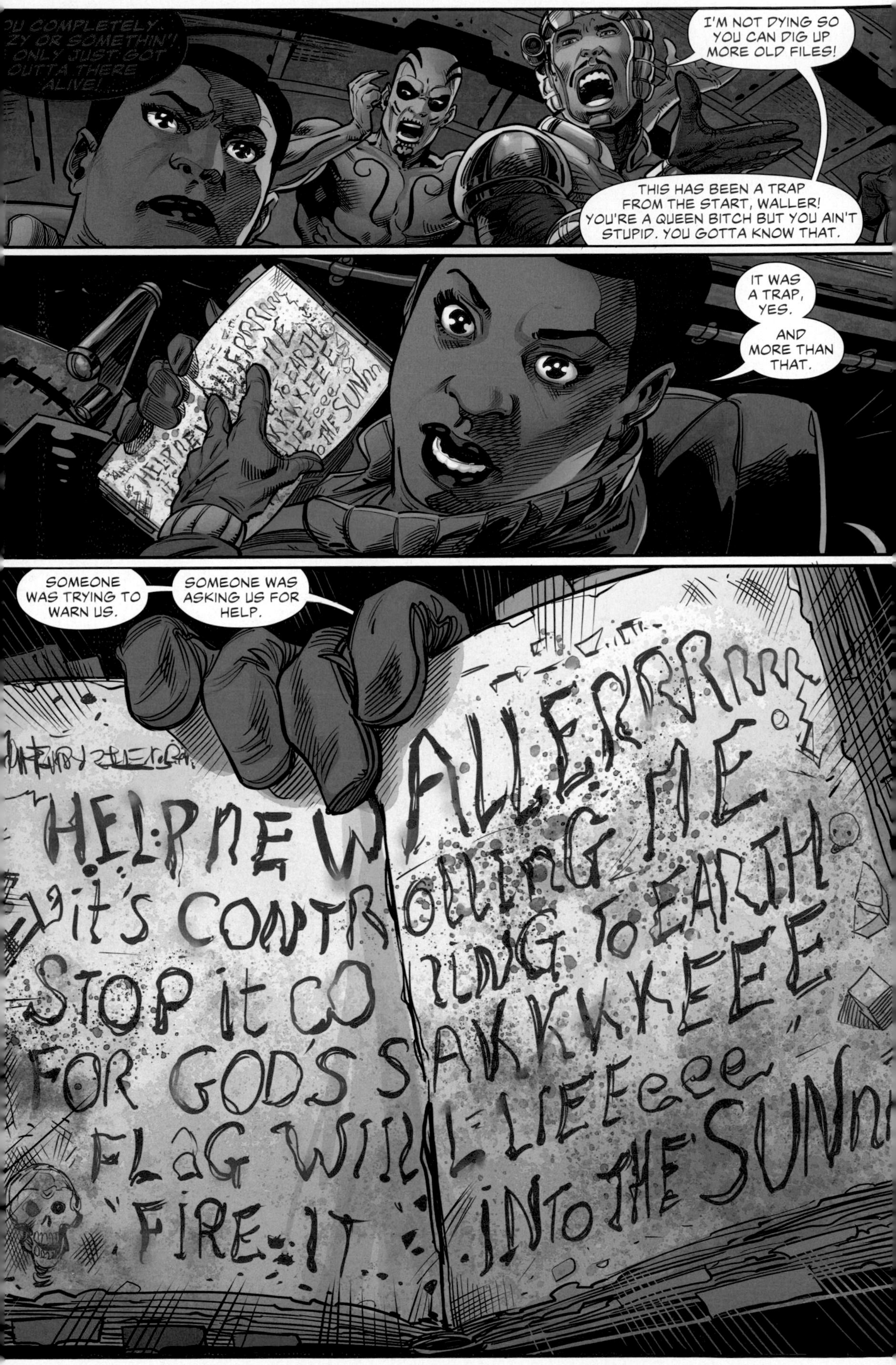
OU COMPLETELY ZY OR SOMETHIN'! ONLY JUST GOT OUTTA THERE ALIVE!
I'M NOT DYING SO YOU CAN DIG UP MORE OLD FILES!
THIS HAS BEEN A TRAP FROM THE START, WALLER! YOU'RE A QUEEN BITCH BUT YOU AIN'T STUPID. YOU GOTTA KNOW THAT.
IT WAS A TRAP, YES.
AND MORE THAN THAT.
SOMEONE WAS TRYING TO WARN US.
SOMEONE WAS ASKING US FOR HELP.
HELP ME WALLERRRR
it's CONTROLLING ME
STOP it COMING TO EARTH
FOR GOD'S SAKKKKEEE
FLAG WILL LIEEeee
FIRE IT INTO THE SUNNn

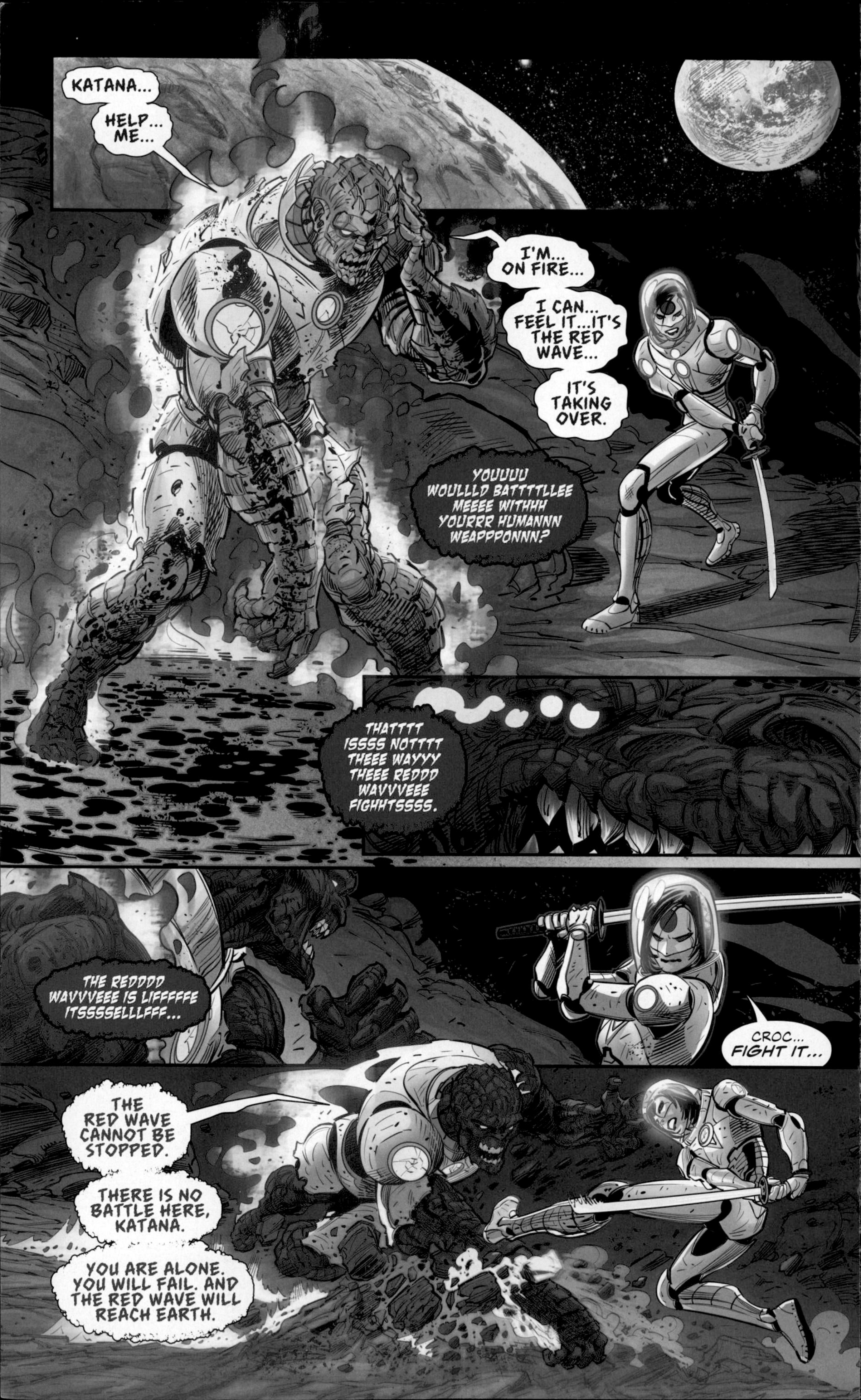
KATANA...
HELP... ME...
I'M... ON FIRE...
I CAN... FEEL IT...IT'S THE RED WAVE...
IT'S TAKING OVER.
YOUUUU WOULLLD BATTTTLLEE MEEEE WITHHH YOURRR HUMANNN WEAPPPONNN?
THATTTT ISSSS NOTTTT THEEE WAYYY THEEE REDDD WAVVVEEE FIGHHTSSSS.
THE REDDDD WAVVVEEE IS LIFFFFFE ITSSSSELLLFFF...
CROC... FIGHT IT...
THE RED WAVE CANNOT BE STOPPED.
THERE IS NO BATTLE HERE, KATANA.
YOU ARE ALONE. YOU WILL FAIL. AND THE RED WAVE WILL REACH EARTH.

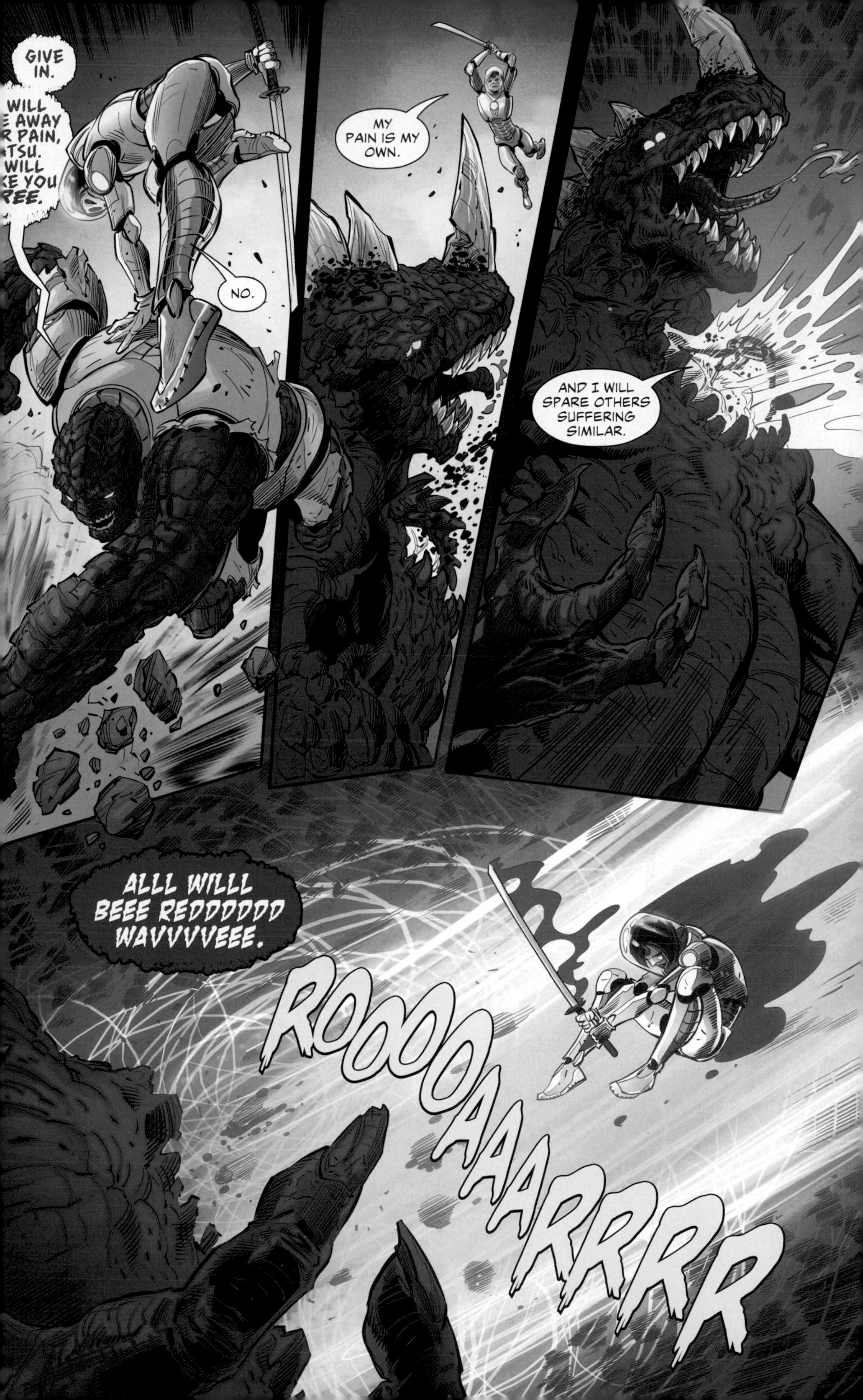
GIVE IN.
WILL
E AWAY
R PAIN,
TSU.
WILL
KE YOU
REE.
NO.
MY PAIN IS MY OWN.
AND I WILL SPARE OTHERS SUFFERING SIMILAR.
ALLL WILLL BEEE REDDDDDD WAVVVVEEE.
ROOOOAAARRRRR

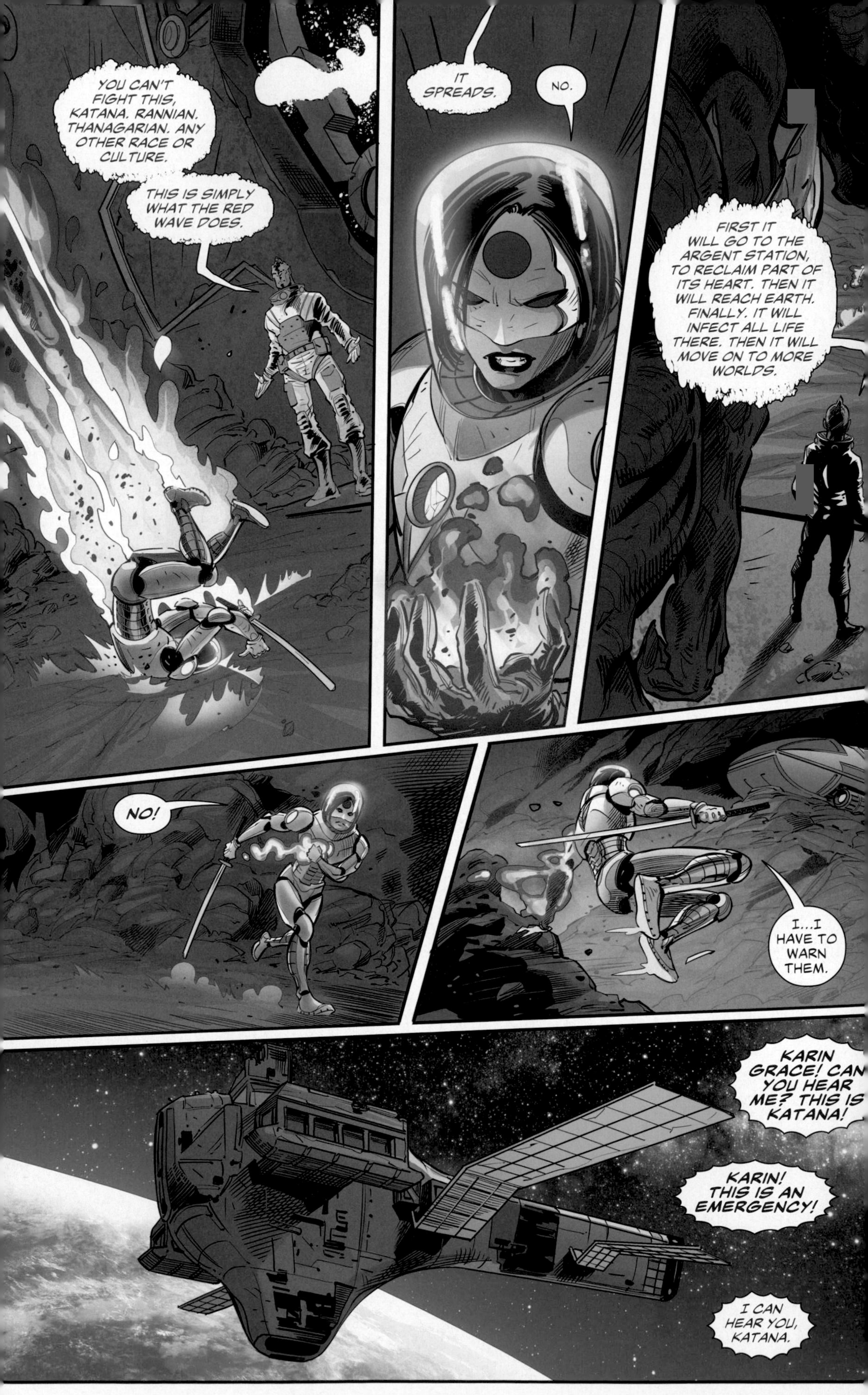
YOU CAN'T FIGHT THIS, KATANA. RANNIAN. THANAGARIAN. ANY OTHER RACE OR CULTURE.
THIS IS SIMPLY WHAT THE RED WAVE DOES.
IT SPREADS.
NO.
FIRST IT WILL GO TO THE ARGENT STATION, TO RECLAIM PART OF ITS HEART. THEN IT WILL REACH EARTH. FINALLY, IT WILL INFECT ALL LIFE THERE. THEN IT WILL MOVE ON TO MORE WORLDS.
NO!
I...I HAVE TO WARN THEM.
KARIN GRACE! CAN YOU HEAR ME? THIS IS KATANA!
KARIN! THIS IS AN EMERGENCY!
I CAN HEAR YOU, KATANA.

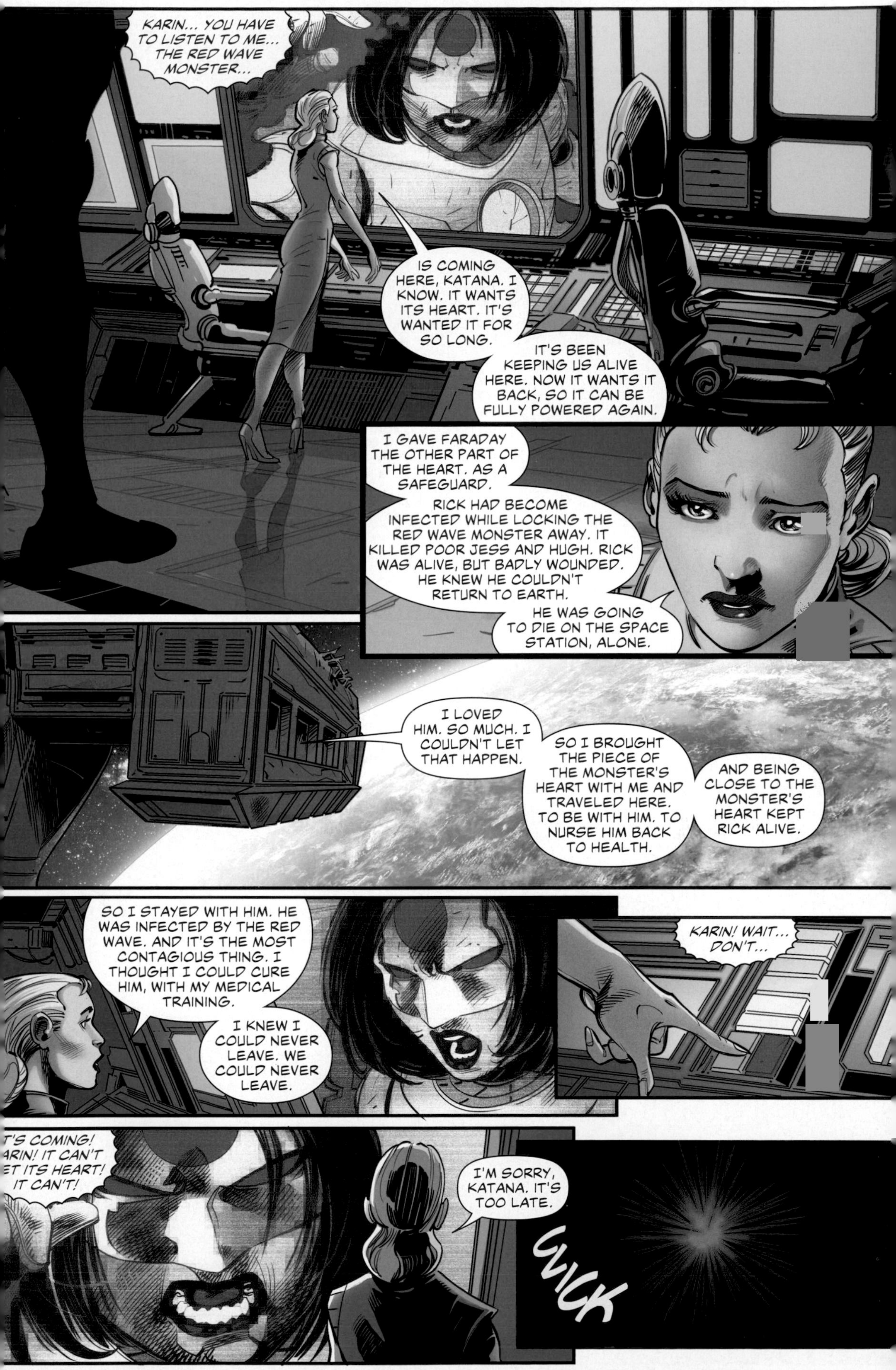
KARIN... YOU HAVE TO LISTEN TO ME... THE RED WAVE MONSTER...
IS COMING HERE, KATANA. I KNOW. IT WANTS ITS HEART. IT'S WANTED IT FOR SO LONG.
IT'S BEEN KEEPING US ALIVE HERE. NOW IT WANTS IT BACK, SO IT CAN BE FULLY POWERED AGAIN.
I GAVE FARADAY THE OTHER PART OF THE HEART. AS A SAFEGUARD.
RICK HAD BECOME INFECTED WHILE LOCKING THE RED WAVE MONSTER AWAY. IT KILLED POOR JESS AND HUGH. RICK WAS ALIVE, BUT BADLY WOUNDED. HE KNEW HE COULDN'T RETURN TO EARTH.
HE WAS GOING TO DIE ON THE SPACE STATION, ALONE.
I LOVED HIM. SO MUCH. I COULDN'T LET THAT HAPPEN.
SO I BROUGHT THE PIECE OF THE MONSTER'S HEART WITH ME AND TRAVELED HERE. TO BE WITH HIM. TO NURSE HIM BACK TO HEALTH.
AND BEING CLOSE TO THE MONSTER'S HEART KEPT RICK ALIVE.
SO I STAYED WITH HIM. HE WAS INFECTED BY THE RED WAVE. AND IT'S THE MOST CONTAGIOUS THING. I THOUGHT I COULD CURE HIM, WITH MY MEDICAL TRAINING.
I KNEW I COULD NEVER LEAVE. WE COULD NEVER LEAVE.
KARIN! WAIT... DON'T...
T'S COMING! ARIN! IT CAN'T ET ITS HEART! IT CAN'T!
I'M SORRY, KATANA. IT'S TOO LATE.
UWICK

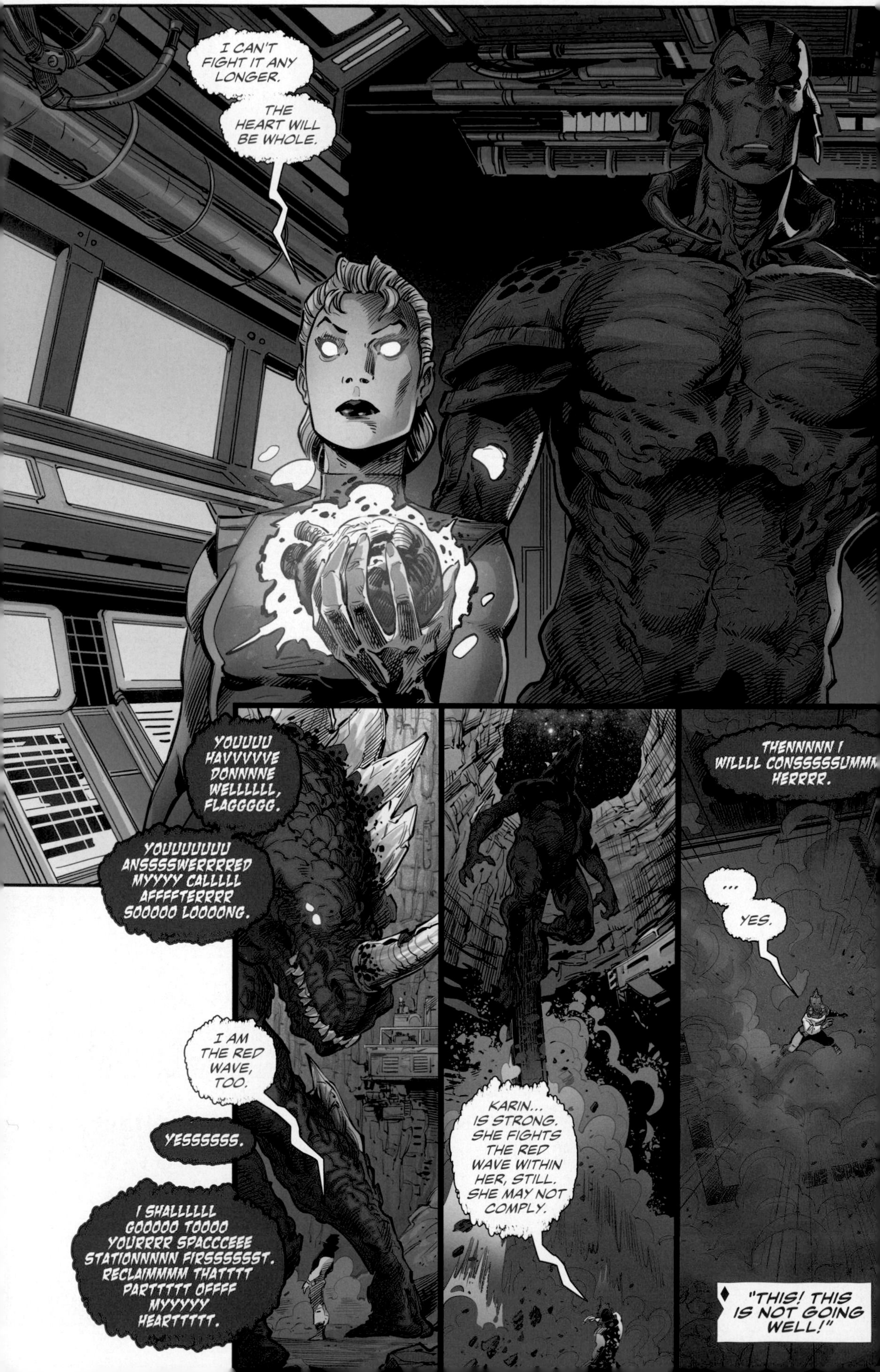
I CAN'T FIGHT IT ANY LONGER.
THE HEART WILL BE WHOLE.
YOUUUU HAVVVVVE DONNNNE WELLLLLL, FLAGGGGG.
YOUUUUUUU ANSSSSWERRRRED MYYYY CALLLLL AFFFFTERRRR SOOOOO LOOOONG.
I AM THE RED WAVE, TOO.
YESSSSSS.
I SHALLLLLL GOOOOO TOOOO YOURRRR SPACCCEEE STATIONNNNN FIRSSSSSST. RECLAIMMMM THATTTT PARTTTTT OFFFF MYYYYY HEARTTTTT.
KARIN... IS STRONG. SHE FIGHTS THE RED WAVE WITHIN HER, STILL. SHE MAY NOT COMPLY.
THENNNNN I WILLLL CONSSSSSUMM HERRRR.
...
YES.
"THIS! THIS IS NOT GOING WELL!"

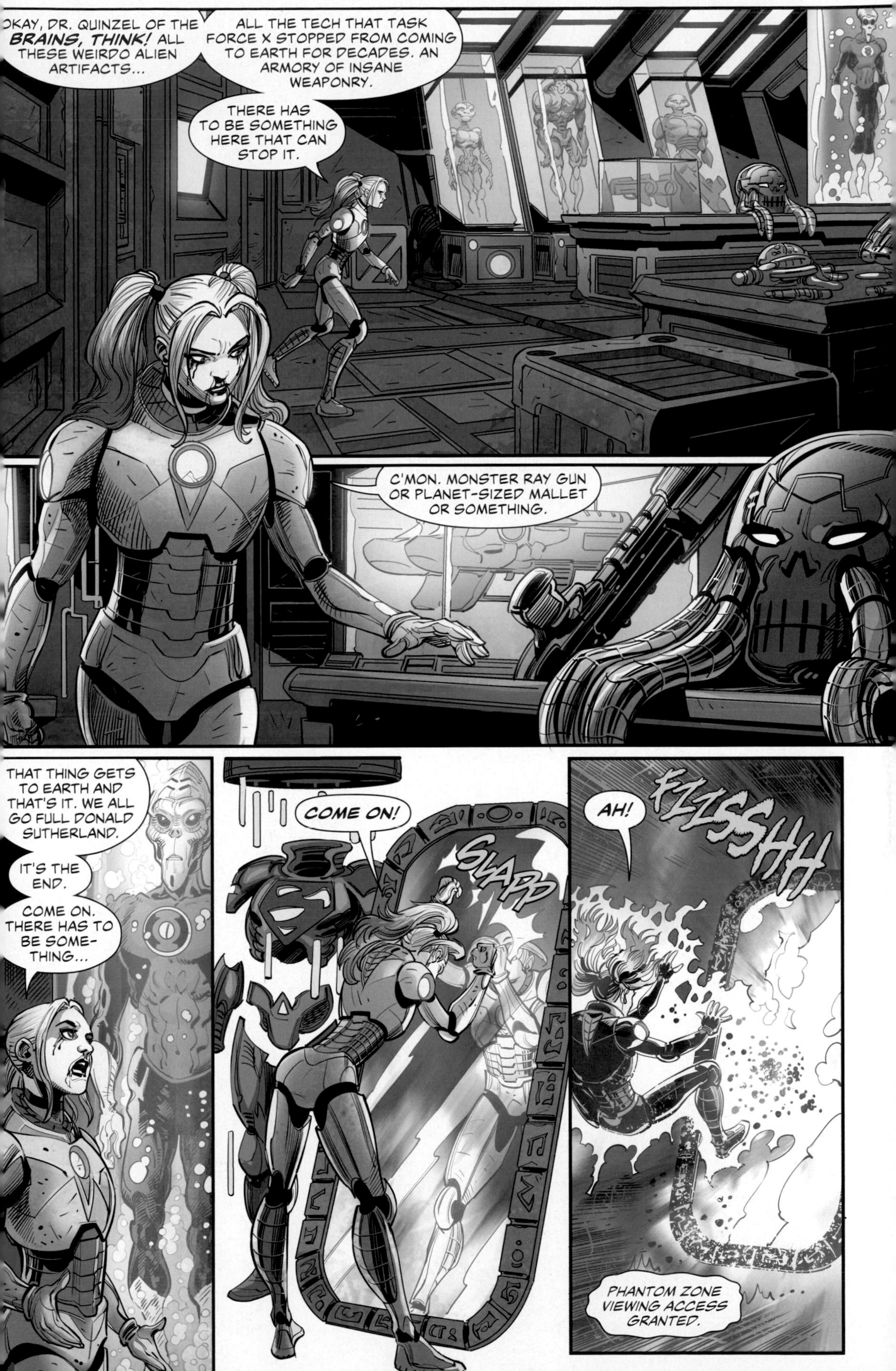
OKAY, DR. QUINZEL OF THE BRAINS, THINK! ALL THESE WEIRDO ALIEN ARTIFACTS...
ALL THE TECH THAT TASK FORCE X STOPPED FROM COMING TO EARTH FOR DECADES. AN ARMORY OF INSANE WEAPONRY.
THERE HAS TO BE SOMETHING HERE THAT CAN STOP IT.
C'MON. MONSTER RAY GUN OR PLANET-SIZED MALLET OR SOMETHING.
THAT THING GETS TO EARTH AND THAT'S IT. WE ALL GO FULL DONALD SUTHERLAND.
IT'S THE END.
COME ON. THERE HAS TO BE SOME-THING...
COME ON!
SLAPP
AH!
FZZSSHH
PHANTOM ZONE VIEWING ACCESS GRANTED.

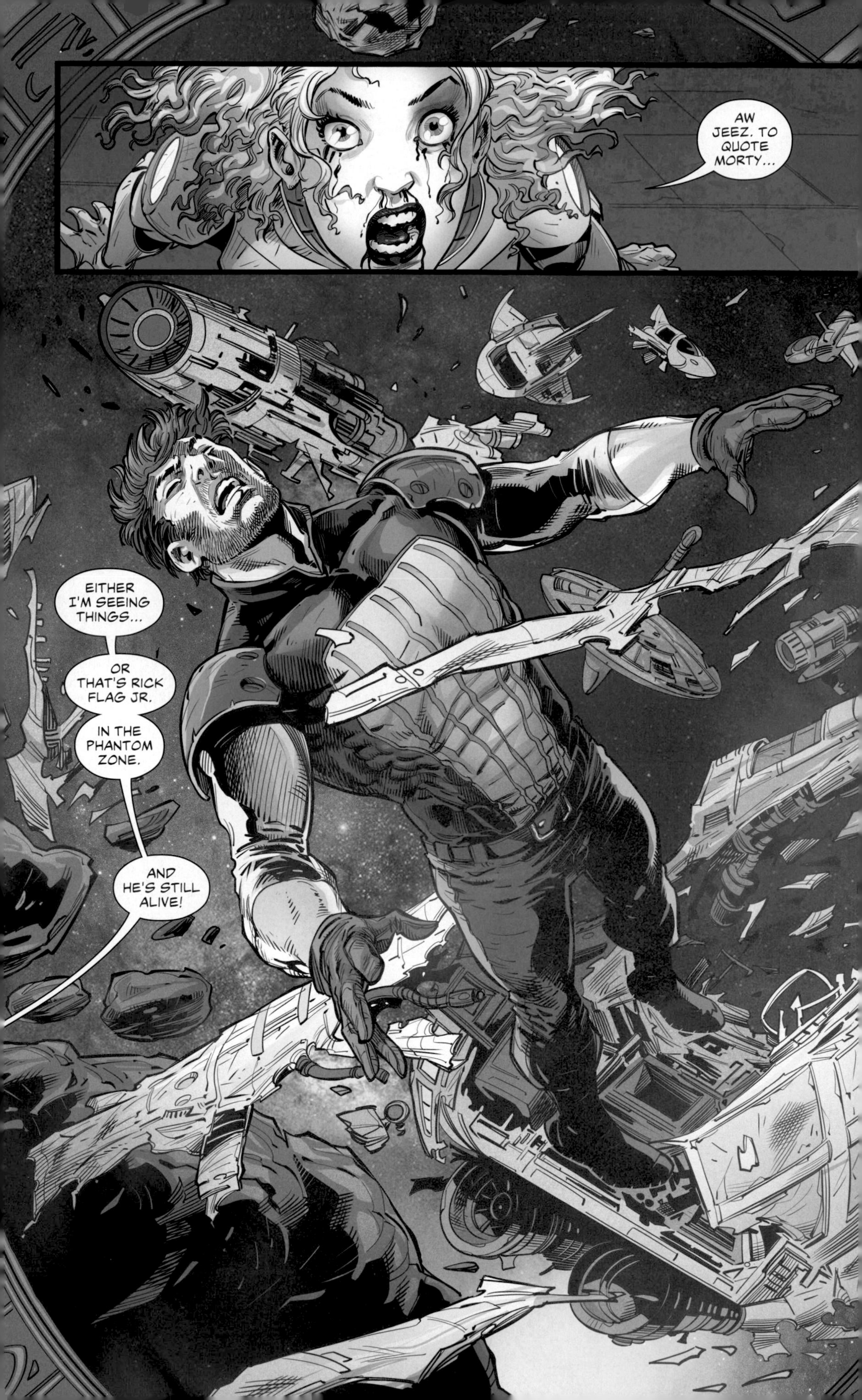
AW JEEZ. TO QUOTE MORTY...
EITHER I'M SEEING THINGS...
OR THAT'S RICK FLAG JR.
IN THE PHANTOM ZONE.
AND HE'S STILL ALIVE!

Armstrong, Aldrin and Michael Collins returned from the moon.

...came back, too... ...ough the public ...'t even know he'd ... gone. No statues ... history books for ...k Force X...

...ING FOR A DAY PART 4

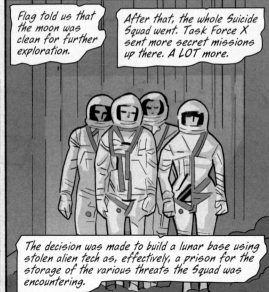

Flag told us that the moon was clean for further exploration.

After that, the whole Suicide Squad went. Task Force X sent more secret missions up there. A LOT more.

The decision was made to build a lunar base using stolen alien tech as, effectively, a prison for the storage of the various threats the Squad was encountering.

A couple of space stations were built...one more barrier to stop anything with too many tentacles getting in.

They were in the heavens. I was in the dirt.

Suited me fine. Meant I didn't have to think about Karin.

I'd run into them once in a while. Bright and Evans...

HEY, IT'S THE BOFFINS! HOW'S SPACE TREATING YOU FELLAS? FIND A PERSONALITY UP THERE?

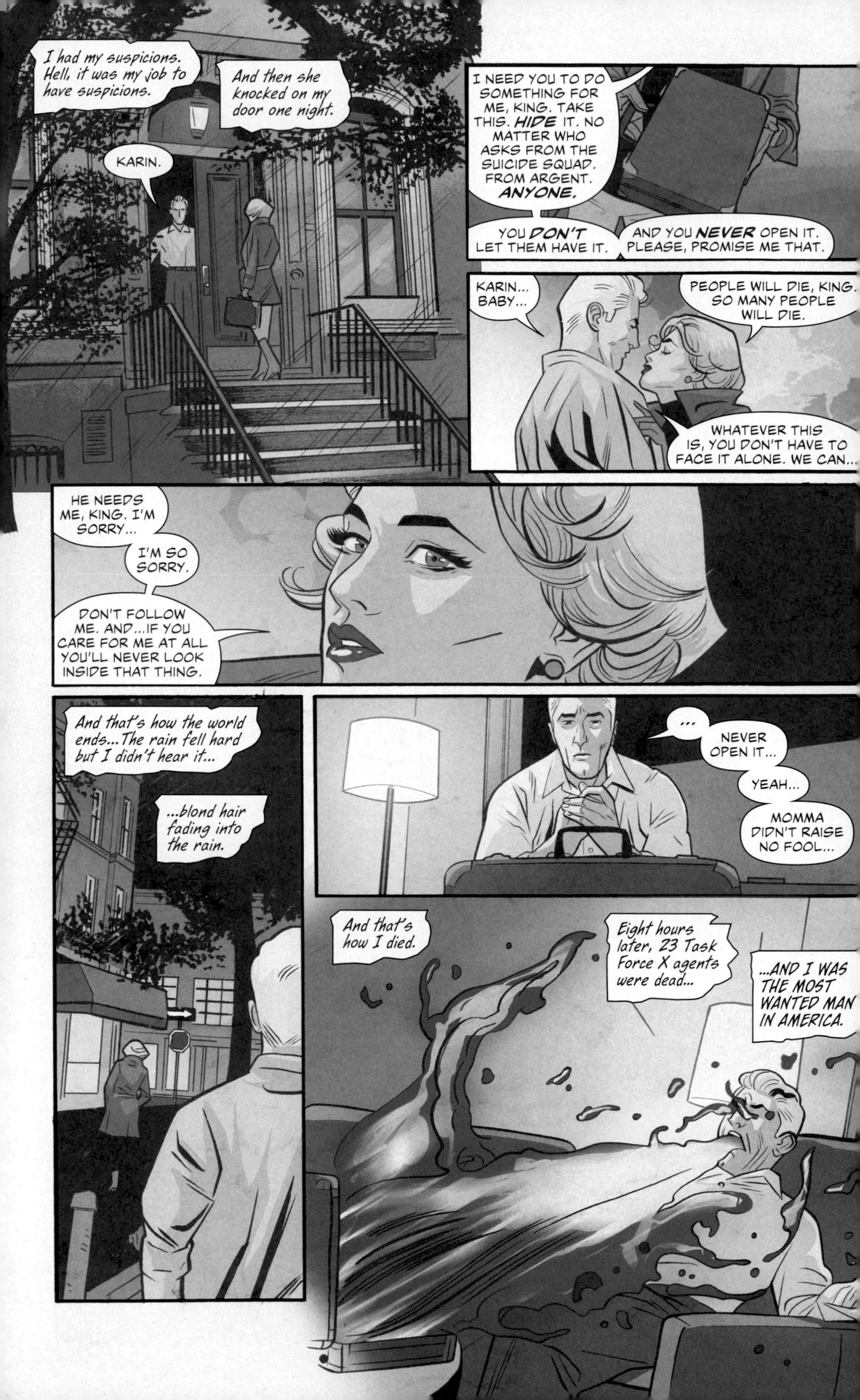
I had my suspicions. Hell, it was my job to have suspicions.
And then she knocked on my door one night.
KARIN.
I NEED YOU TO DO SOMETHING FOR ME, KING. TAKE THIS. HIDE IT. NO MATTER WHO ASKS FROM THE SUICIDE SQUAD. FROM ARGENT. ANYONE.
YOU DON'T LET THEM HAVE IT.
AND YOU NEVER OPEN IT. PLEASE, PROMISE ME THAT.
KARIN... BABY...
PEOPLE WILL DIE, KING. SO MANY PEOPLE WILL DIE.
WHATEVER THIS IS, YOU DON'T HAVE TO FACE IT ALONE. WE CAN...
HE NEEDS ME, KING. I'M SORRY...
I'M SO SORRY.
DON'T FOLLOW ME. AND...IF YOU CARE FOR ME AT ALL YOU'LL NEVER LOOK INSIDE THAT THING.
And that's how the world ends...The rain fell hard but I didn't hear it...
...blond hair fading into the rain.
...
NEVER OPEN IT...
YEAH...
MOMMA DIDN'T RAISE NO FOOL...
And that's how I died.
Eight hours later, 23 Task Force X agents were dead...
...AND I WAS THE MOST WANTED MAN IN AMERICA.

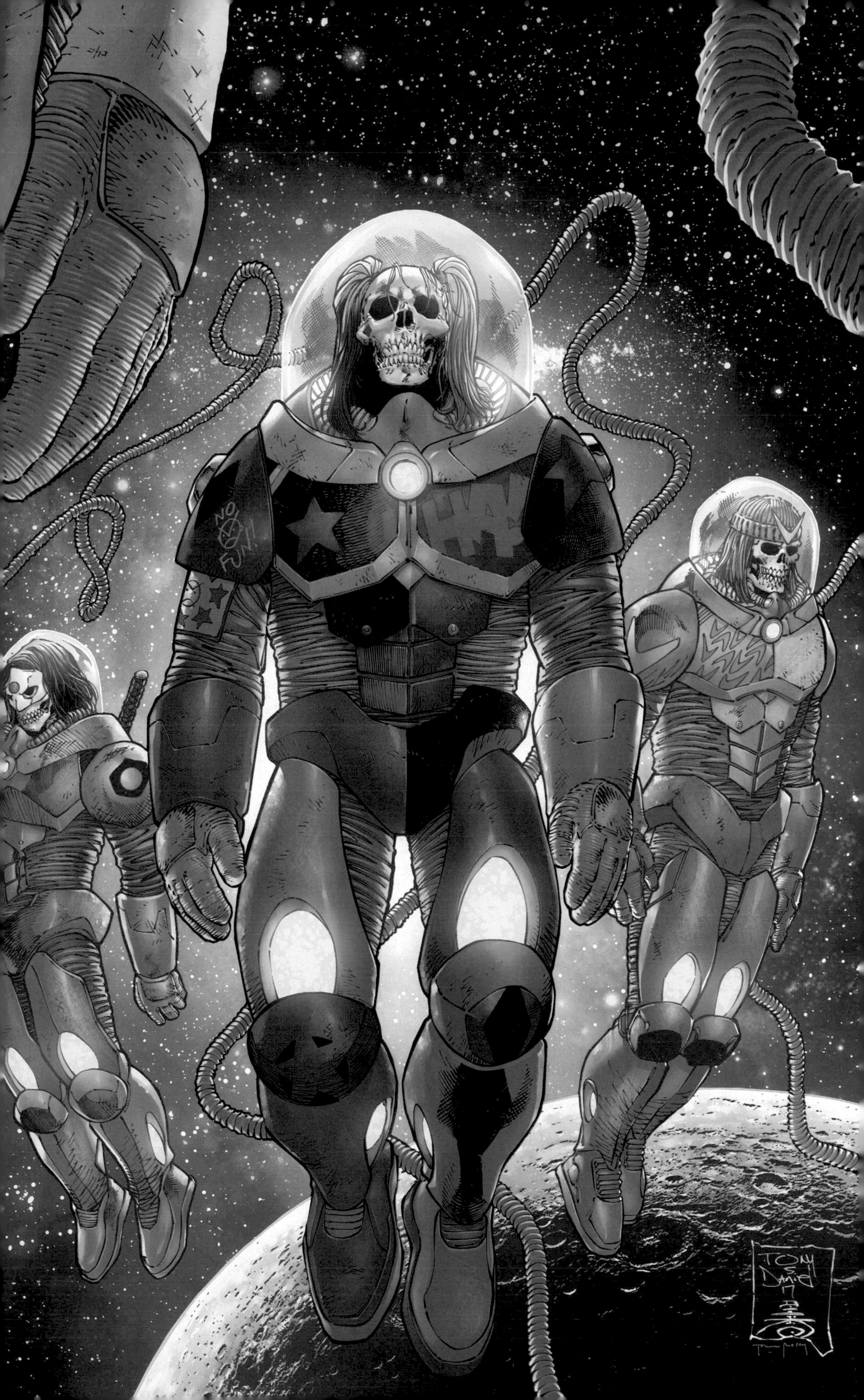
NO FUN!!

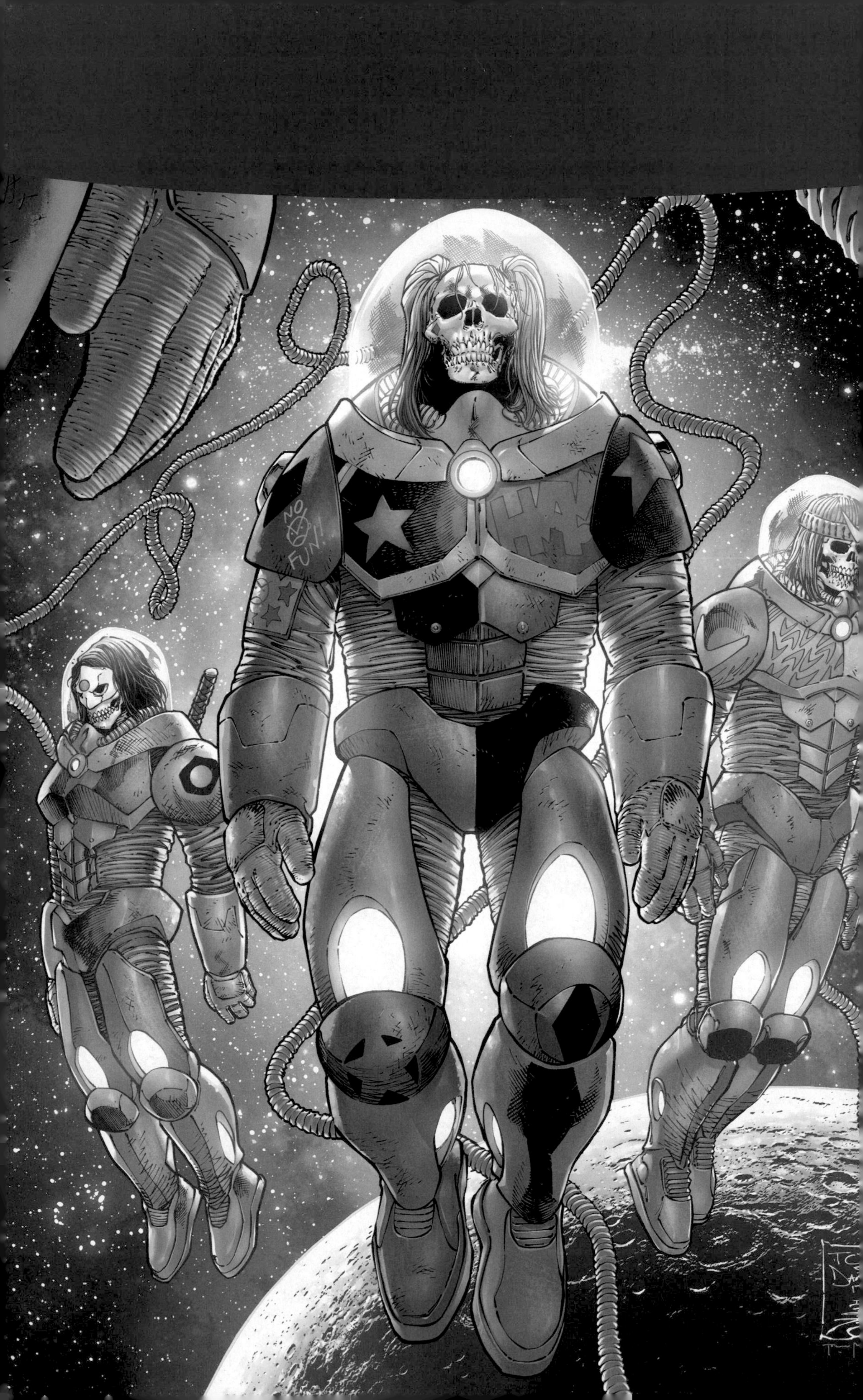
NO FUN!!

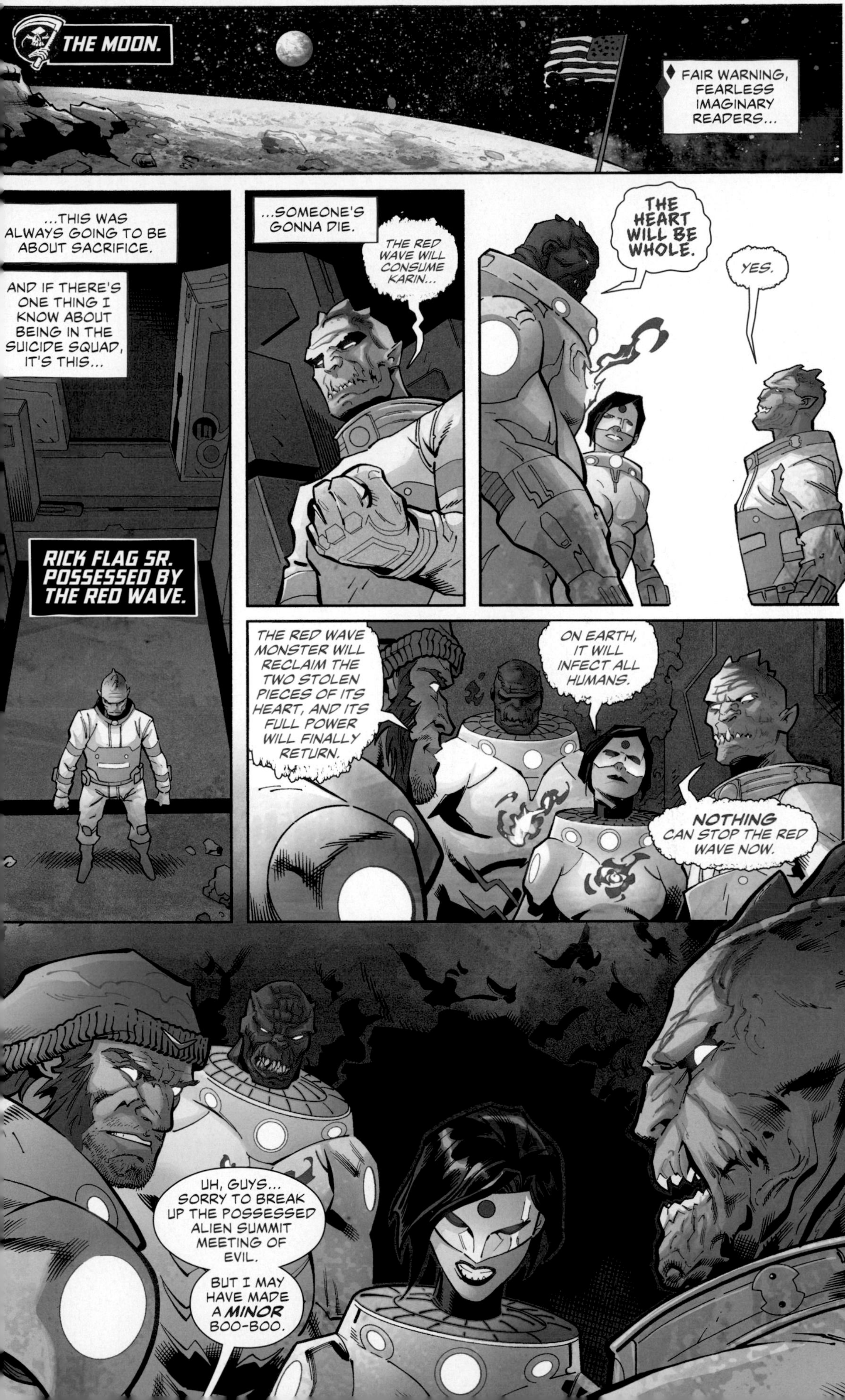
THE MOON.
FAIR WARNING, FEARLESS IMAGINARY READERS...
...THIS WAS ALWAYS GOING TO BE ABOUT SACRIFICE.
AND IF THERE'S ONE THING I KNOW ABOUT BEING IN THE SUICIDE SQUAD, IT'S THIS...
...SOMEONE'S GONNA DIE.
THE RED WAVE WILL CONSUME KARIN...
THE HEART WILL BE WHOLE.
YES.
RICK FLAG SR. POSSESSED BY THE RED WAVE.
THE RED WAVE MONSTER WILL RECLAIM THE TWO STOLEN PIECES OF ITS HEART, AND ITS FULL POWER WILL FINALLY RETURN.
ON EARTH, IT WILL INFECT ALL HUMANS.
NOTHING CAN STOP THE RED WAVE NOW.
UH, GUYS... SORRY TO BREAK UP THE POSSESSED ALIEN SUMMIT MEETING OF EVIL.
BUT I MAY HAVE MADE A MINOR BOO-BOO.

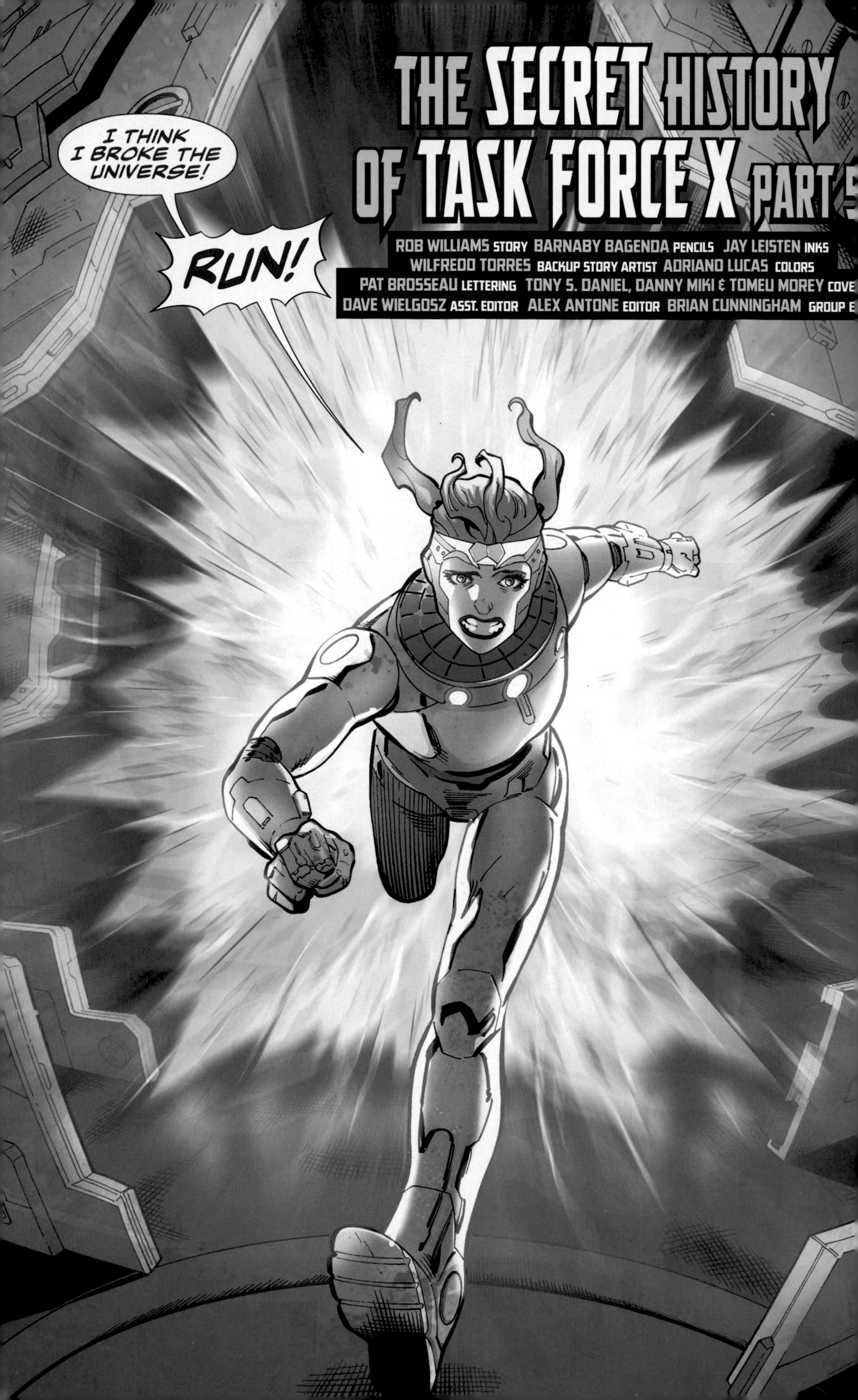
THE SECRET HISTORY OF TASK FORCE X PART 5
ROB WILLIAMS STORY BARNABY BAGENDA PENCILS JAY LEISTEN INKS
WILFREDO TORRES BACKUP STORY ARTIST ADRIANO LUCAS COLORS
PAT BROSSEAU LETTERING TONY S. DANIEL, DANNY MIKI & TOMEU MOREY COVE
DAVE WIELGOSZ ASST. EDITOR ALEX ANTONE EDITOR BRIAN CUNNINGHAM GROUP E
I THINK I BROKE THE UNIVERSE!
RUN!

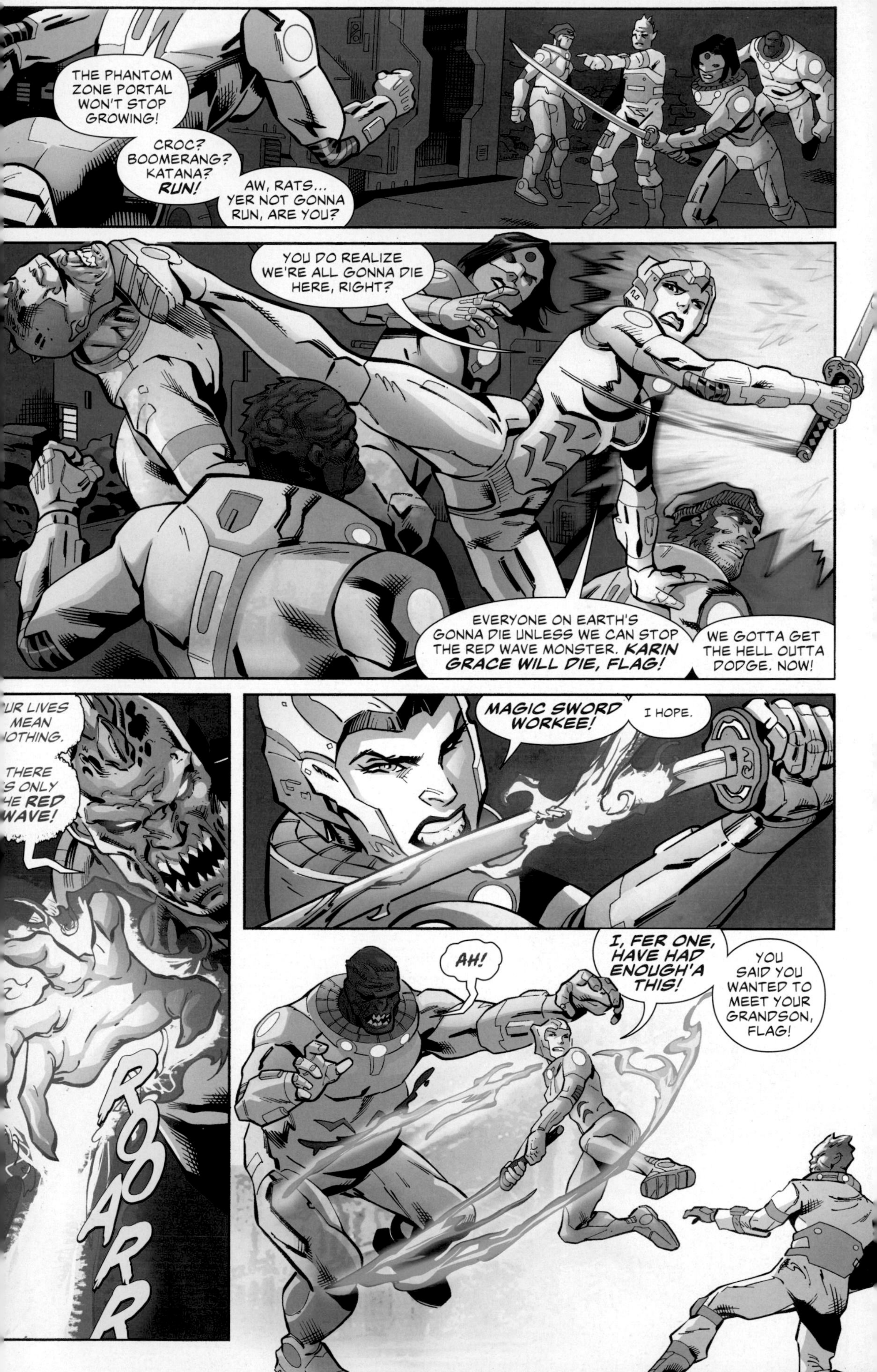
THE PHANTOM ZONE PORTAL WON'T STOP GROWING!
CROC? BOOMERANG? KATANA? RUN!
AW, RATS... YER NOT GONNA RUN, ARE YOU?
YOU DO REALIZE WE'RE ALL GONNA DIE HERE, RIGHT?
EVERYONE ON EARTH'S GONNA DIE UNLESS WE CAN STOP THE RED WAVE MONSTER. KARIN GRACE WILL DIE, FLAG!
WE GOTTA GET THE HELL OUTTA DODGE. NOW!
UR LIVES MEAN OTHING.
THERE S ONLY HE RED WAVE!
ROOARRR
MAGIC SWORD WORKEE!
I HOPE.
AH!
I, FER ONE, HAVE HAD ENOUGH'A THIS!
YOU SAID YOU WANTED TO MEET YOUR GRANDSON, FLAG!

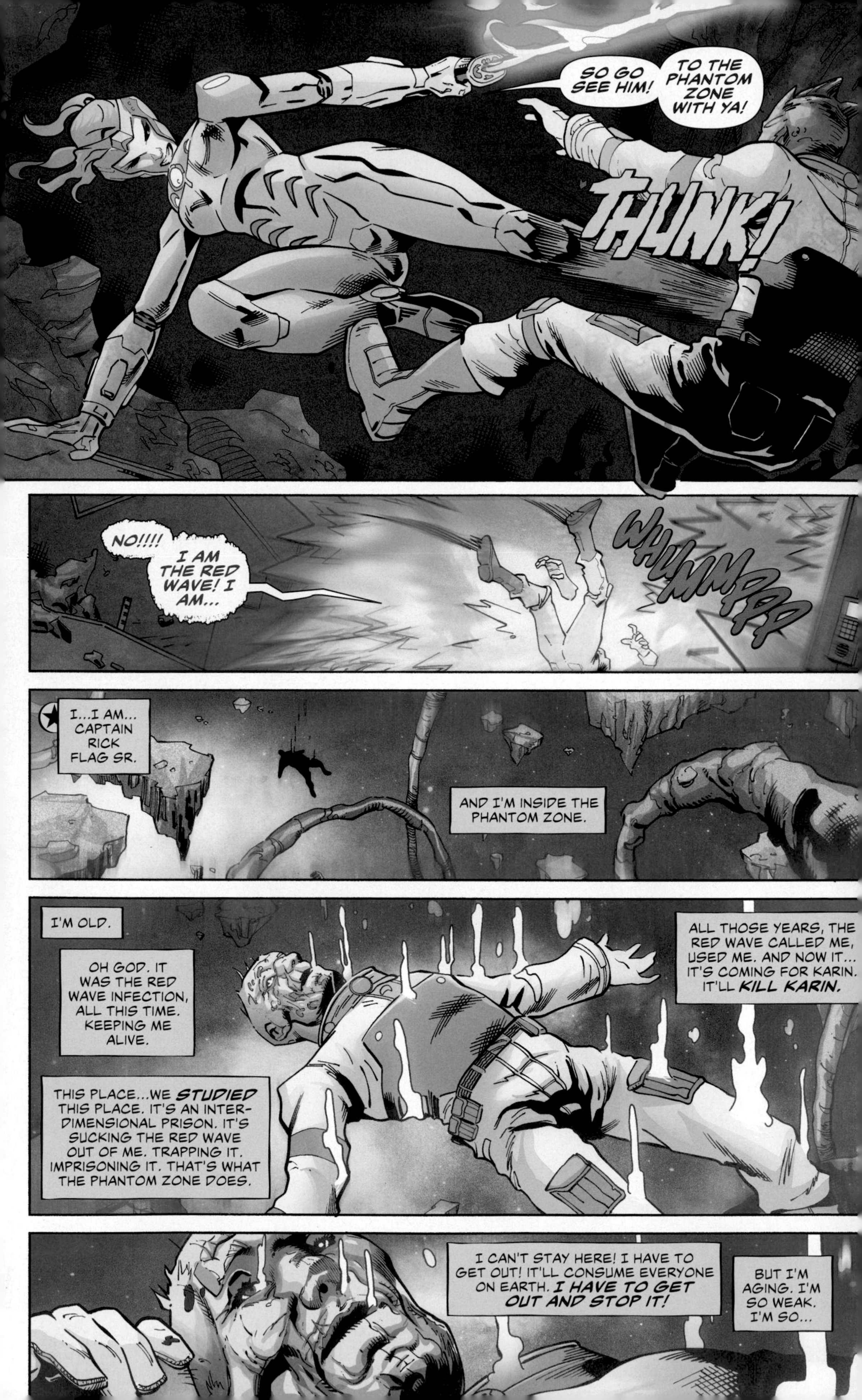
SO GO SEE HIM!
TO THE PHANTOM ZONE WITH YA!
THUNK!
NO!!!!
I AM THE RED WAVE! I AM...
WHUMMPPP
I...I AM... CAPTAIN RICK FLAG SR.
AND I'M INSIDE THE PHANTOM ZONE.
I'M OLD.
OH GOD. IT WAS THE RED WAVE INFECTION, ALL THIS TIME. KEEPING ME ALIVE.
THIS PLACE...WE STUDIED THIS PLACE. IT'S AN INTER-DIMENSIONAL PRISON. IT'S SUCKING THE RED WAVE OUT OF ME. TRAPPING IT. IMPRISONING IT. THAT'S WHAT THE PHANTOM ZONE DOES.
ALL THOSE YEARS, THE RED WAVE CALLED ME, USED ME. AND NOW IT... IT'S COMING FOR KARIN. IT'LL KILL KARIN.
I CAN'T STAY HERE! I HAVE TO GET OUT! IT'LL CONSUME EVERYONE ON EARTH. I HAVE TO GET OUT AND STOP IT!
BUT I'M AGING. I'M SO WEAK. I'M SO...

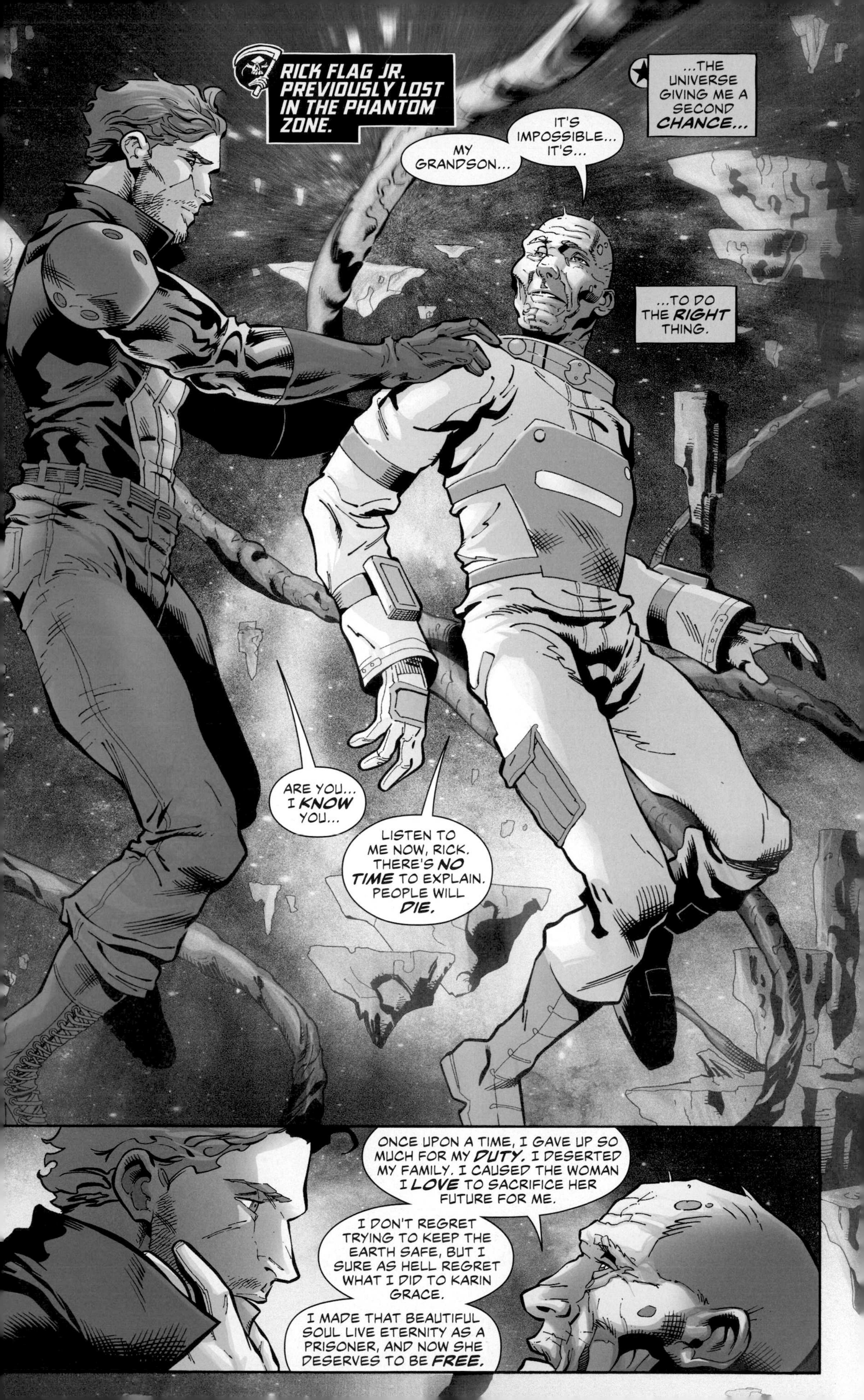
RICK FLAG JR. PREVIOUSLY LOST IN THE PHANTOM ZONE.
MY GRANDSON...
IT'S IMPOSSIBLE... IT'S...
...THE UNIVERSE GIVING ME A SECOND CHANCE...
...TO DO THE RIGHT THING.
ARE YOU... I KNOW YOU...
LISTEN TO ME NOW, RICK. THERE'S NO TIME TO EXPLAIN. PEOPLE WILL DIE.
ONCE UPON A TIME, I GAVE UP SO MUCH FOR MY DUTY. I DESERTED MY FAMILY. I CAUSED THE WOMAN I LOVE TO SACRIFICE HER FUTURE FOR ME.
I DON'T REGRET TRYING TO KEEP THE EARTH SAFE, BUT I SURE AS HELL REGRET WHAT I DID TO KARIN GRACE.
I MADE THAT BEAUTIFUL SOUL LIVE ETERNITY AS A PRISONER, AND NOW SHE DESERVES TO BE FREE.

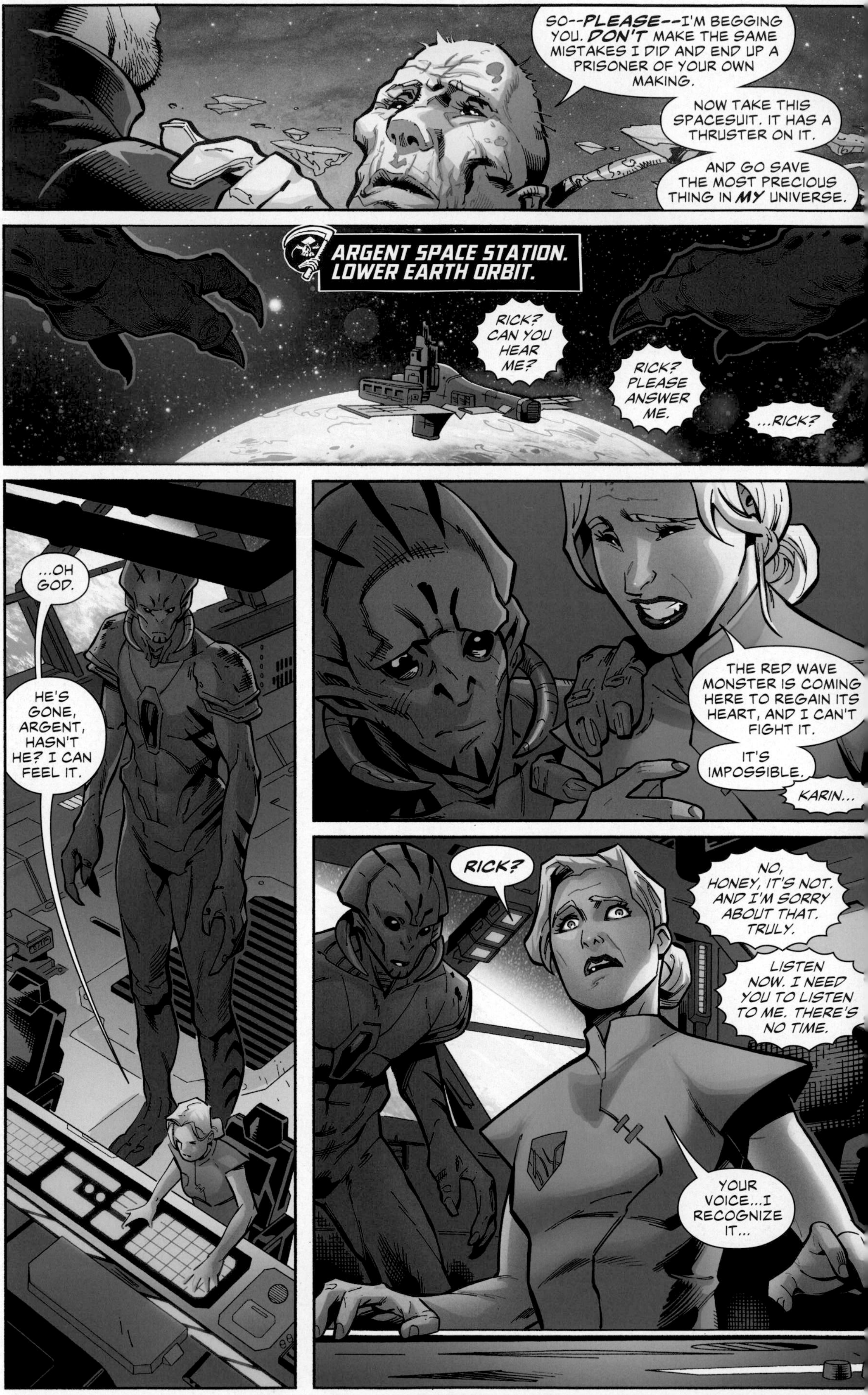
SO--PLEASE--I'M BEGGING YOU. DON'T MAKE THE SAME MISTAKES I DID AND END UP A PRISONER OF YOUR OWN MAKING.
NOW TAKE THIS SPACESUIT. IT HAS A THRUSTER ON IT.
AND GO SAVE THE MOST PRECIOUS THING IN MY UNIVERSE.
ARGENT SPACE STATION. LOWER EARTH ORBIT.
RICK? CAN YOU HEAR ME?
RICK? PLEASE ANSWER ME.
...RICK?
...OH GOD.
HE'S GONE, ARGENT, HASN'T HE? I CAN FEEL IT.
THE RED WAVE MONSTER IS COMING HERE TO REGAIN ITS HEART, AND I CAN'T FIGHT IT.
IT'S IMPOSSIBLE.
KARIN...
RICK?
NO, HONEY, IT'S NOT. AND I'M SORRY ABOUT THAT. TRULY.
LISTEN NOW. I NEED YOU TO LISTEN TO ME. THERE'S NO TIME.
YOUR VOICE...I RECOGNIZE IT...

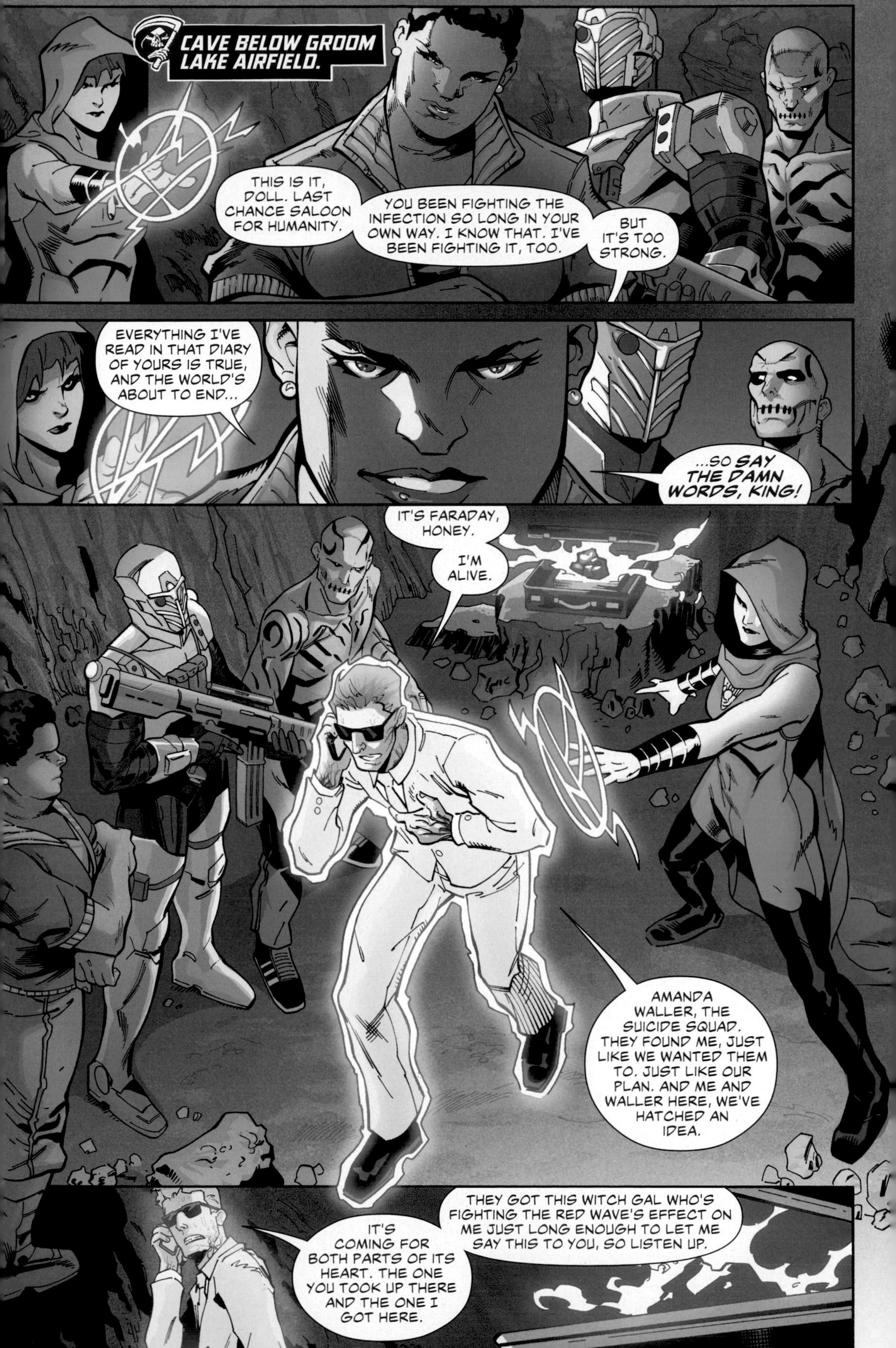
CAVE BELOW GROOM LAKE AIRFIELD.
THIS IS IT, DOLL. LAST CHANCE SALOON FOR HUMANITY.
YOU BEEN FIGHTING THE INFECTION SO LONG IN YOUR OWN WAY. I KNOW THAT. I'VE BEEN FIGHTING IT, TOO.
BUT IT'S TOO STRONG.
EVERYTHING I'VE READ IN THAT DIARY OF YOURS IS TRUE, AND THE WORLD'S ABOUT TO END...
...SO SAY THE DAMN WORDS, KING!
IT'S FARADAY, HONEY.
I'M ALIVE.
AMANDA WALLER, THE SUICIDE SQUAD. THEY FOUND ME, JUST LIKE WE WANTED THEM TO. JUST LIKE OUR PLAN. AND ME AND WALLER HERE, WE'VE HATCHED AN IDEA.
THEY GOT THIS WITCH GAL WHO'S FIGHTING THE RED WAVE'S EFFECT ON ME JUST LONG ENOUGH TO LET ME SAY THIS TO YOU, SO LISTEN UP.
IT'S COMING FOR BOTH PARTS OF ITS HEART. THE ONE YOU TOOK UP THERE AND THE ONE I GOT HERE.

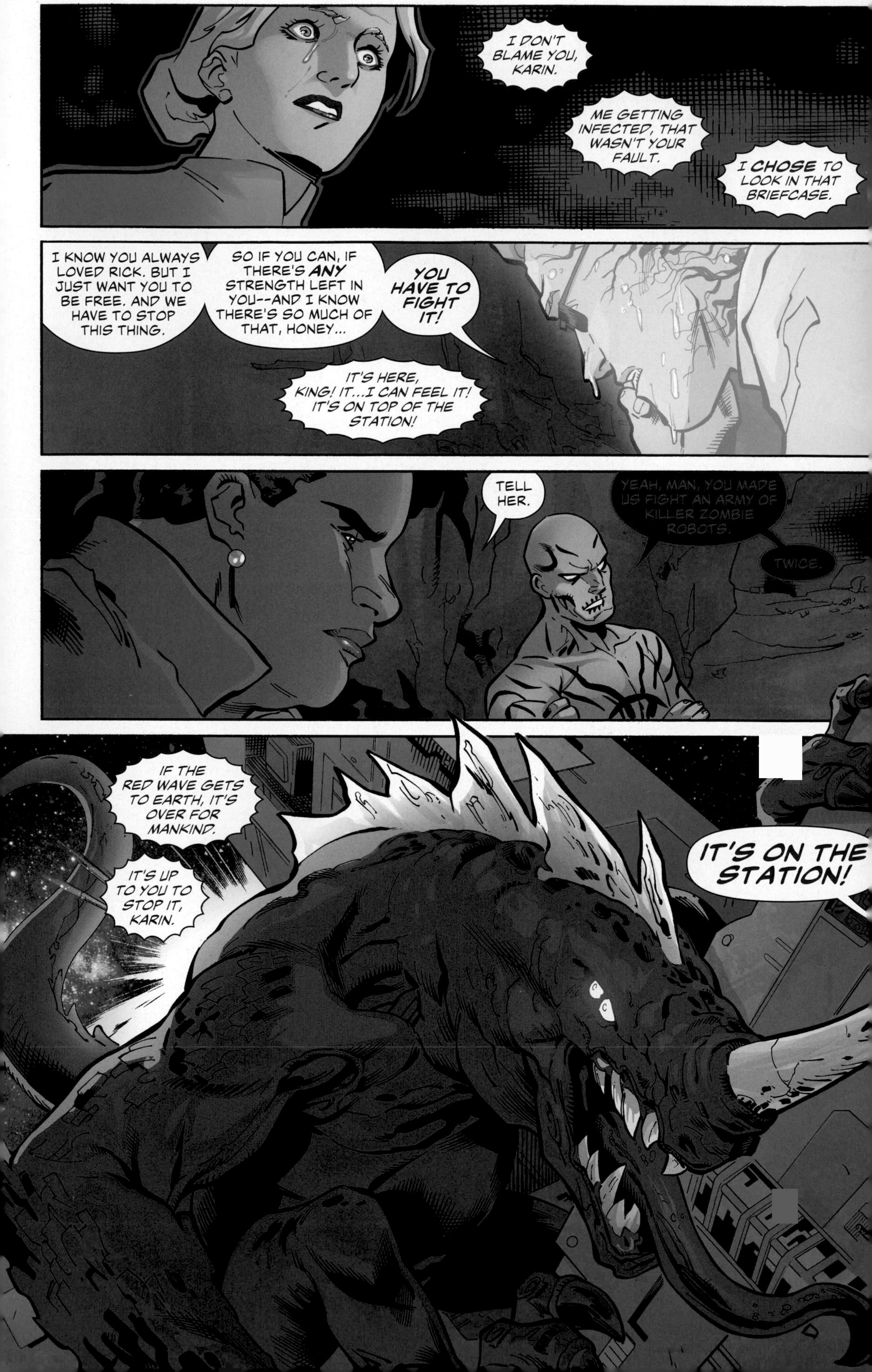
I DON'T BLAME YOU, KARIN.
ME GETTING INFECTED, THAT WASN'T YOUR FAULT.
I **CHOSE** TO LOOK IN THAT BRIEFCASE.
I KNOW YOU ALWAYS LOVED RICK. BUT I JUST WANT YOU TO BE FREE. AND WE HAVE TO STOP THIS THING.
SO IF YOU CAN, IF THERE'S ***ANY*** STRENGTH LEFT IN YOU--AND I KNOW THERE'S SO MUCH OF THAT, HONEY...
YOU HAVE TO FIGHT IT!
IT'S HERE, KING! IT...I CAN FEEL IT! IT'S ON TOP OF THE STATION!
TELL HER.
YEAH, MAN, YOU MADE US FIGHT AN ARMY OF KILLER ZOMBIE ROBOTS.
TWICE.
IF THE RED WAVE GETS TO EARTH, IT'S OVER FOR MANKIND.
IT'S UP TO YOU TO STOP IT, KARIN.
IT'S ON THE STATION!

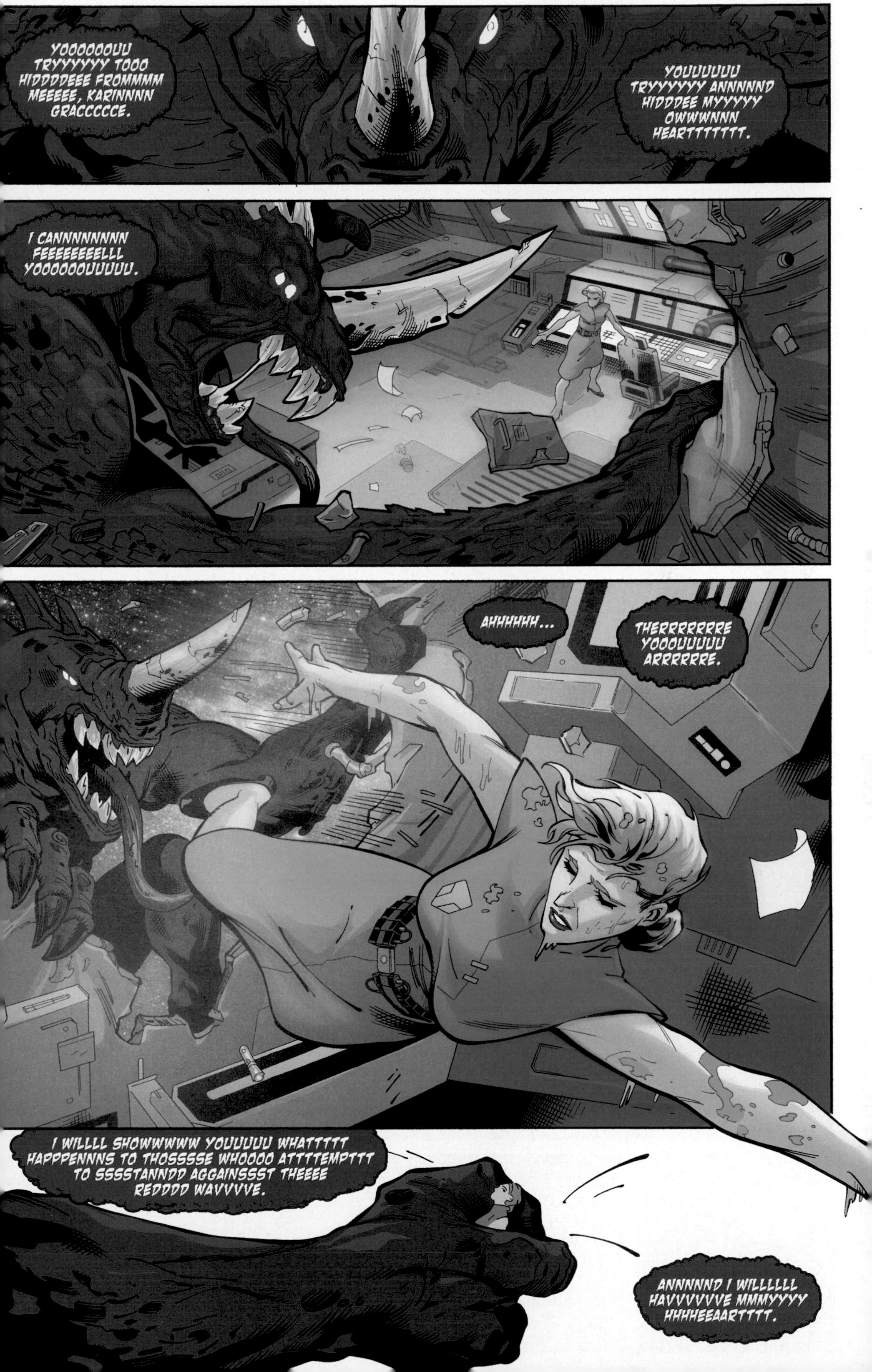
YOOOOOOUU TRYYYYYY TOOO HIDDDDEEE FROMMMM MEEEEE, KARINNNN GRACCCCCE.
YOUUUUUU TRYYYYYY ANNNNND HIDDDEE MYYYYY OWWWNNN HEARTTTTTTT.
I CANNNNNNNN FEEEEEEEELLL YOOOOOOUUUUU.
AHHHHHH...
THERRRRRRE YOOOUUUUU ARRRRRRE.
I WILLLL SHOWWWWW YOUUUUU WHATTTTT HAPPPENNNS TO THOSSSSE WHOOOO ATTTTEMPTTT TO SSSSTANNDD AGGAINSSST THEEEE REDDDD WAVVVVE.
ANNNNND I WILLLLLL HAVVVVVVE MMMYYYYY HHHHEEAARTTTT.

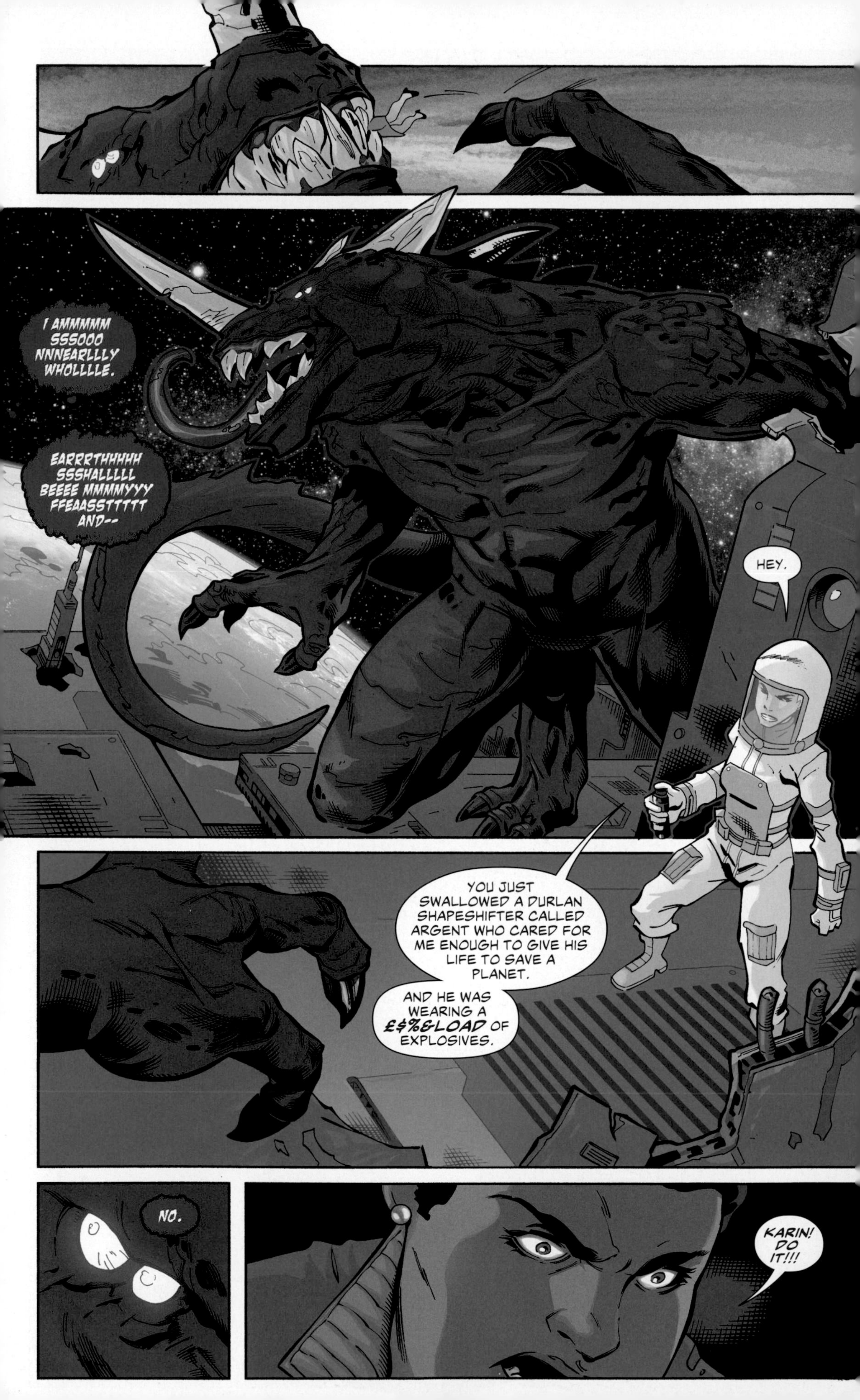
I AMMMMM SSSOOO NNNEARLLLY WHOLLLLE.
EARRRTHHHHH SSSHALLLLL BEEEE MMMMYYY FFEAASSTTTTT AND--
HEY.
YOU JUST SWALLOWED A DURLAN SHAPESHIFTER CALLED ARGENT WHO CARED FOR ME ENOUGH TO GIVE HIS LIFE TO SAVE A PLANET.
AND HE WAS WEARING A £$%&LOAD OF EXPLOSIVES.
NO.
KARIN! DO IT!!!

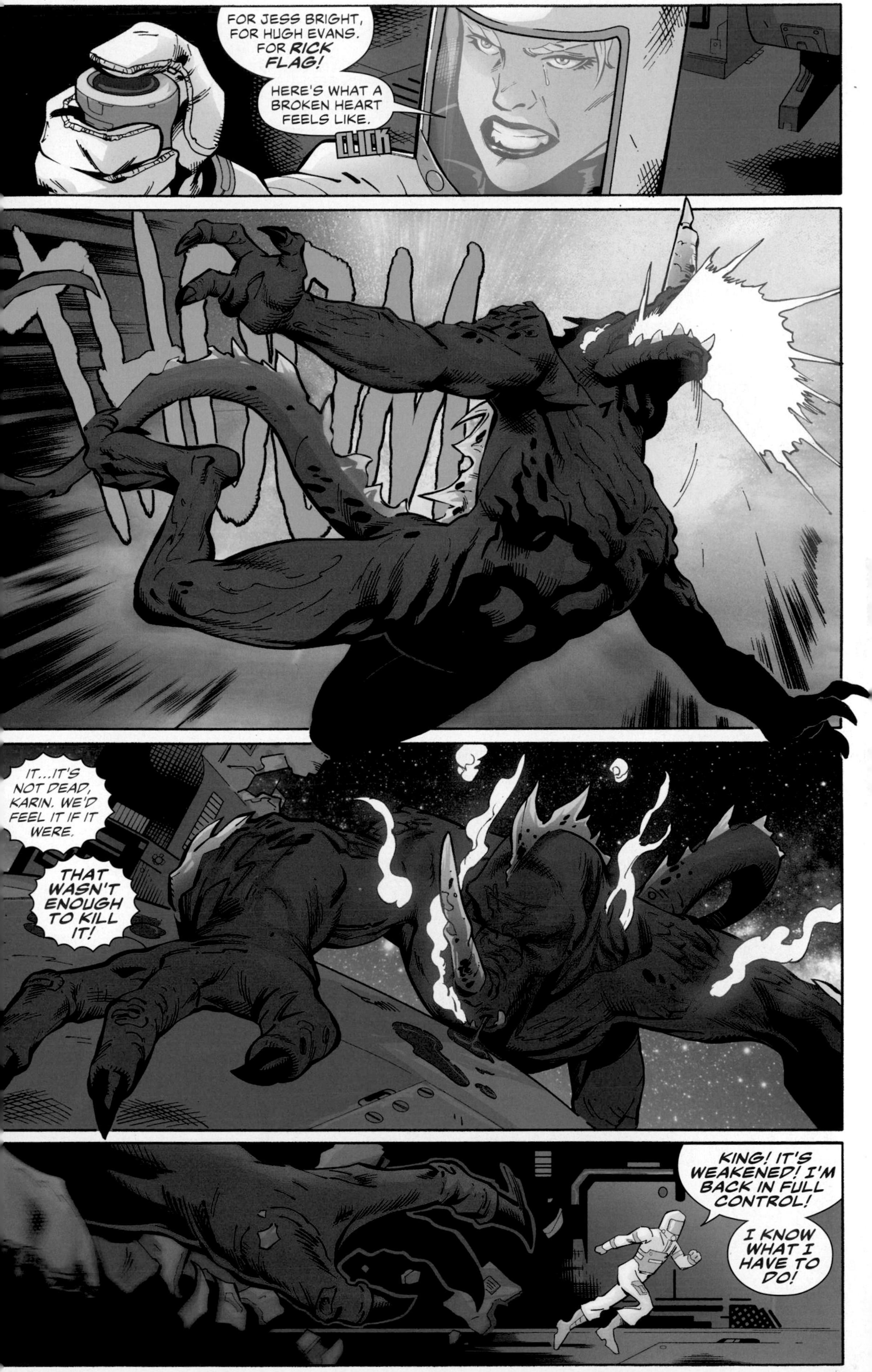
FOR JESS BRIGHT, FOR HUGH EVANS. FOR RICK FLAG!
HERE'S WHAT A BROKEN HEART FEELS LIKE.
CLICK
IT...IT'S NOT DEAD, KARIN. WE'D FEEL IT IF IT WERE.
THAT WASN'T ENOUGH TO KILL IT!
KING! IT'S WEAKENED! I'M BACK IN FULL CONTROL!
I KNOW WHAT I HAVE TO DO!

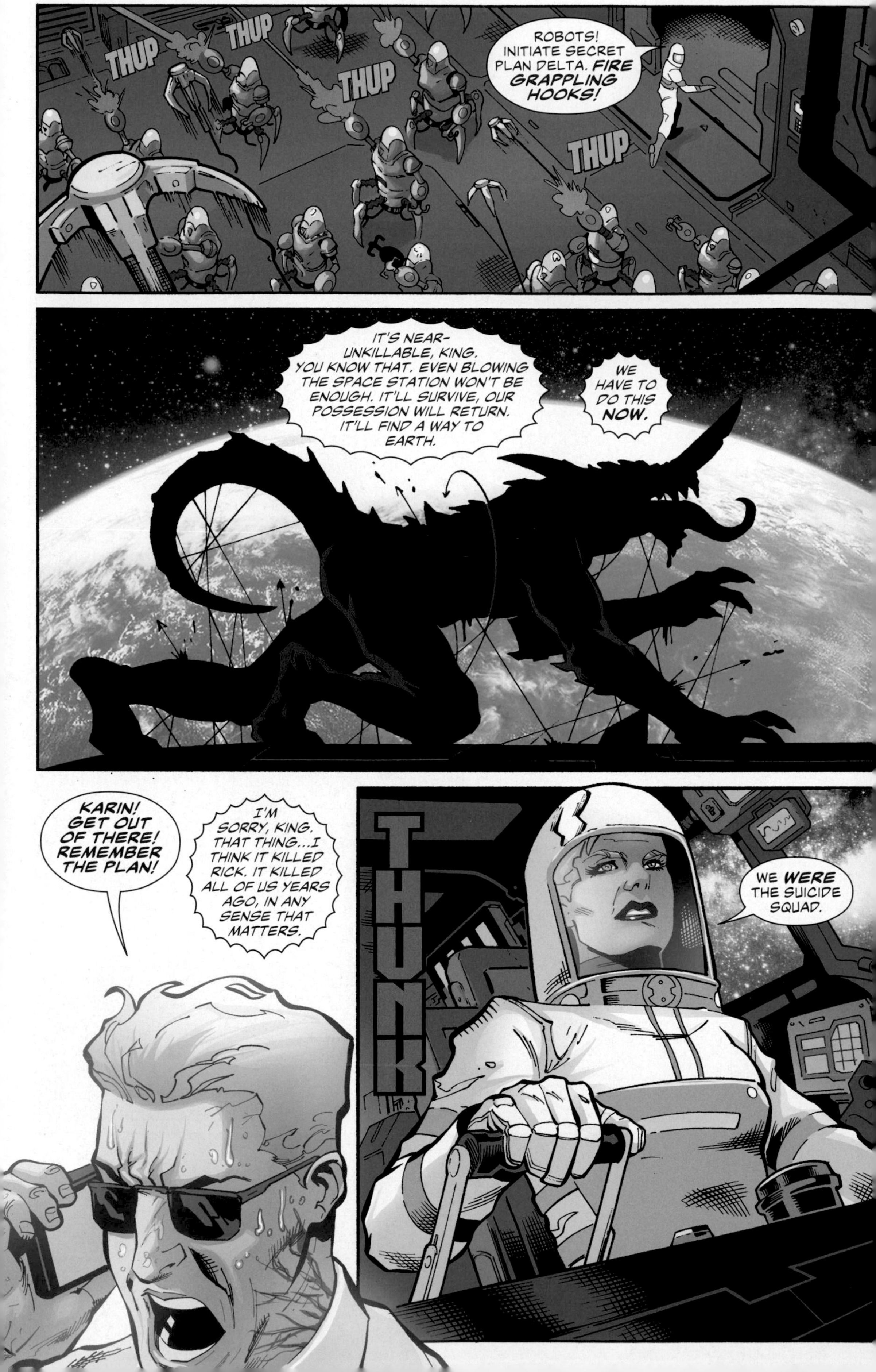
THUP
THUP
THUP
ROBOTS! INITIATE SECRET PLAN DELTA. FIRE GRAPPLING HOOKS!
THUP
IT'S NEAR-UNKILLABLE, KING. YOU KNOW THAT. EVEN BLOWING THE SPACE STATION WON'T BE ENOUGH. IT'LL SURVIVE, OUR POSSESSION WILL RETURN. IT'LL FIND A WAY TO EARTH.
WE HAVE TO DO THIS NOW.
KARIN! GET OUT OF THERE! REMEMBER THE PLAN!
I'M SORRY, KING. THAT THING...I THINK IT KILLED RICK. IT KILLED ALL OF US YEARS AGO, IN ANY SENSE THAT MATTERS.
THUNK
WE WERE THE SUICIDE SQUAD.

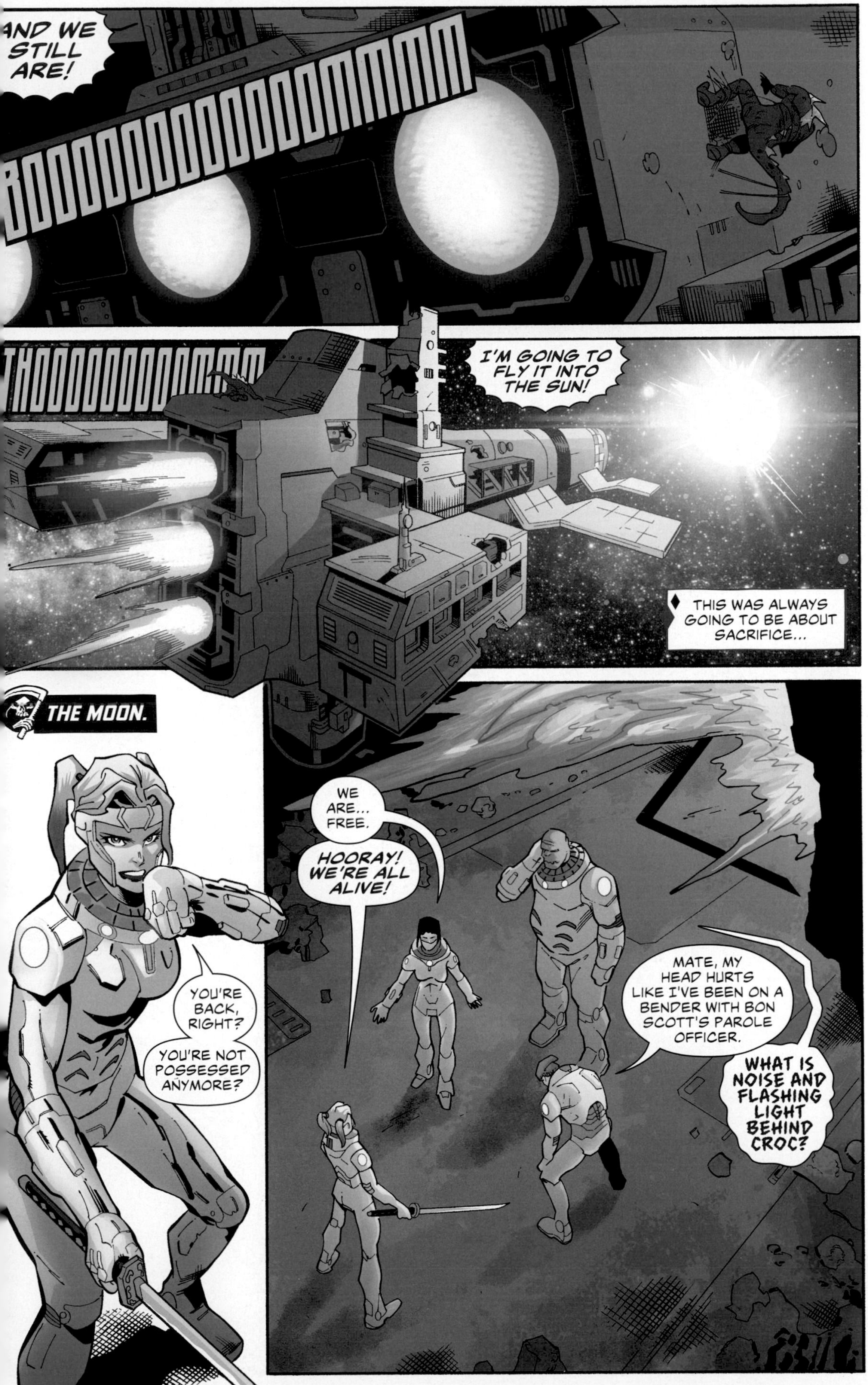
AND WE STILL ARE!
BOOOOOOOOOOOOOMMMMM
THOOOOOOOOMMMM
I'M GOING TO FLY IT INTO THE SUN!
THIS WAS ALWAYS GOING TO BE ABOUT SACRIFICE...
THE MOON.
YOU'RE BACK, RIGHT?
YOU'RE NOT POSSESSED ANYMORE?
WE ARE... FREE.
HOORAY! WE'RE ALL ALIVE!
MATE, MY HEAD HURTS LIKE I'VE BEEN ON A BENDER WITH BON SCOTT'S PAROLE OFFICER.
WHAT IS NOISE AND FLASHING LIGHT BEHIND CROC?

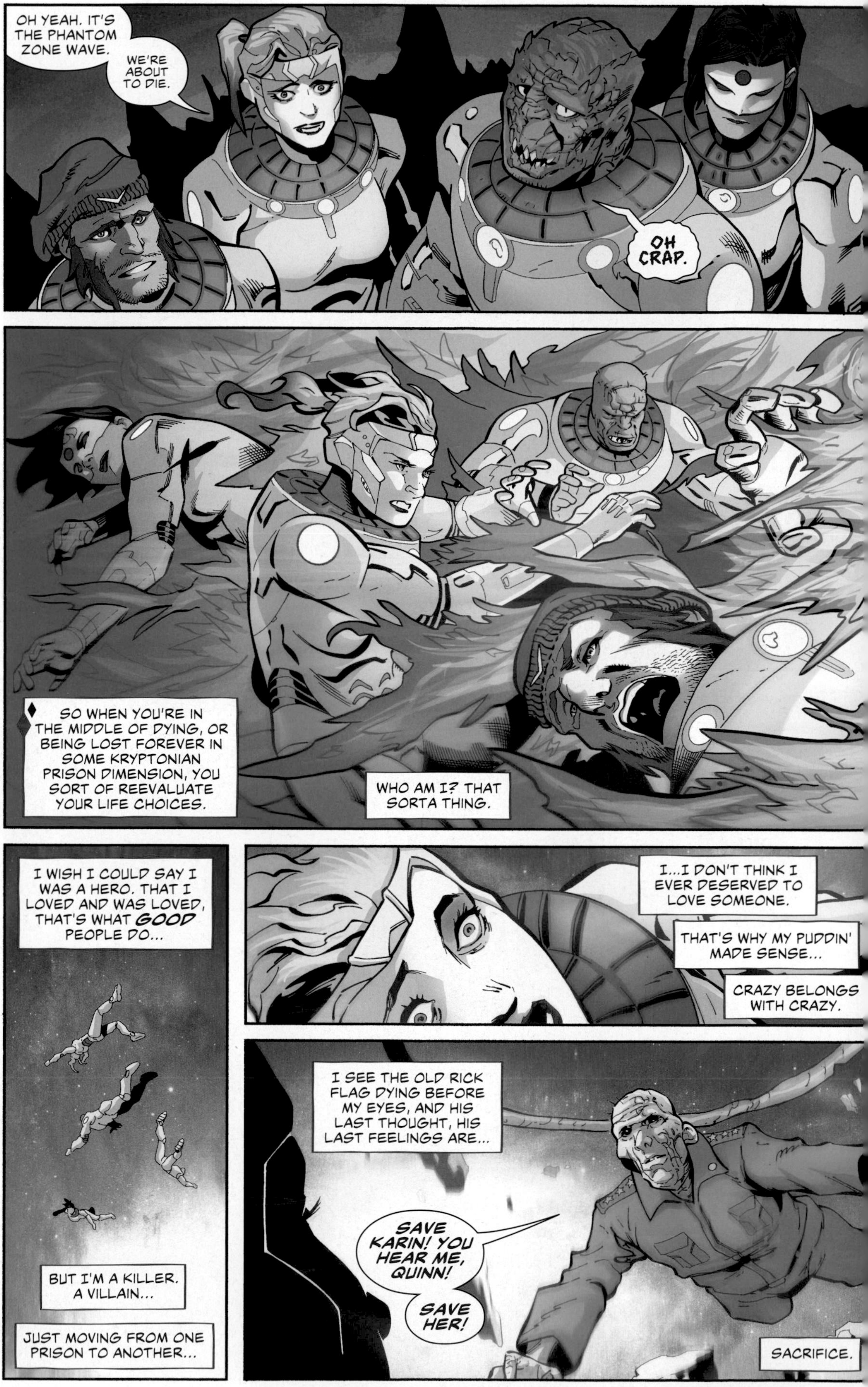
OH YEAH. IT'S THE PHANTOM ZONE WAVE.
WE'RE ABOUT TO DIE.
OH CRAP.
SO WHEN YOU'RE IN THE MIDDLE OF DYING, OR BEING LOST FOREVER IN SOME KRYPTONIAN PRISON DIMENSION, YOU SORT OF REEVALUATE YOUR LIFE CHOICES.
WHO AM I? THAT SORTA THING.
I WISH I COULD SAY I WAS A HERO. THAT I LOVED AND WAS LOVED, THAT'S WHAT GOOD PEOPLE DO...
BUT I'M A KILLER. A VILLAIN...
JUST MOVING FROM ONE PRISON TO ANOTHER...
I...I DON'T THINK I EVER DESERVED TO LOVE SOMEONE.
THAT'S WHY MY PUDDIN' MADE SENSE...
CRAZY BELONGS WITH CRAZY.
I SEE THE OLD RICK FLAG DYING BEFORE MY EYES, AND HIS LAST THOUGHT, HIS LAST FEELINGS ARE...
SAVE KARIN! YOU HEAR ME, QUINN!
SAVE HER!
SACRIFICE.

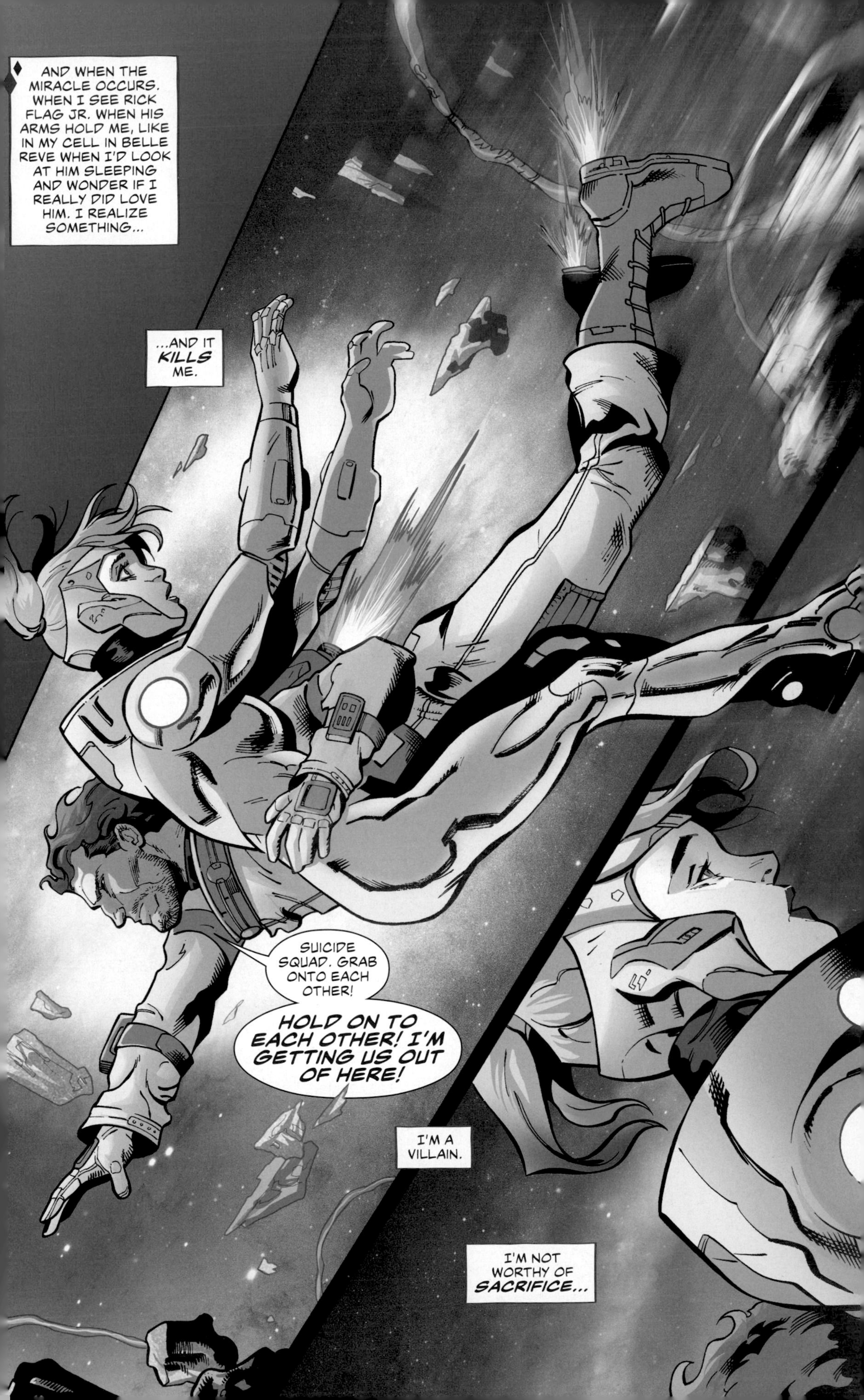
AND WHEN THE MIRACLE OCCURS. WHEN I SEE RICK FLAG JR. WHEN HIS ARMS HOLD ME, LIKE IN MY CELL IN BELLE REVE WHEN I'D LOOK AT HIM SLEEPING AND WONDER IF I REALLY DID LOVE HIM. I REALIZE SOMETHING...
...AND IT KILLS ME.
SUICIDE SQUAD. GRAB ONTO EACH OTHER!
HOLD ON TO EACH OTHER! I'M GETTING US OUT OF HERE!
I'M A VILLAIN.
I'M NOT WORTHY OF SACRIFICE...

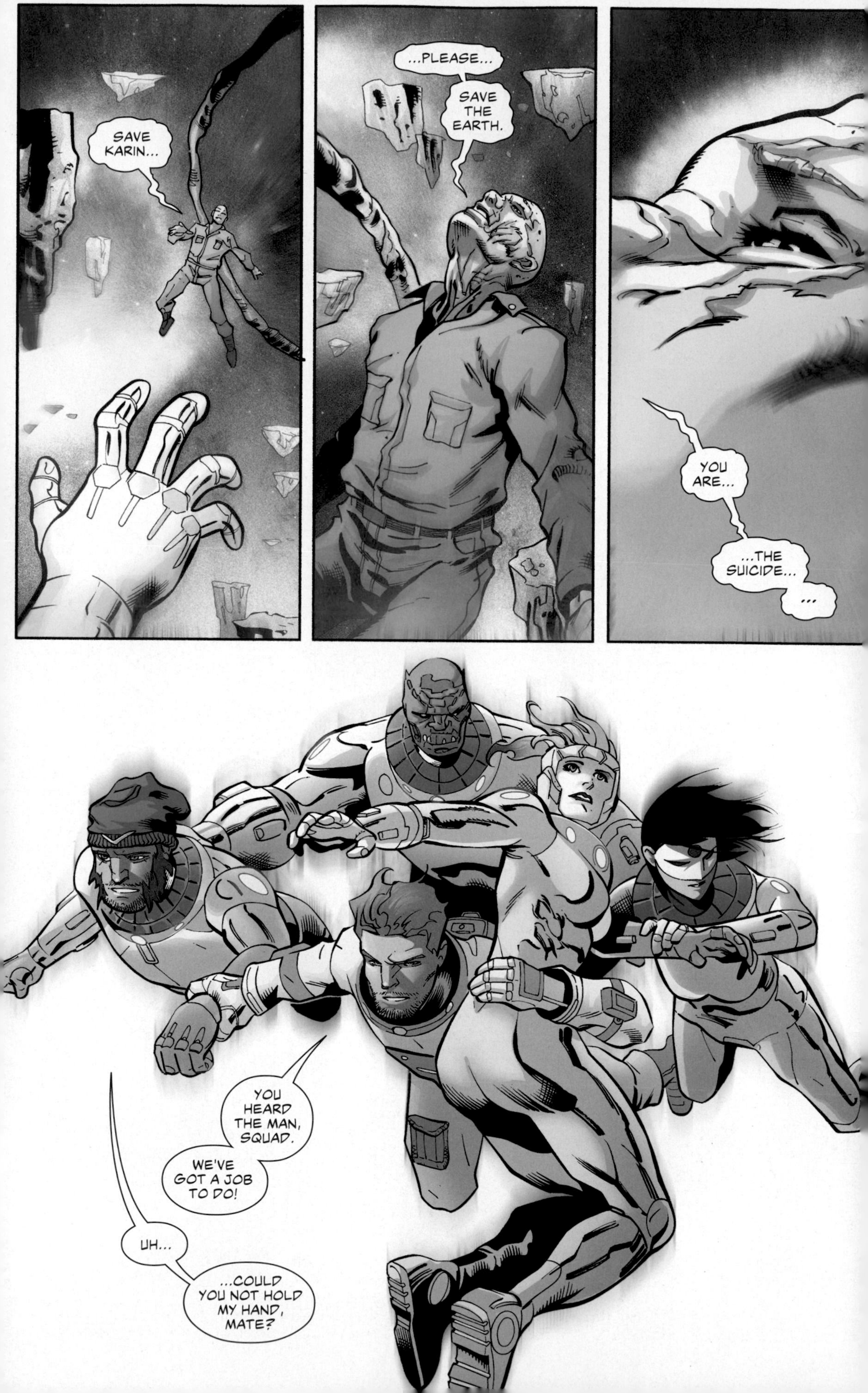
SAVE KARIN...
...PLEASE...
SAVE THE EARTH.
YOU ARE...
...THE SUICIDE...
...
YOU HEARD THE MAN, SQUAD.
WE'VE GOT A JOB TO DO!
UH...
...COULD YOU NOT HOLD MY HAND, MATE?

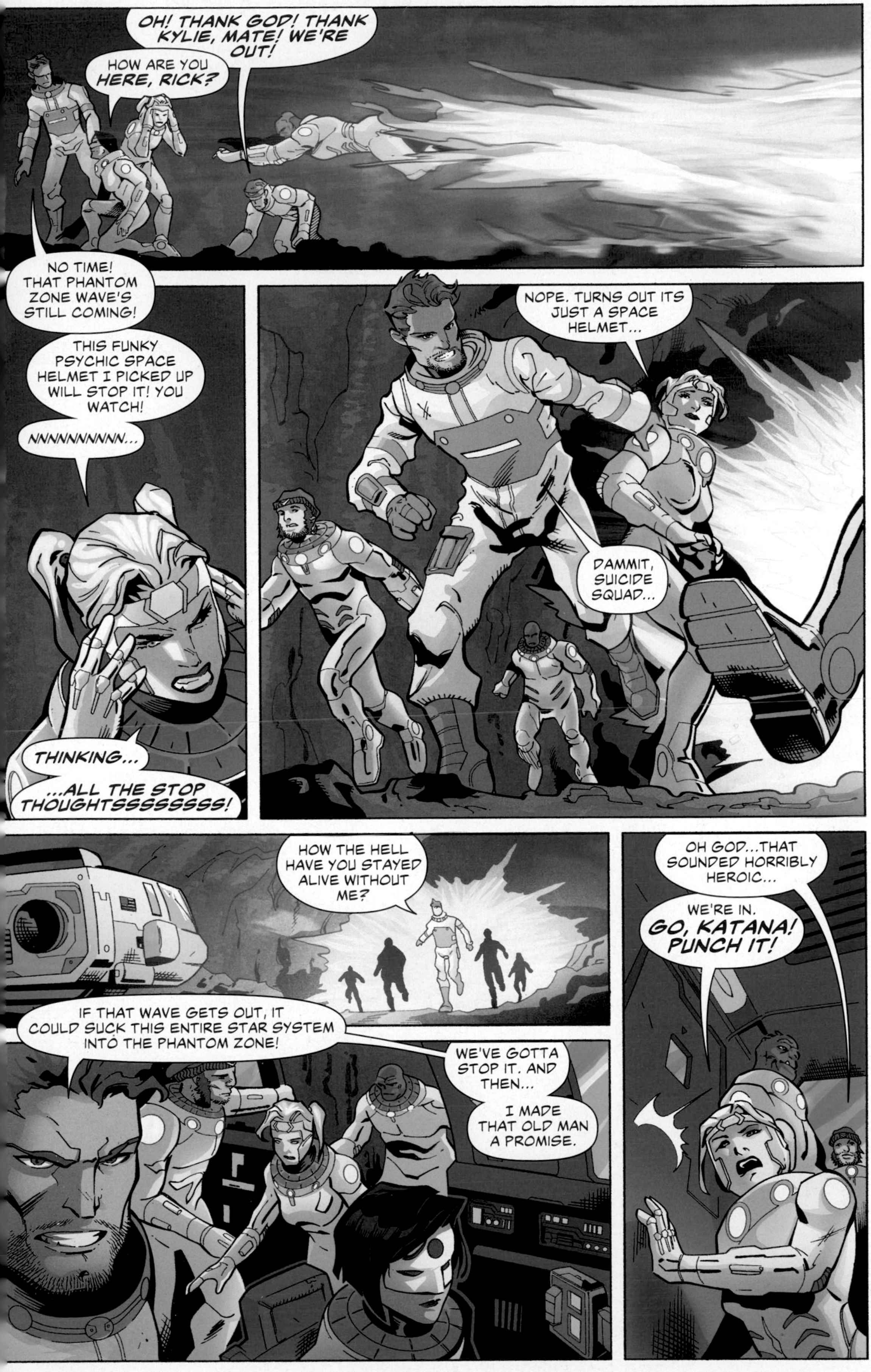
OH! THANK GOD! THANK KYLIE, MATE! WE'RE OUT!
HOW ARE YOU HERE, RICK?
NO TIME! THAT PHANTOM ZONE WAVE'S STILL COMING!
THIS FUNKY PSYCHIC SPACE HELMET I PICKED UP WILL STOP IT! YOU WATCH!
NNNNNNNNNN...
THINKING...
...ALL THE STOP THOUGHTSSSSSSSS!
NOPE. TURNS OUT ITS JUST A SPACE HELMET...
DAMMIT, SUICIDE SQUAD...
HOW THE HELL HAVE YOU STAYED ALIVE WITHOUT ME?
IF THAT WAVE GETS OUT, IT COULD SUCK THIS ENTIRE STAR SYSTEM INTO THE PHANTOM ZONE!
WE'VE GOTTA STOP IT. AND THEN...
I MADE THAT OLD MAN A PROMISE.
OH GOD...THAT SOUNDED HORRIBLY HEROIC...
WE'RE IN. GO, KATANA! PUNCH IT!

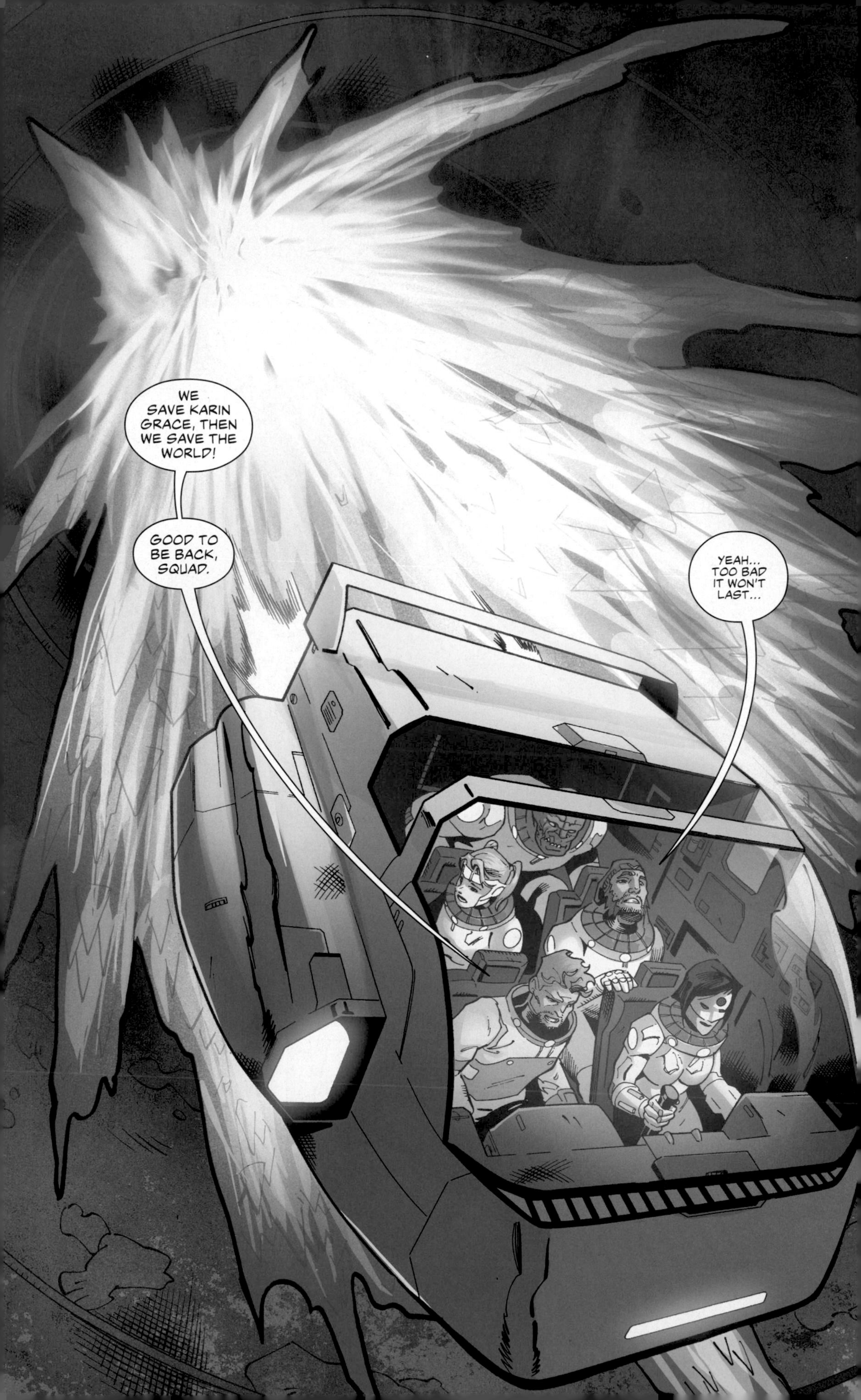
WE SAVE KARIN GRACE, THEN WE SAVE THE WORLD!
GOOD TO BE BACK, SQUAD.
YEAH... TOO BAD IT WON'T LAST...

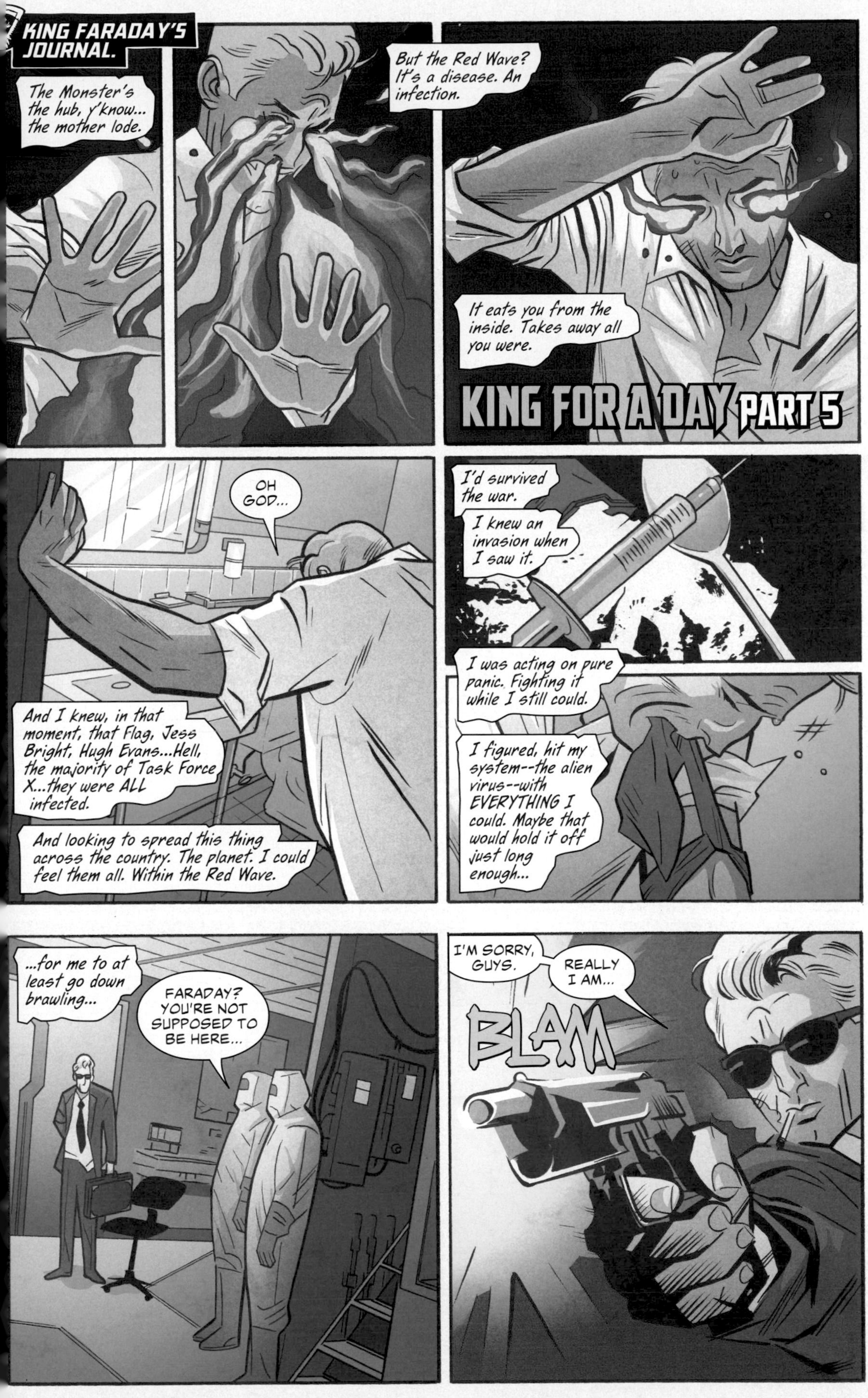
KING FARADAY'S JOURNAL.
The Monster's the hub, y'know... the mother lode.
But the Red Wave? It's a disease. An infection.
It eats you from the inside. Takes away all you were.
KING FOR A DAY PART 5
OH GOD...
And I knew, in that moment, that Flag, Jess Bright, Hugh Evans...Hell, the majority of Task Force X...they were ALL infected.
And looking to spread this thing across the country. The planet. I could feel them all. Within the Red Wave.
I'd survived the war.
I knew an invasion when I saw it.
I was acting on pure panic. Fighting it while I still could.
I figured, hit my system--the alien virus--with EVERYTHING I could. Maybe that would hold it off just long enough...
...for me to at least go down brawling...
FARADAY? YOU'RE NOT SUPPOSED TO BE HERE...
I'M SORRY, GUYS.
REALLY I AM...
BLAM

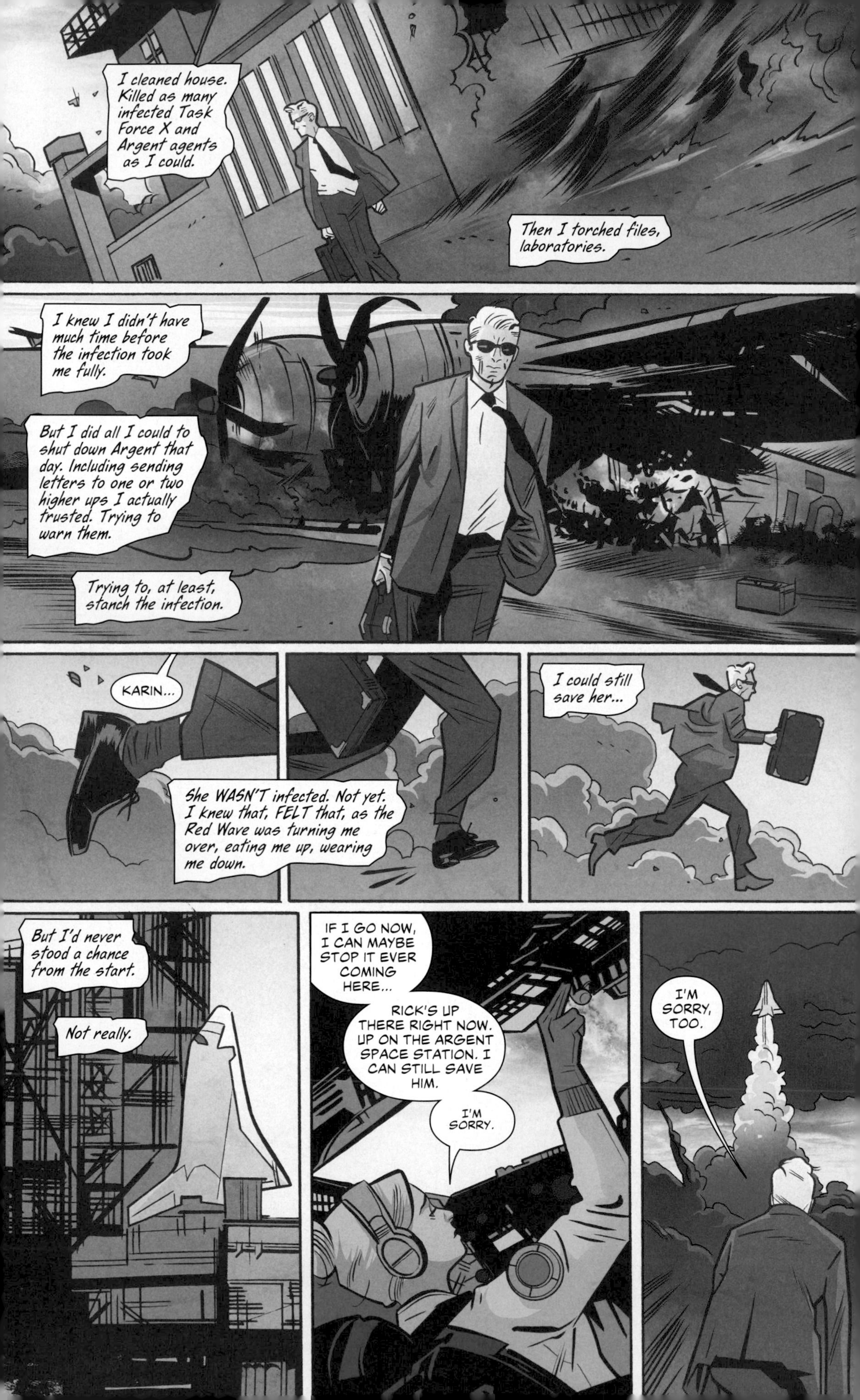
I cleaned house. Killed as many infected Task Force X and Argent agents as I could.
Then I torched files, laboratories.
I knew I didn't have much time before the infection took me fully.
But I did all I could to shut down Argent that day. Including sending letters to one or two higher ups I actually trusted. Trying to warn them.
Trying to, at least, stanch the infection.
KARIN...
She WASN'T infected. Not yet. I knew that, FELT that, as the Red Wave was turning me over, eating me up, wearing me down.
I could still save her...
But I'd never stood a chance from the start.
Not really.
IF I GO NOW, I CAN MAYBE STOP IT EVER COMING HERE...
RICK'S UP THERE RIGHT NOW. UP ON THE ARGENT SPACE STATION. I CAN STILL SAVE HIM.
I'M SORRY.
I'M SORRY, TOO.

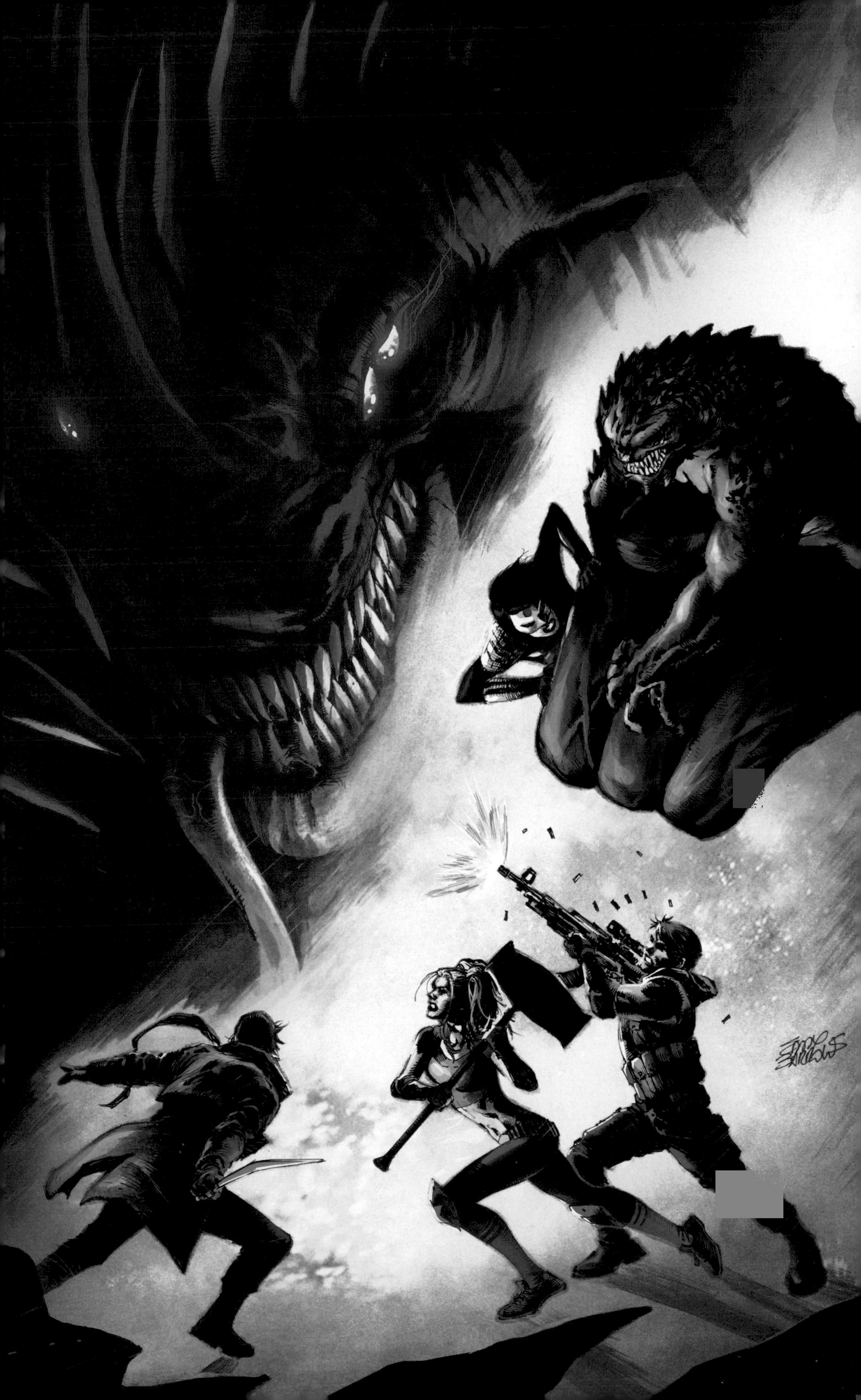

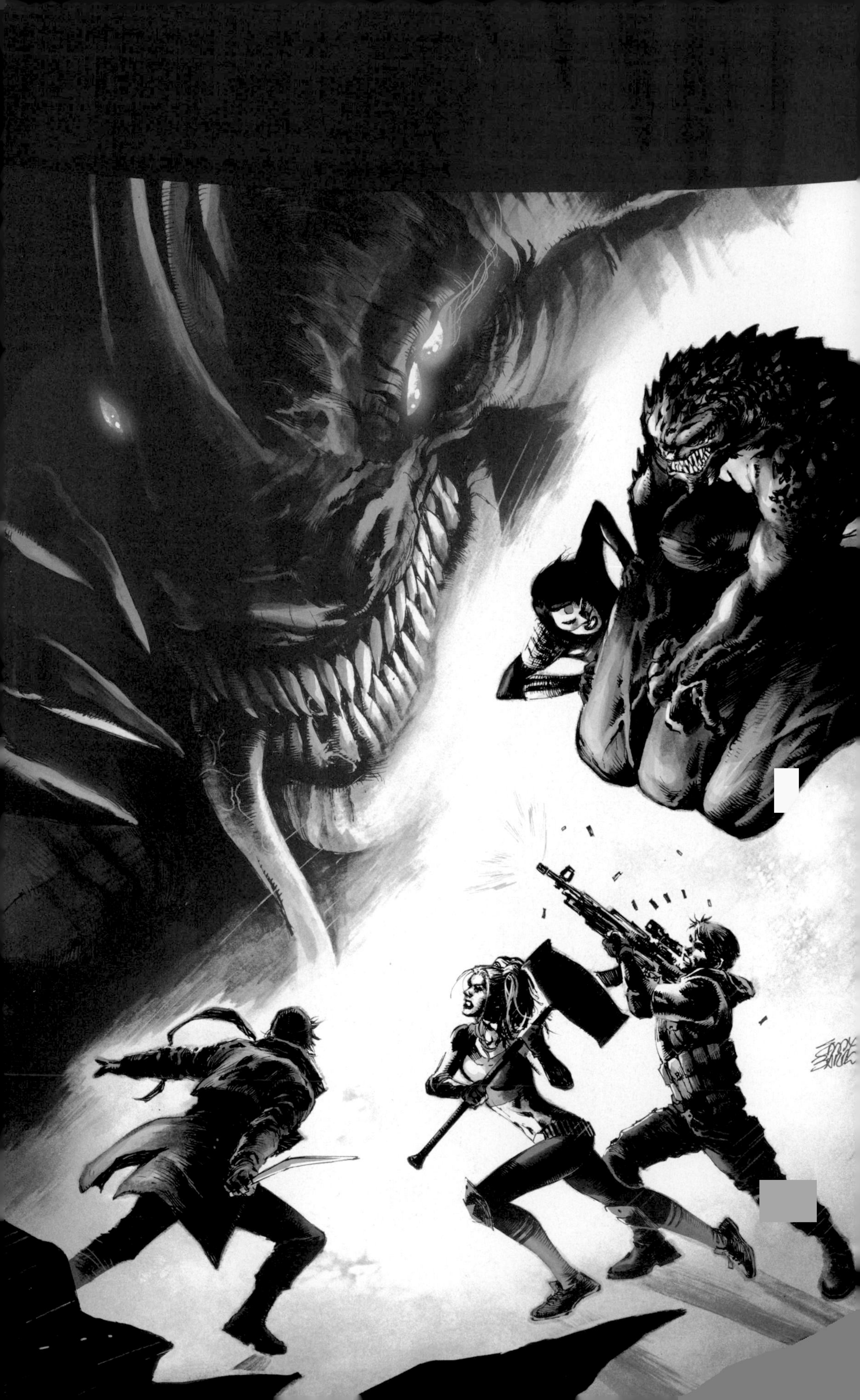

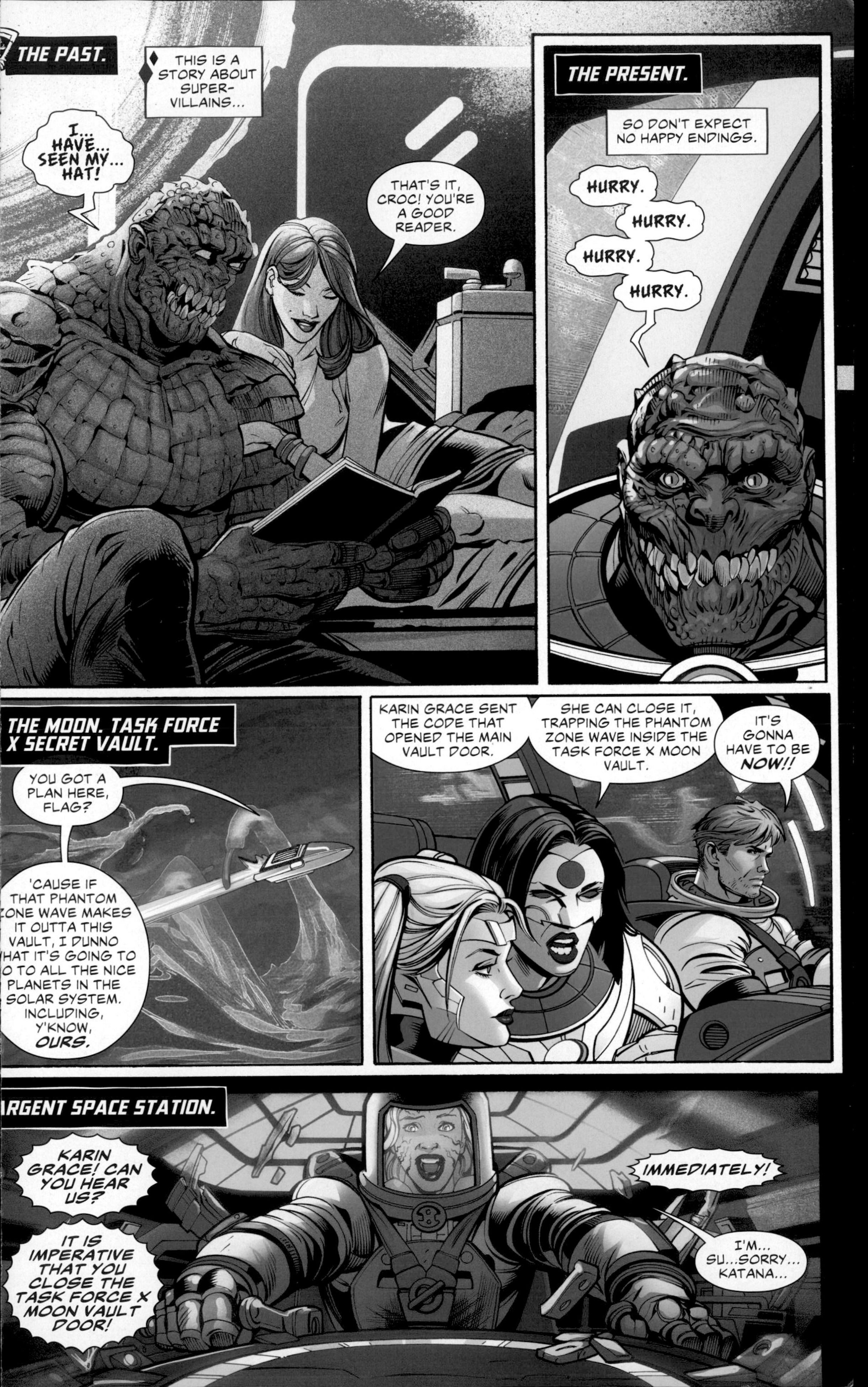
THE PAST.
THIS IS A STORY ABOUT SUPER-VILLAINS...
I... HAVE... SEEN MY... HAT!
THAT'S IT, CROC! YOU'RE A GOOD READER.
THE PRESENT.
SO DON'T EXPECT NO HAPPY ENDINGS.
HURRY.
HURRY.
HURRY.
HURRY.
THE MOON. TASK FORCE X SECRET VAULT.
YOU GOT A PLAN HERE, FLAG?
'CAUSE IF THAT PHANTOM ZONE WAVE MAKES IT OUTTA THIS VAULT, I DUNNO WHAT IT'S GOING TO DO TO ALL THE NICE PLANETS IN THE SOLAR SYSTEM. INCLUDING, Y'KNOW, OURS.
KARIN GRACE SENT THE CODE THAT OPENED THE MAIN VAULT DOOR.
SHE CAN CLOSE IT, TRAPPING THE PHANTOM ZONE WAVE INSIDE THE TASK FORCE X MOON VAULT.
IT'S GONNA HAVE TO BE NOW!!
ARGENT SPACE STATION.
KARIN GRACE! CAN YOU HEAR US?
IT IS IMPERATIVE THAT YOU CLOSE THE TASK FORCE X MOON VAULT DOOR!
IMMEDIATELY!
I'M... SU...SORRY... KATANA...

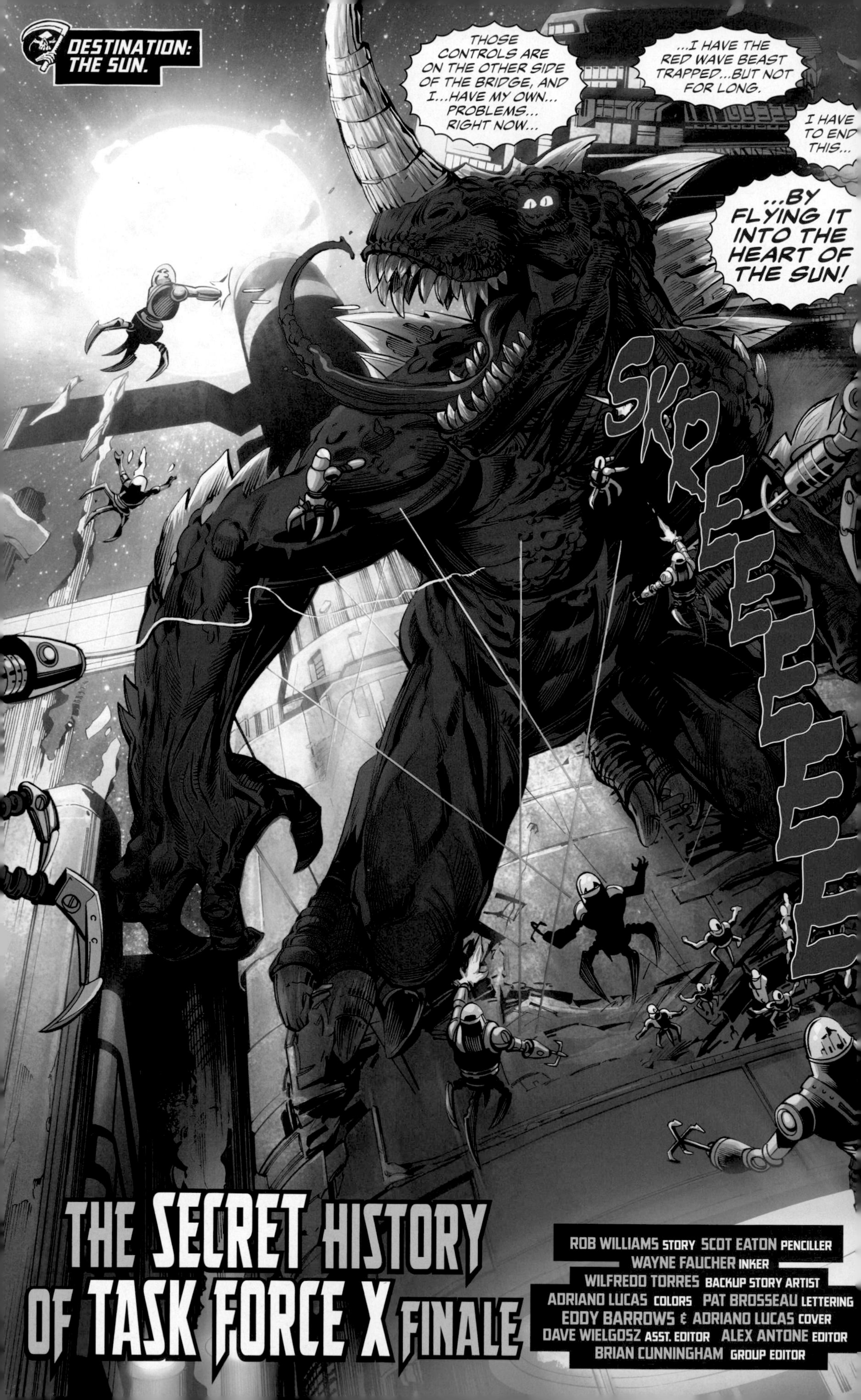
DESTINATION: THE SUN.
THOSE CONTROLS ARE ON THE OTHER SIDE OF THE BRIDGE, AND I...HAVE MY OWN... PROBLEMS... RIGHT NOW...
...I HAVE THE RED WAVE BEAST TRAPPED...BUT NOT FOR LONG.
I HAVE TO END THIS...
...BY FLYING IT INTO THE HEART OF THE SUN!
SKREEEEEEE
THE SECRET HISTORY OF TASK FORCE X FINALE
ROB WILLIAMS STORY SCOT EATON PENCILLER
WAYNE FAUCHER INKER
WILFREDO TORRES BACKUP STORY ARTIST
ADRIANO LUCAS COLORS PAT BROSSEAU LETTERING
EDDY BARROWS & ADRIANO LUCAS COVER
DAVE WIELGOSZ ASST. EDITOR ALEX ANTONE EDITOR
BRIAN CUNNINGHAM GROUP EDITOR

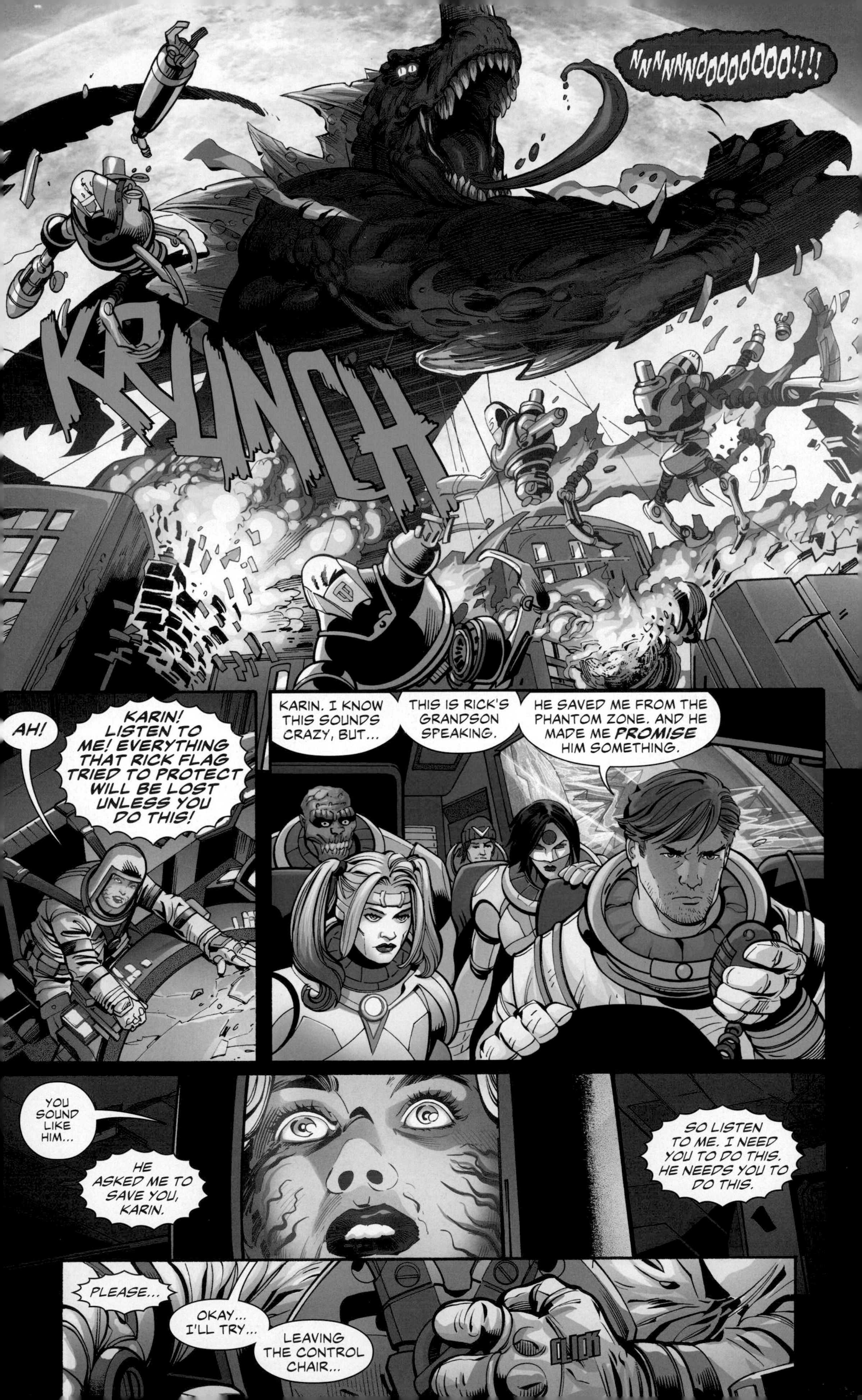
NNNNNNOOOOOOOO!!!!
KRUNCH
AH!
KARIN! LISTEN TO ME! EVERYTHING THAT RICK FLAG TRIED TO PROTECT WILL BE LOST UNLESS YOU DO THIS!
KARIN. I KNOW THIS SOUNDS CRAZY, BUT...
THIS IS RICK'S GRANDSON SPEAKING.
HE SAVED ME FROM THE PHANTOM ZONE. AND HE MADE ME PROMISE HIM SOMETHING.
YOU SOUND LIKE HIM...
HE ASKED ME TO SAVE YOU, KARIN.
SO LISTEN TO ME. I NEED YOU TO DO THIS. HE NEEDS YOU TO DO THIS.
PLEASE...
OKAY... I'LL TRY...
LEAVING THE CONTROL CHAIR...
CLICK

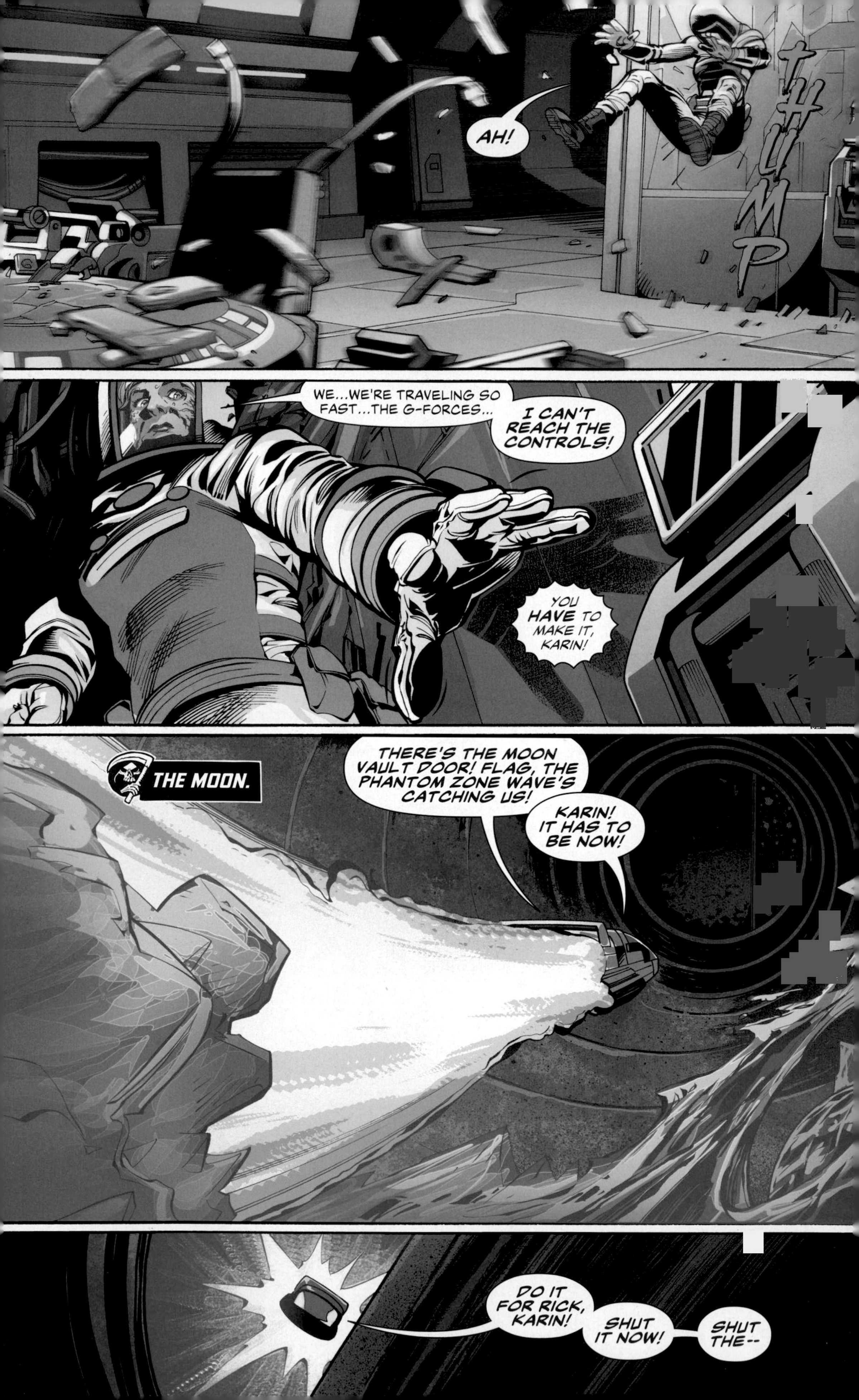
AH!
THUMP
WE...WE'RE TRAVELING SO FAST...THE G-FORCES...
I CAN'T REACH THE CONTROLS!
YOU HAVE TO MAKE IT, KARIN!
THE MOON.
THERE'S THE MOON VAULT DOOR! FLAG, THE PHANTOM ZONE WAVE'S CATCHING US!
KARIN! IT HAS TO BE NOW!
DO IT FOR RICK, KARIN!
SHUT IT NOW!
SHUT THE--

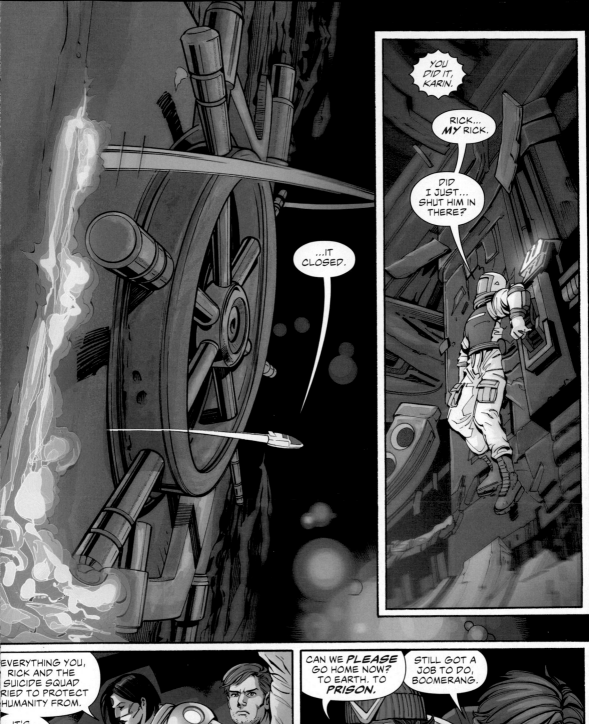

...IT CLOSED.

YOU DID IT, KARIN.

RICK... *MY* RICK.

DID I JUST... SHUT HIM IN THERE?

EVERYTHING YOU, RICK AND THE SUICIDE SQUAD TRIED TO PROTECT HUMANITY FROM.

IT'S LOCKED AWAY NOW. FOREVER.

CAN WE *PLEASE* GO HOME NOW? TO EARTH. TO *PRISON.*

STILL GOT A JOB TO DO, BOOMERANG.

...OH GOOD... WE'RE DOING HERO THINGS.

KARIN, WE HAVE YOUR POSITION...

BEHOLD THE STRONG-JAWED AMERICAN HERO, RETURNED FROM THE DEAD...

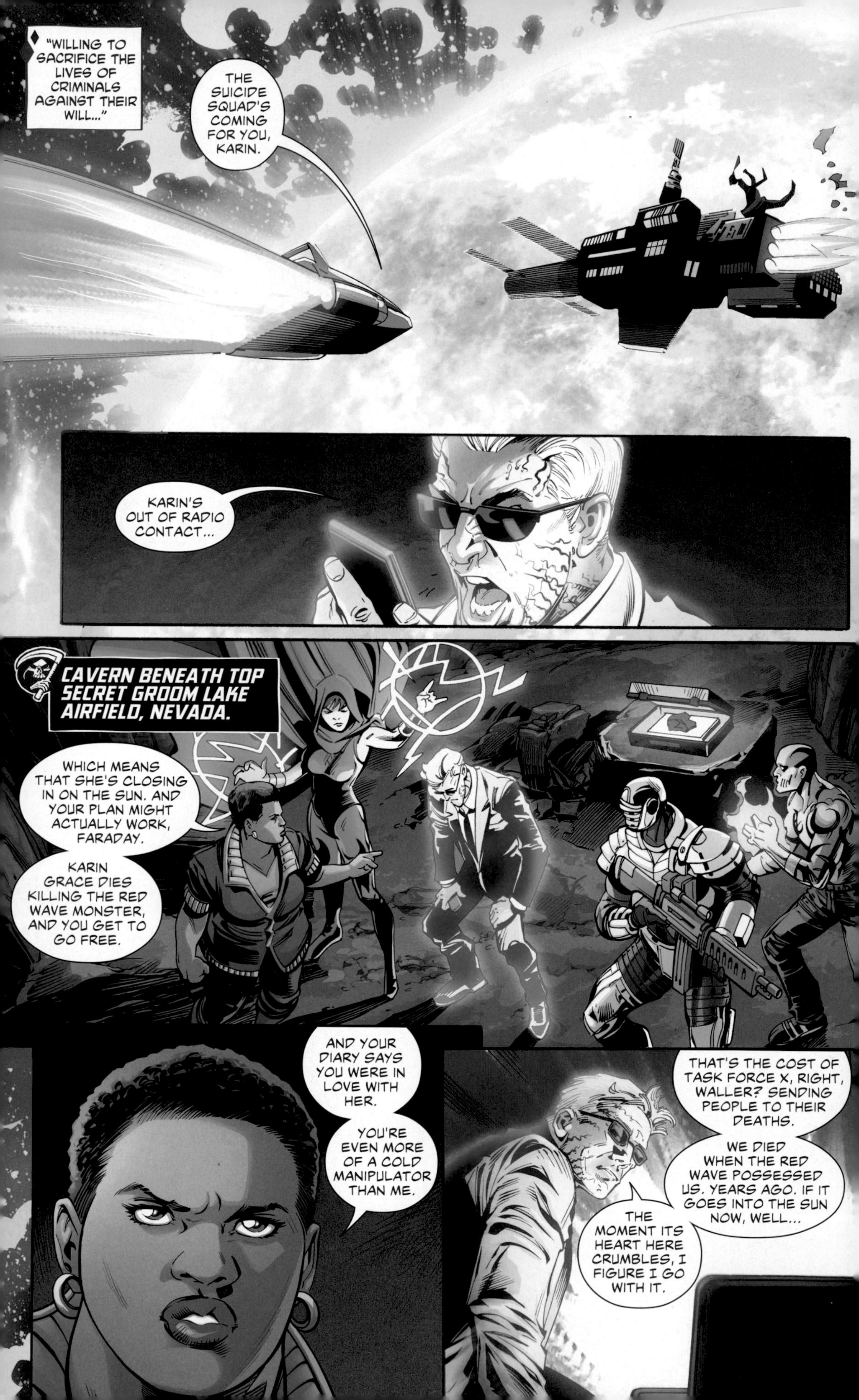
"WILLING TO SACRIFICE THE LIVES OF CRIMINALS AGAINST THEIR WILL..."
THE SUICIDE SQUAD'S COMING FOR YOU, KARIN.
KARIN'S OUT OF RADIO CONTACT...
CAVERN BENEATH TOP SECRET GROOM LAKE AIRFIELD, NEVADA.
WHICH MEANS THAT SHE'S CLOSING IN ON THE SUN. AND YOUR PLAN MIGHT ACTUALLY WORK, FARADAY.
KARIN GRACE DIES KILLING THE RED WAVE MONSTER, AND YOU GET TO GO FREE.
AND YOUR DIARY SAYS YOU WERE IN LOVE WITH HER.
YOU'RE EVEN MORE OF A COLD MANIPULATOR THAN ME.
THAT'S THE COST OF TASK FORCE X, RIGHT, WALLER? SENDING PEOPLE TO THEIR DEATHS.
WE DIED WHEN THE RED WAVE POSSESSED US. YEARS AGO. IF IT GOES INTO THE SUN NOW, WELL...
THE MOMENT ITS HEART HERE CRUMBLES, I FIGURE I GO WITH IT.

THE RED WAVE MONSTER'S HURT FROM WHATEVER KARIN'S DONE TO IT. WEAKENED. BUT IT'S NOT OUT.

KARIN'S ABLE TO STAY IN CONTROL, JUST. SHE'S ALWAYS BEEN THE STRONGEST OF US.

THANKS TO YOUR WITCH THERE, THIS IS THE FIRST TIME I'VE BEEN IN FULL CONTROL OF MYSELF FOR YEARS.

THIS PIECE OF THE RED WAVE'S HEART IS WHAT'S BEEN KEEPING YOU ALIVE? CONTROLLING YOU?

A PRISON SENTENCE. I COULDN'T LEAVE THIS PLACE UNLESS I TOOK IT WITH ME, WHICH WOULD'VE INFECTED MORE PEOPLE. SO: IMMORTALITY, TRAPPED IN A JUNKYARD OF OLD WARBIRDS.

...I'M A GHOST.

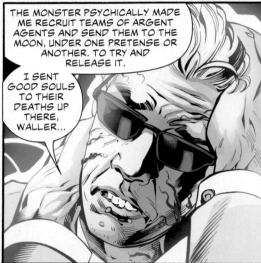

THE MONSTER PSYCHICALLY MADE ME RECRUIT TEAMS OF ARGENT AGENTS AND SEND THEM TO THE MOON, UNDER ONE PRETENSE OR ANOTHER. TO TRY AND RELEASE IT.

I SENT GOOD SOULS TO THEIR DEATHS UP THERE, WALLER...

AND THEN YOU FINALLY CAME TO US?

YOU WERE MY FINAL HAND, YEAH. I COULD FEEL THE MONSTER'S STRENGTH GROWING. IT WAS NOW OR NEVER. I THOUGHT YOU AND YOUR OUTFIT COULD KILL IT. AND YOUR SQUAD, WELL...

THEY'RE EXPENDABLE...

NO...

NO! THE FUTURE! I... IT TWISTS BEFORE ME! IT SHOWS ITSELF!

ENCHANTRESS?

HE'S KILLED WAYLON...

HE'S KILLED CROC.

◆ "FLAG, I HATE TO MENTION THIS, BUT...

"YOU DO KNOW WE'RE ON FIRE, RIGHT?"

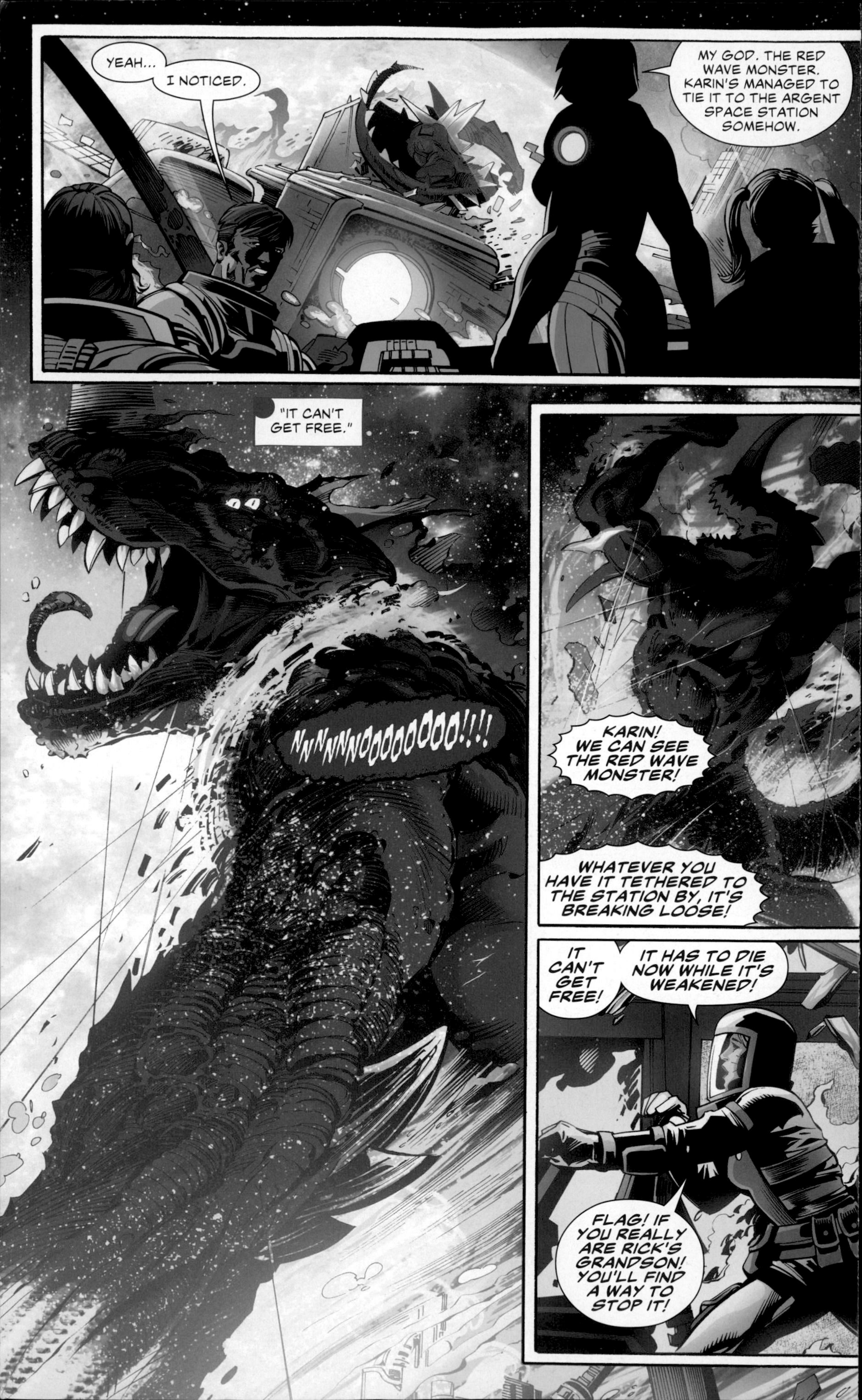
YEAH... I NOTICED.
MY GOD. THE RED WAVE MONSTER. KARIN'S MANAGED TO TIE IT TO THE ARGENT SPACE STATION SOMEHOW.
"IT CAN'T GET FREE."
NNNNNOOOOOOOO!!!!
KARIN! WE CAN SEE THE RED WAVE MONSTER!
WHATEVER YOU HAVE IT TETHERED TO THE STATION BY, IT'S BREAKING LOOSE!
IT CAN'T GET FREE!
IT HAS TO DIE NOW WHILE IT'S WEAKENED!
FLAG! IF YOU REALLY ARE RICK'S GRANDSON! YOU'LL FIND A WAY TO STOP IT!

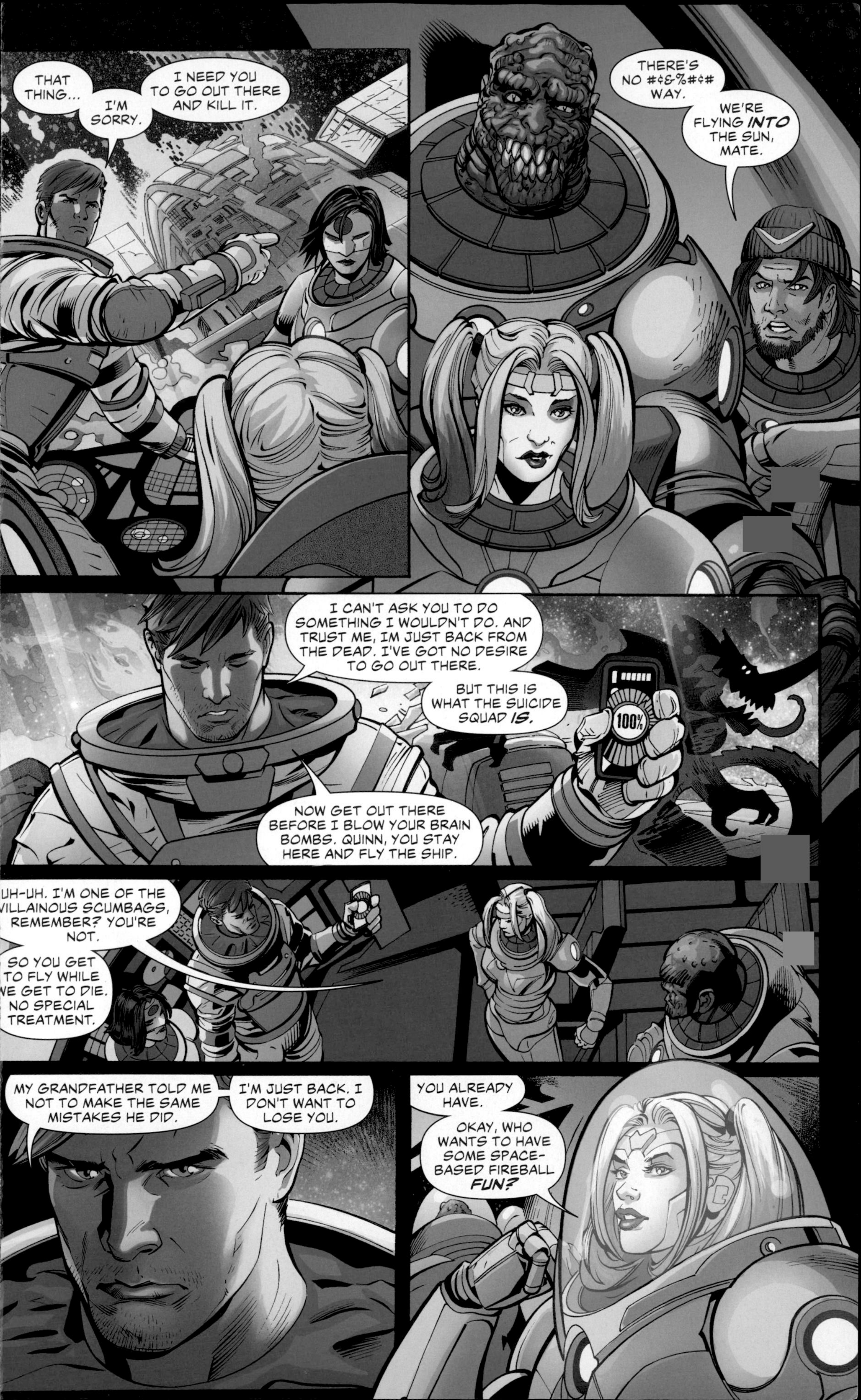
THAT THING...
I NEED YOU TO GO OUT THERE AND KILL IT.
I'M SORRY.
THERE'S NO #¢&%#¢# WAY.
WE'RE FLYING *INTO* THE SUN, MATE.
I CAN'T ASK YOU TO DO SOMETHING I WOULDN'T DO. AND TRUST ME, IM JUST BACK FROM THE DEAD. I'VE GOT NO DESIRE TO GO OUT THERE.
BUT THIS IS WHAT THE SUICIDE SQUAD *IS.*
100%
NOW GET OUT THERE BEFORE I BLOW YOUR BRAIN BOMBS. QUINN, YOU STAY HERE AND FLY THE SHIP.
UH-UH. I'M ONE OF THE VILLAINOUS SCUMBAGS, REMEMBER? YOU'RE NOT.
SO YOU GET TO FLY WHILE WE GET TO DIE. NO SPECIAL TREATMENT.
MY GRANDFATHER TOLD ME NOT TO MAKE THE SAME MISTAKES HE DID.
I'M JUST BACK. I DON'T WANT TO LOSE YOU.
YOU ALREADY HAVE.
OKAY, WHO WANTS TO HAVE SOME SPACE-BASED FIREBALL *FUN?*

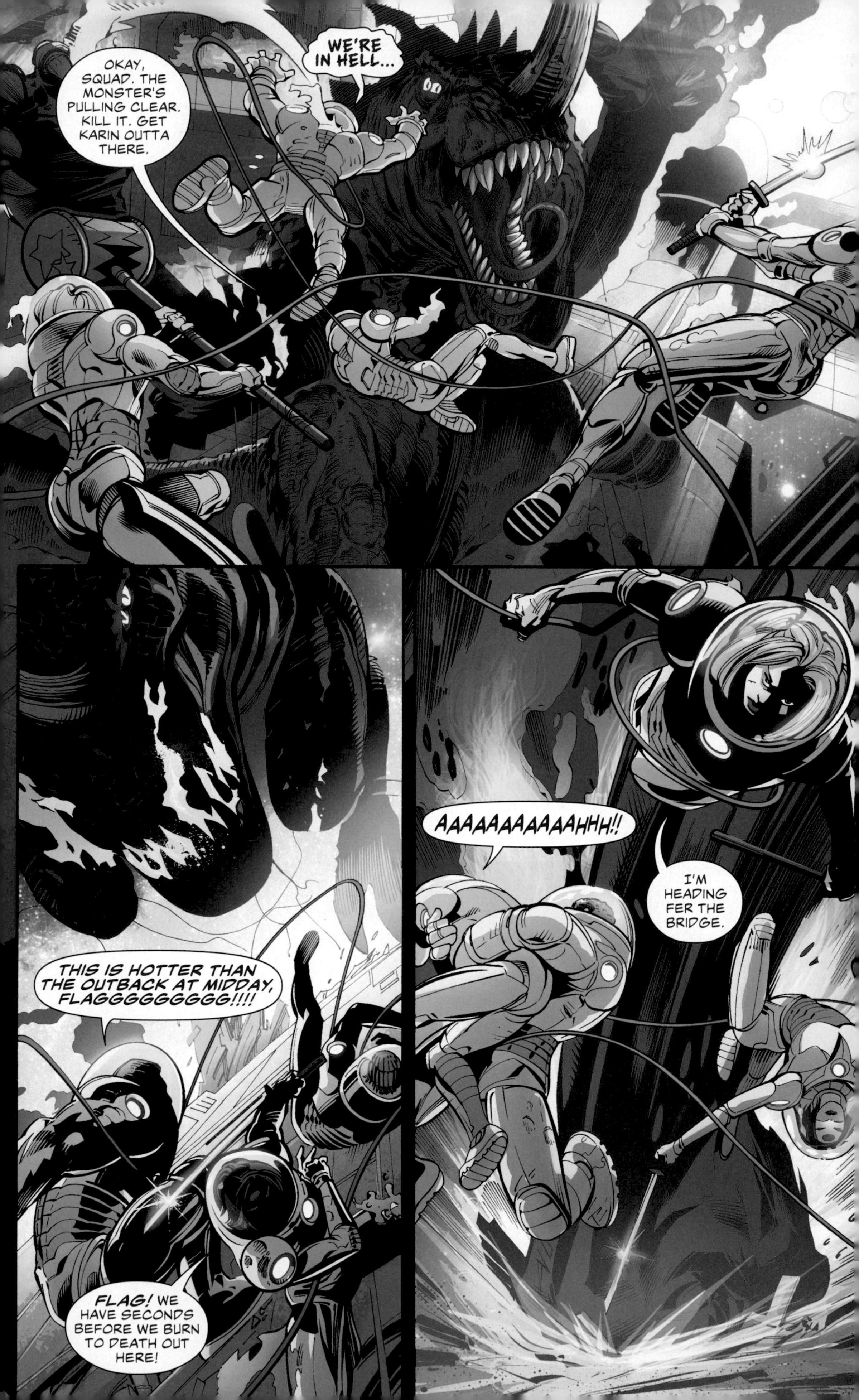

OKAY, SQUAD. THE MONSTER'S PULLING CLEAR. KILL IT. GET KARIN OUTTA THERE.
WE'RE IN HELL...
THIS IS HOTTER THAN THE OUTBACK AT MIDDAY, FLAGGGGGGGGG!!!!
FLAG! WE HAVE SECONDS BEFORE WE BURN TO DEATH OUT HERE!
AAAAAAAAAAAHHH!!
I'M HEADING FER THE BRIDGE.

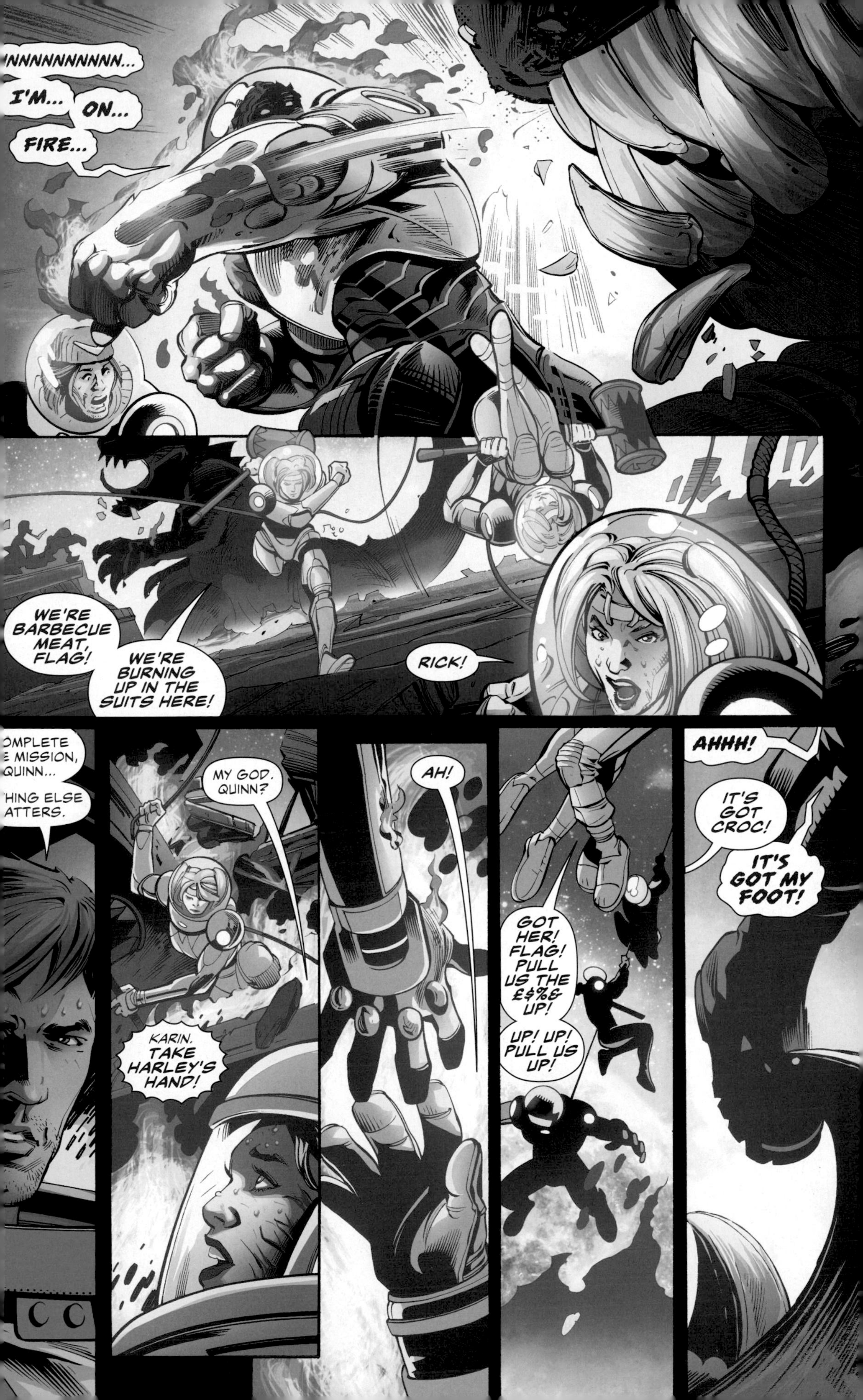
NNNNNNNNNN...
I'M... ON...
FIRE...
WE'RE BARBECUE MEAT, FLAG!
WE'RE BURNING UP IN THE SUITS HERE!
RICK!
OMPLETE E MISSION, QUINN...
THING ELSE ATTERS.
MY GOD. QUINN?
KARIN. TAKE HARLEY'S HAND!
AH!
GOT HER! FLAG! PULL US THE £$%& UP!
UP! UP! PULL US UP!
AHHH!
IT'S GOT CROC!
IT'S GOT MY FOOT!

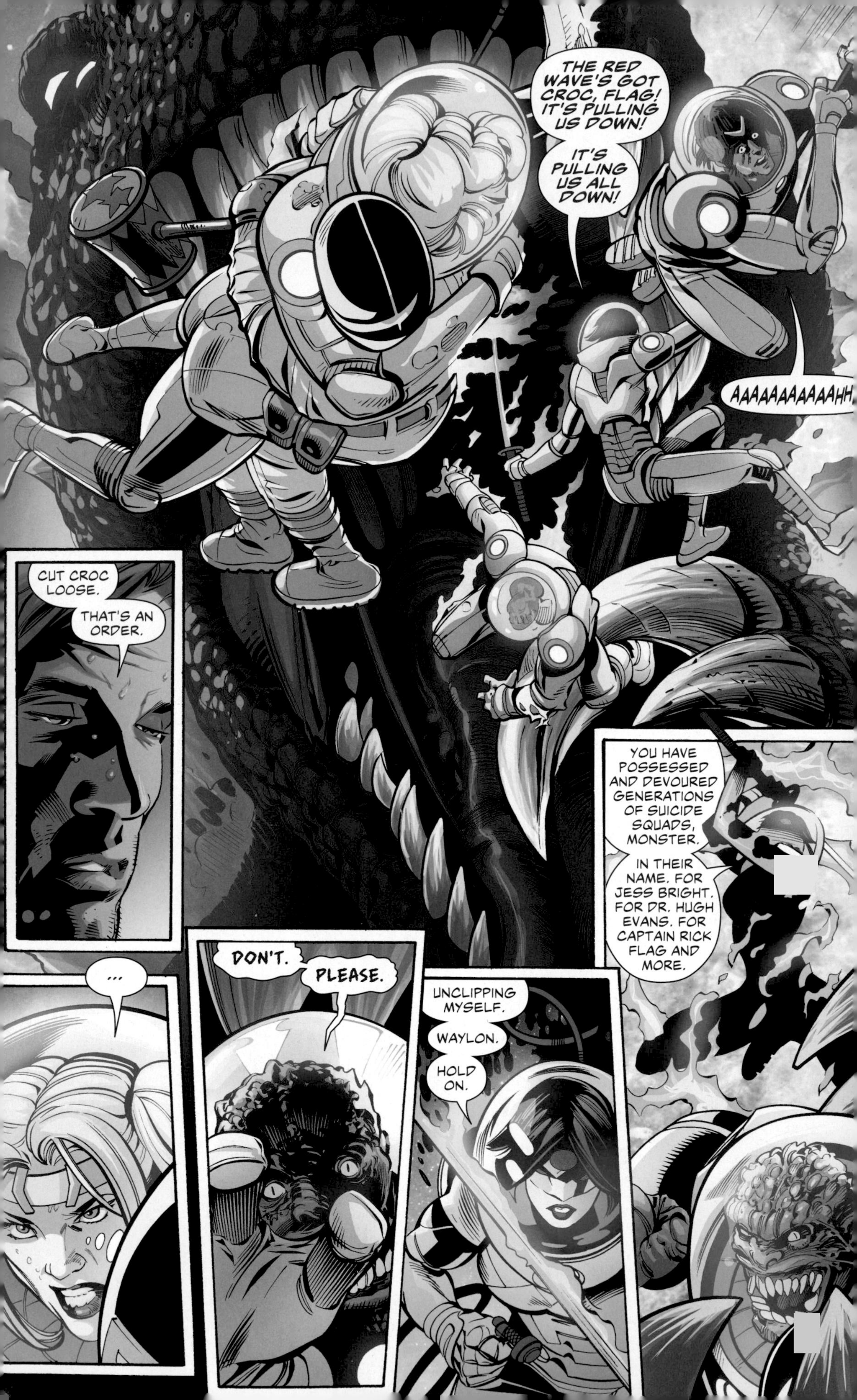
THE RED WAVE'S GOT CROC, FLAG! IT'S PULLING US DOWN!
IT'S PULLING US ALL DOWN!
AAAAAAAAAAHH
CUT CROC LOOSE.
THAT'S AN ORDER.
YOU HAVE POSSESSED AND DEVOURED GENERATIONS OF SUICIDE SQUADS, MONSTER.
IN THEIR NAME. FOR JESS BRIGHT. FOR DR. HUGH EVANS. FOR CAPTAIN RICK FLAG AND MORE.
...
DON'T.
PLEASE.
UNCLIPPING MYSELF.
WAYLON.
HOLD ON.

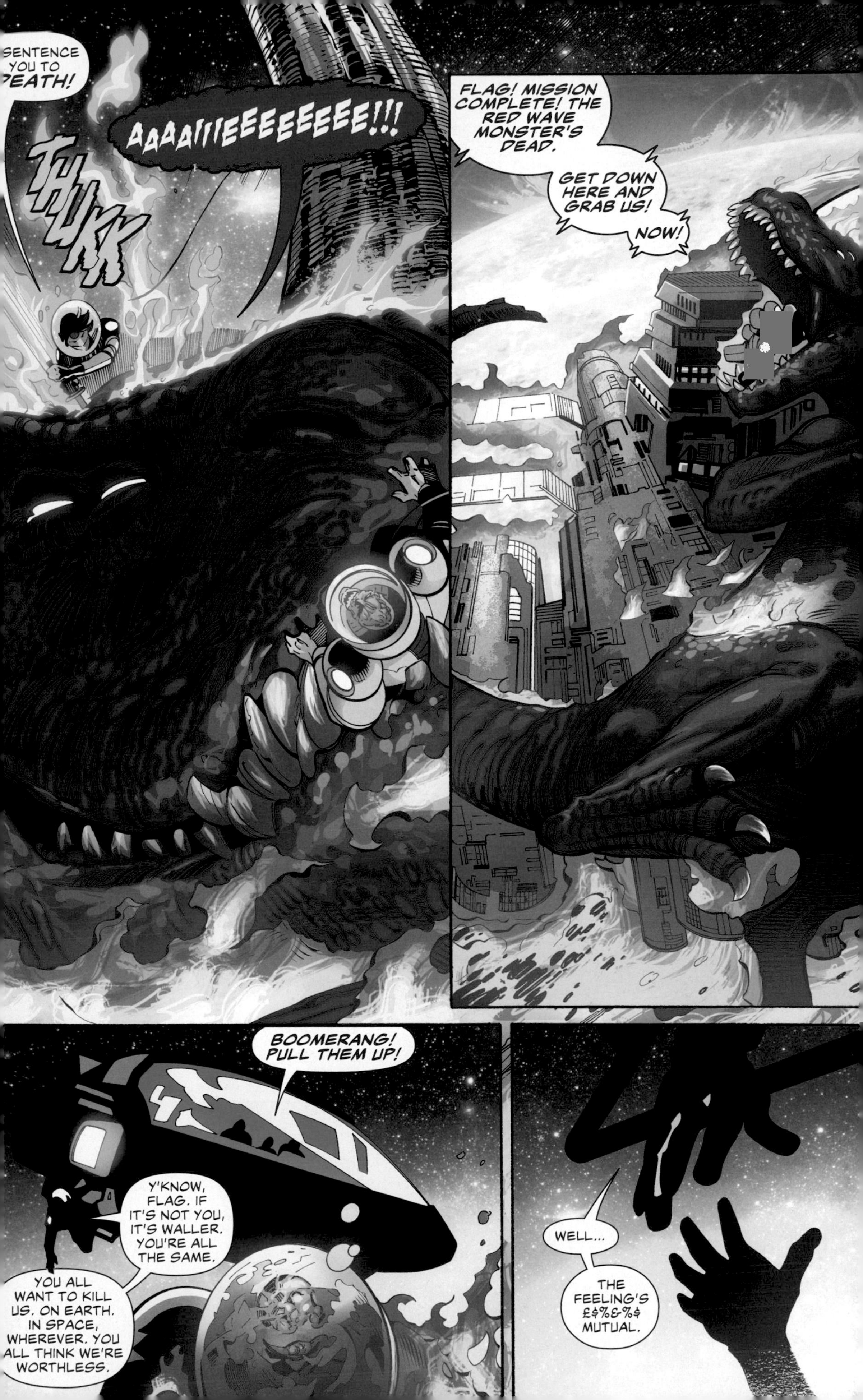
SENTENCE YOU TO DEATH!
AAAAIIIEEEEEEEEE!!!
THUKK
FLAG! MISSION COMPLETE! THE RED WAVE MONSTER'S DEAD.
GET DOWN HERE AND GRAB US!
NOW!
BOOMERANG! PULL THEM UP!
Y'KNOW, FLAG. IF IT'S NOT YOU, IT'S WALLER. YOU'RE ALL THE SAME.
YOU ALL WANT TO KILL US. ON EARTH. IN SPACE, WHEREVER. YOU ALL THINK WE'RE WORTHLESS.
WELL...
THE FEELING'S £$%&%$ MUTUAL.

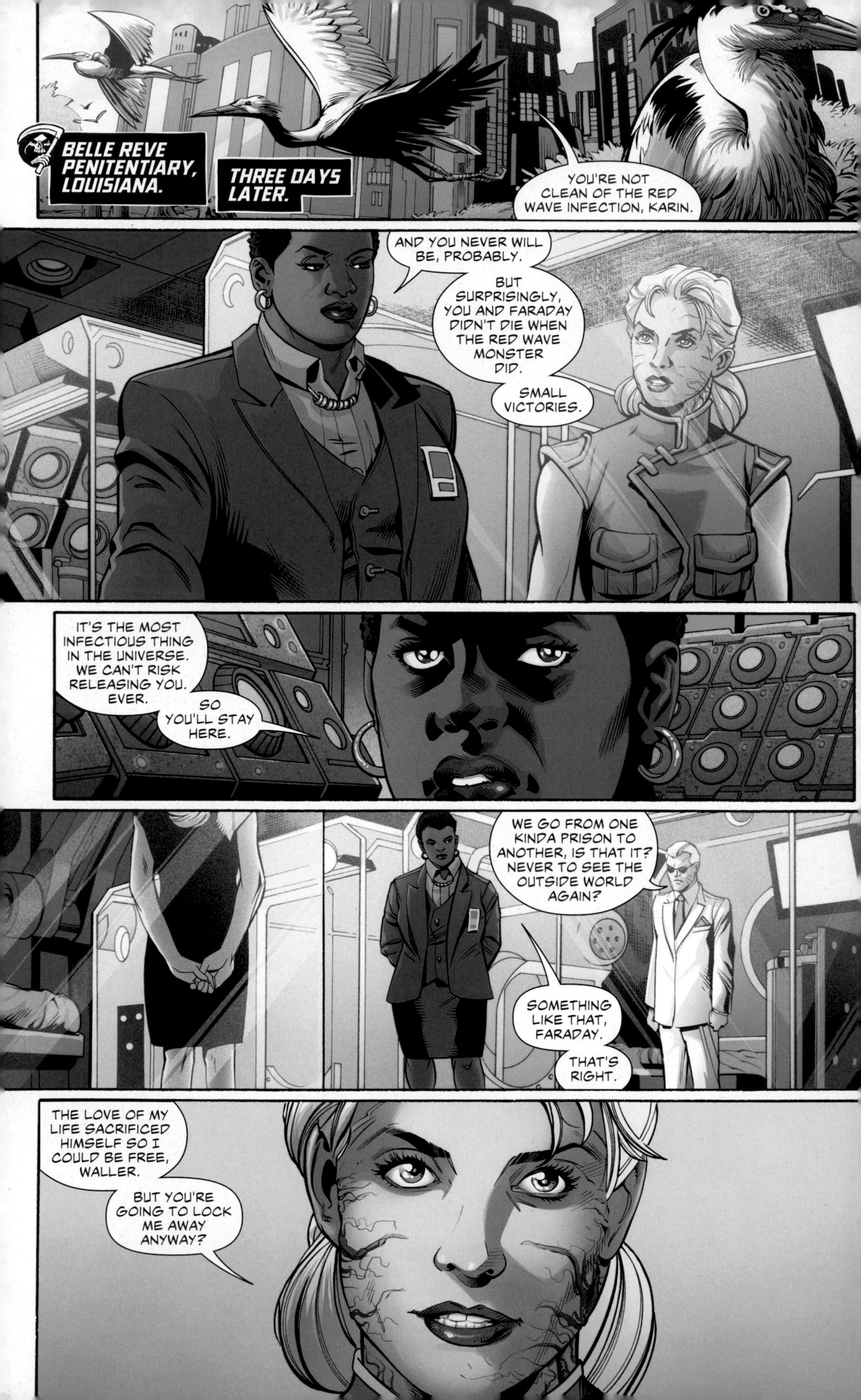
BELLE REVE PENITENTIARY, LOUISIANA.
THREE DAYS LATER.
YOU'RE NOT CLEAN OF THE RED WAVE INFECTION, KARIN.
AND YOU NEVER WILL BE, PROBABLY.
BUT SURPRISINGLY, YOU AND FARADAY DIDN'T DIE WHEN THE RED WAVE MONSTER DID.
SMALL VICTORIES.
IT'S THE MOST INFECTIOUS THING IN THE UNIVERSE. WE CAN'T RISK RELEASING YOU. EVER.
SO YOU'LL STAY HERE.
WE GO FROM ONE KINDA PRISON TO ANOTHER, IS THAT IT? NEVER TO SEE THE OUTSIDE WORLD AGAIN?
SOMETHING LIKE THAT, FARADAY.
THAT'S RIGHT.
THE LOVE OF MY LIFE SACRIFICED HIMSELF SO I COULD BE FREE, WALLER.
BUT YOU'RE GOING TO LOCK ME AWAY ANYWAY?

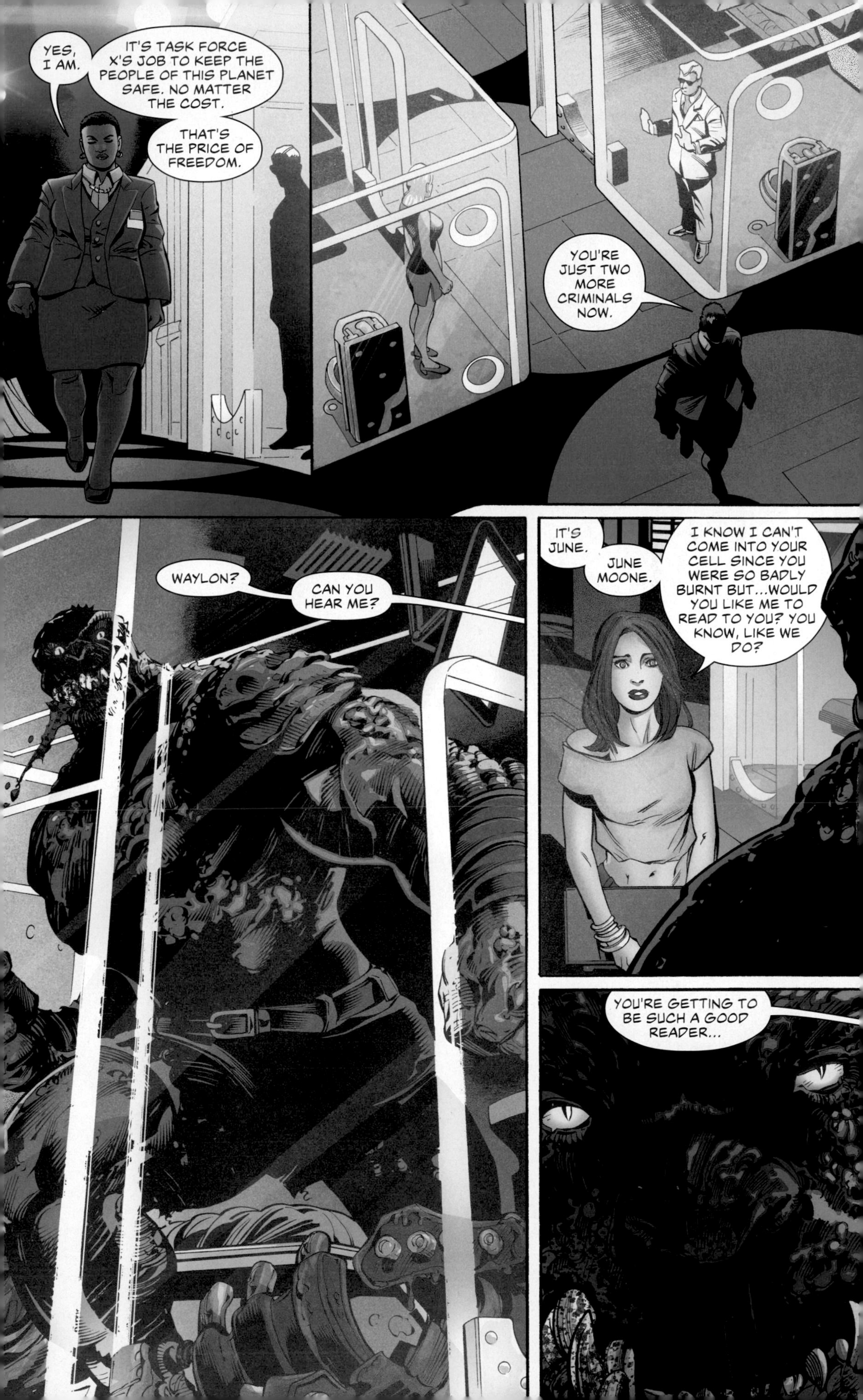
YES, I AM.
IT'S TASK FORCE X'S JOB TO KEEP THE PEOPLE OF THIS PLANET SAFE. NO MATTER THE COST.
THAT'S THE PRICE OF FREEDOM.
YOU'RE JUST TWO MORE CRIMINALS NOW.
WAYLON?
CAN YOU HEAR ME?
IT'S JUNE.
JUNE MOONE.
I KNOW I CAN'T COME INTO YOUR CELL SINCE YOU WERE SO BADLY BURNT BUT...WOULD YOU LIKE ME TO READ TO YOU? YOU KNOW, LIKE WE DO?
YOU'RE GETTING TO BE SUCH A GOOD READER...

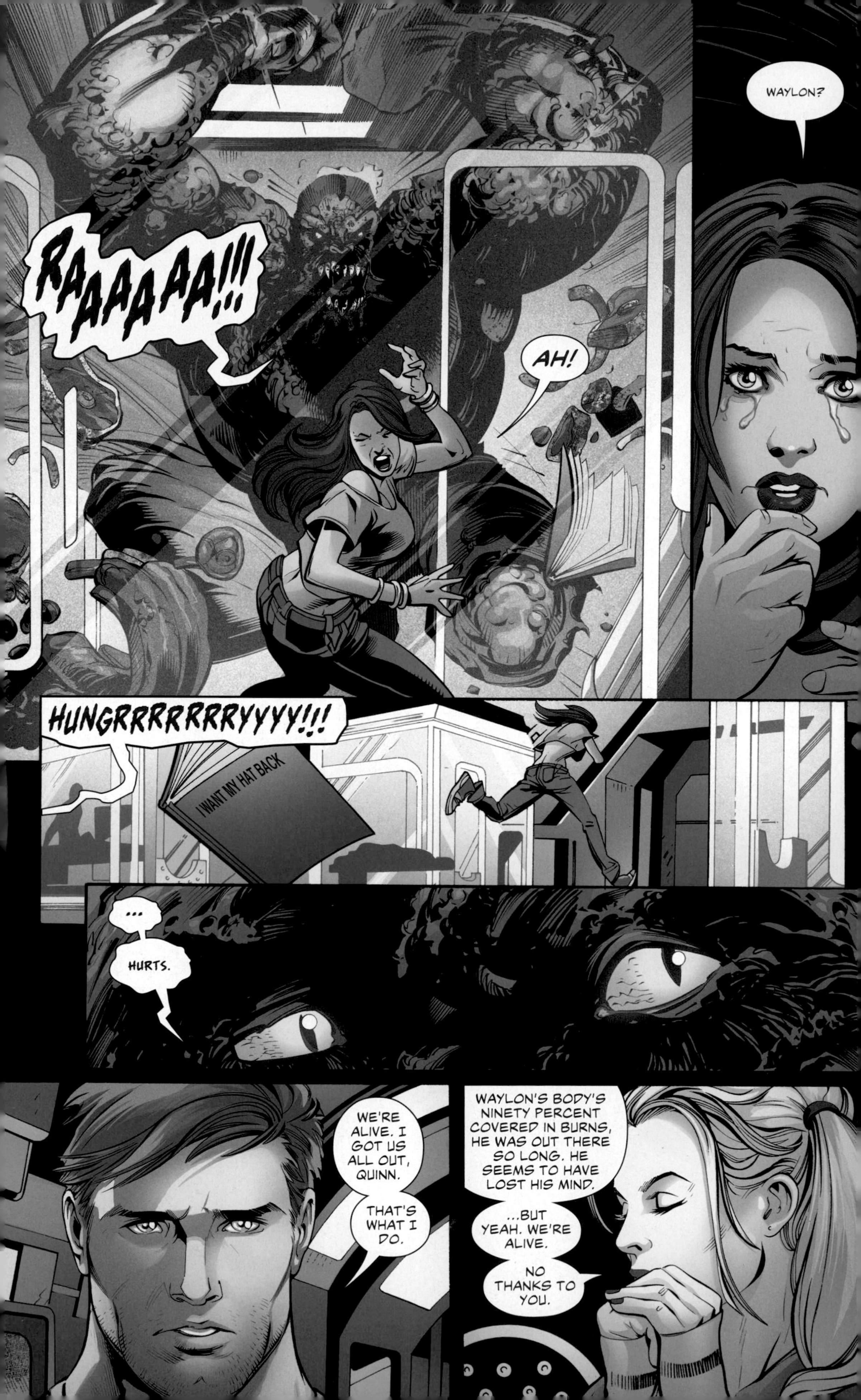
WAYLON?
RAAAAAA!!!
AH!
HUNGRRRRRRRYYYY!!!
I WANT MY HAT BACK
...
HURTS.
WE'RE ALIVE. I GOT US ALL OUT, QUINN.
THAT'S WHAT I DO.
WAYLON'S BODY'S NINETY PERCENT COVERED IN BURNS, HE WAS OUT THERE SO LONG. HE SEEMS TO HAVE LOST HIS MIND.
...BUT YEAH. WE'RE ALIVE.
NO THANKS TO YOU.

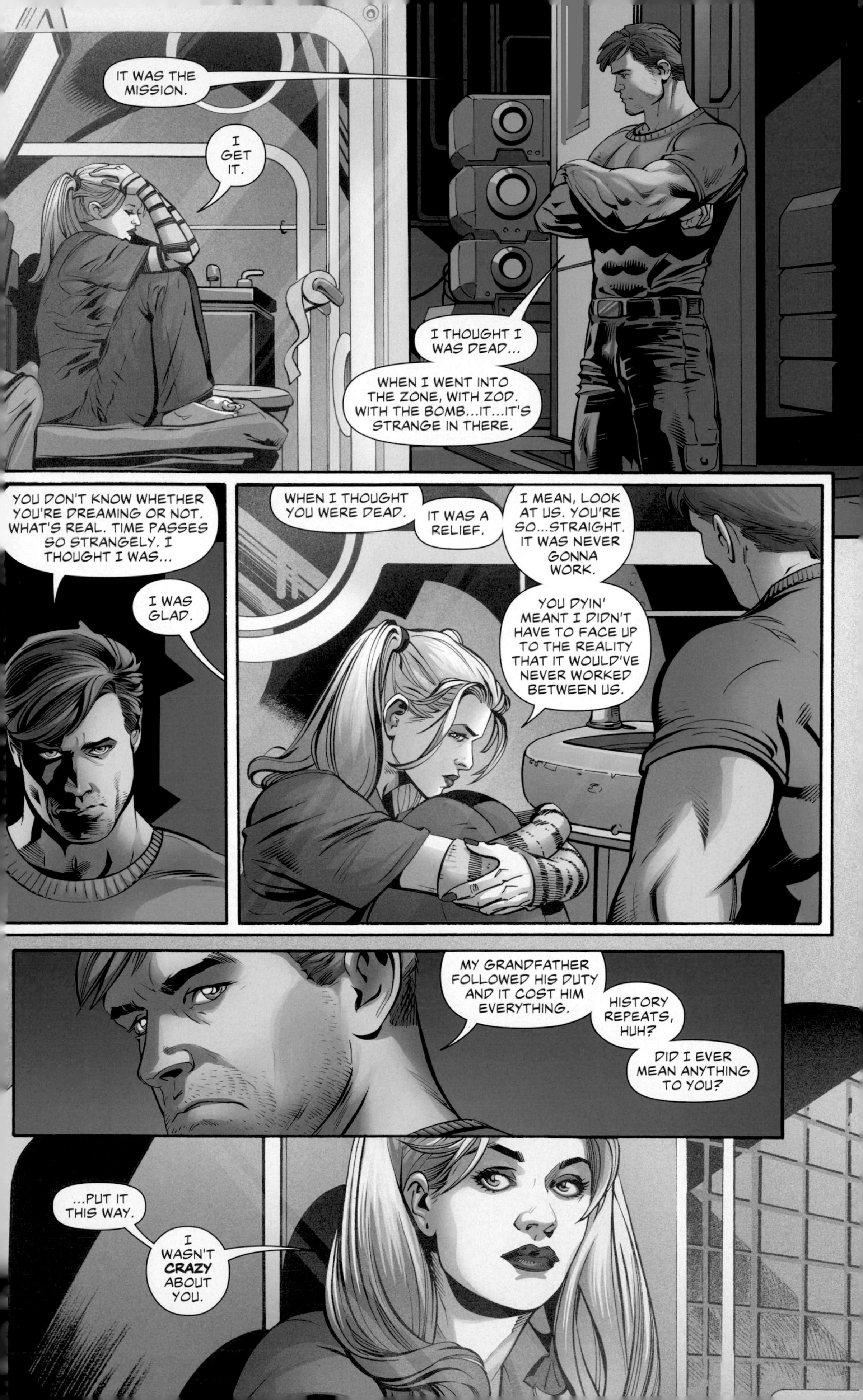
IT WAS THE MISSION.
I GET IT.
I THOUGHT I WAS DEAD...
WHEN I WENT INTO THE ZONE, WITH ZOD. WITH THE BOMB...IT...IT'S STRANGE IN THERE.
YOU DON'T KNOW WHETHER YOU'RE DREAMING OR NOT. WHAT'S REAL. TIME PASSES SO STRANGELY. I THOUGHT I WAS...
I WAS GLAD.
WHEN I THOUGHT YOU WERE DEAD.
IT WAS A RELIEF.
I MEAN, LOOK AT US. YOU'RE SO...STRAIGHT. IT WAS NEVER GONNA WORK.
YOU DYIN' MEANT I DIDN'T HAVE TO FACE UP TO THE REALITY THAT IT WOULD'VE NEVER WORKED BETWEEN US.
MY GRANDFATHER FOLLOWED HIS DUTY AND IT COST HIM EVERYTHING.
HISTORY REPEATS, HUH?
DID I EVER MEAN ANYTHING TO YOU?
...PUT IT THIS WAY.
I WASN'T **CRAZY** ABOUT YOU.

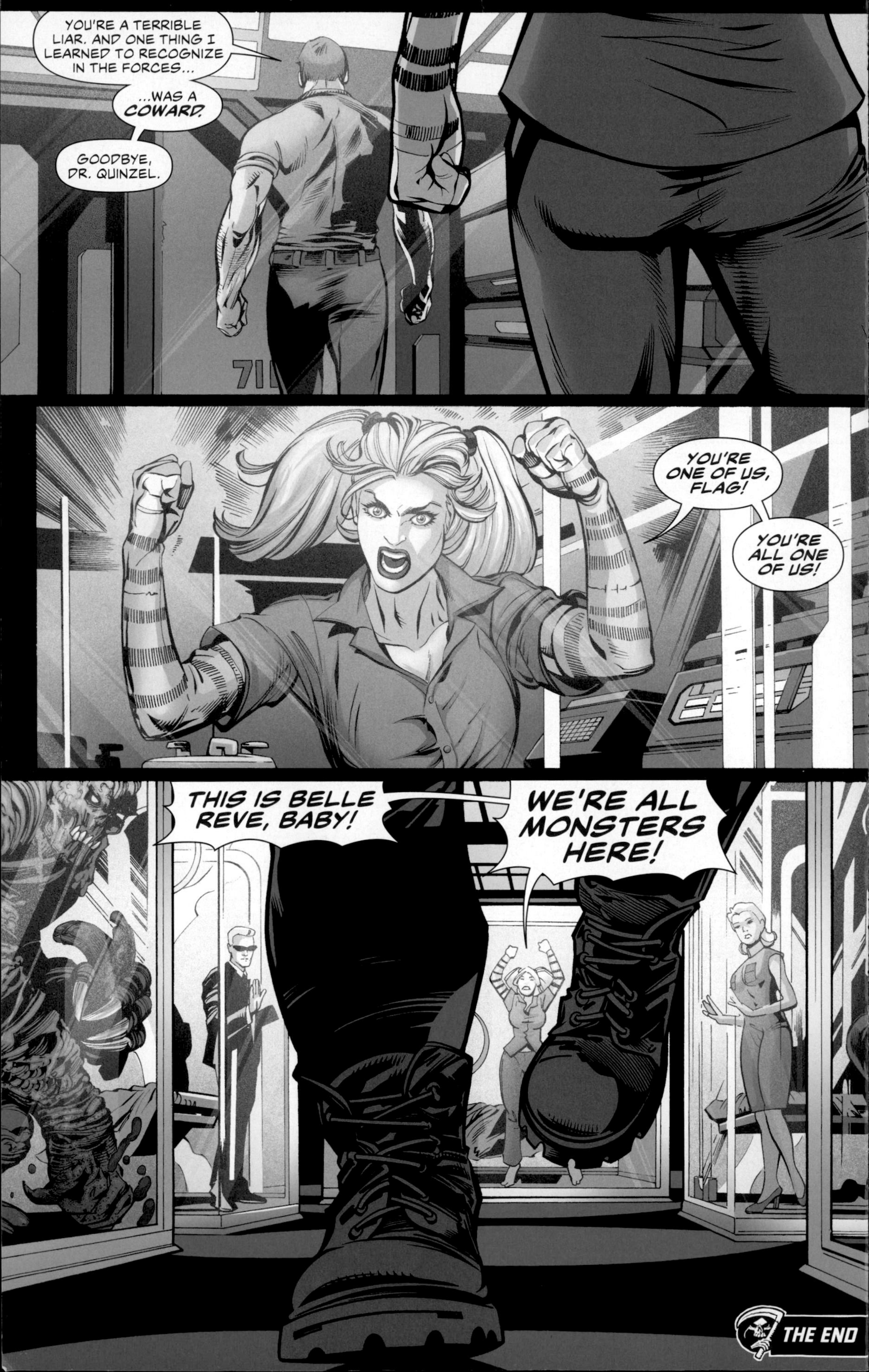
YOU'RE A TERRIBLE LIAR. AND ONE THING I LEARNED TO RECOGNIZE IN THE FORCES...
...WAS A COWARD.
GOODBYE, DR. QUINZEL.
YOU'RE ONE OF US, FLAG!
YOU'RE ALL ONE OF US!
THIS IS BELLE REVE, BABY!
WE'RE ALL MONSTERS HERE!
THE END

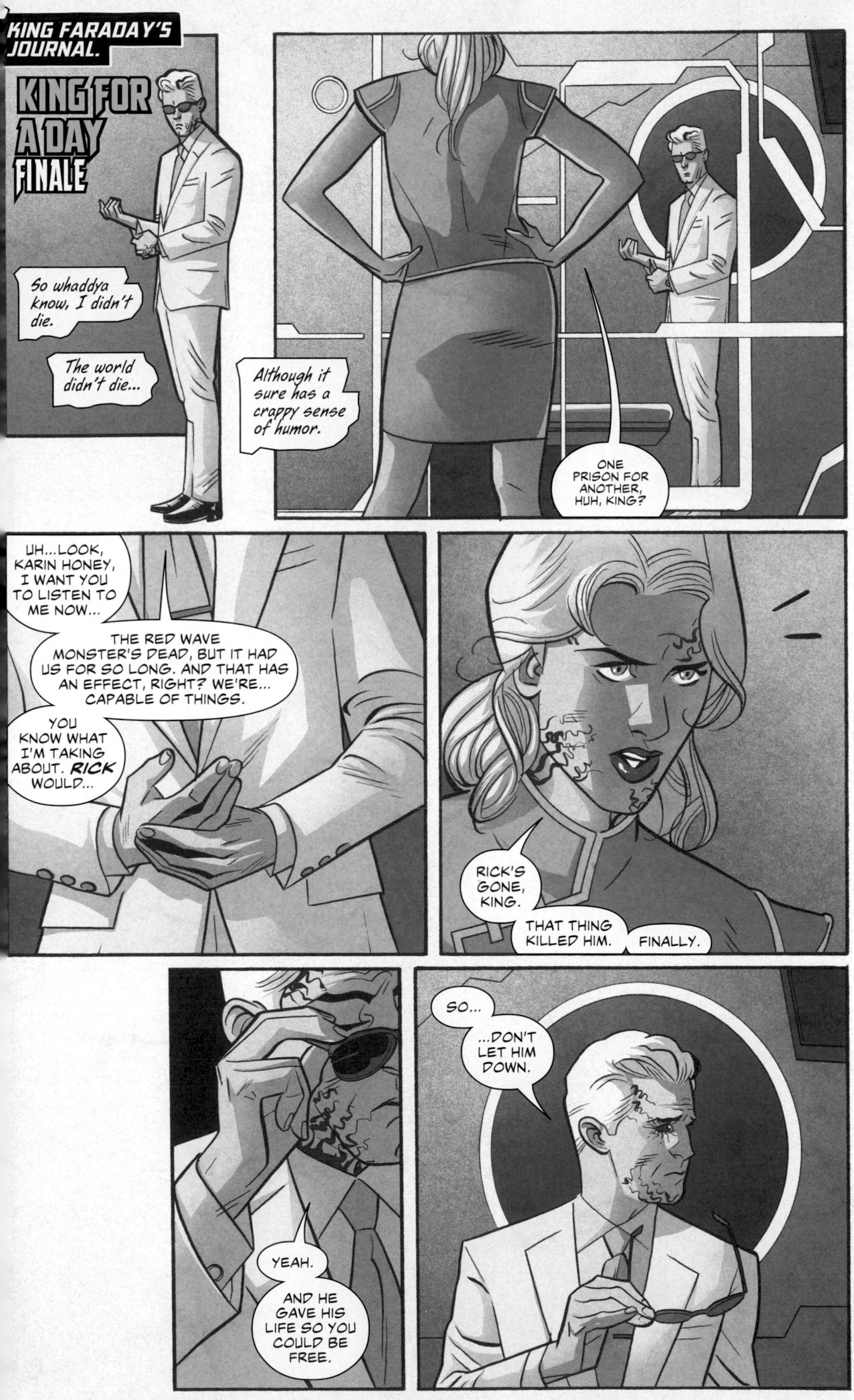
KING FARADAY'S JOURNAL.
KING FOR A DAY FINALE
So whaddya know, I didn't die.
The world didn't die...
Although it sure has a crappy sense of humor.
ONE PRISON FOR ANOTHER, HUH, KING?
UH...LOOK, KARIN HONEY, I WANT YOU TO LISTEN TO ME NOW...
THE RED WAVE MONSTER'S DEAD, BUT IT HAD US FOR SO LONG. AND THAT HAS AN EFFECT, RIGHT? WE'RE... CAPABLE OF THINGS.
YOU KNOW WHAT I'M TAKING ABOUT. RICK WOULD...
RICK'S GONE, KING.
THAT THING KILLED HIM.
FINALLY.
YEAH.
AND HE GAVE HIS LIFE SO YOU COULD BE FREE.
SO...
...DON'T LET HIM DOWN.

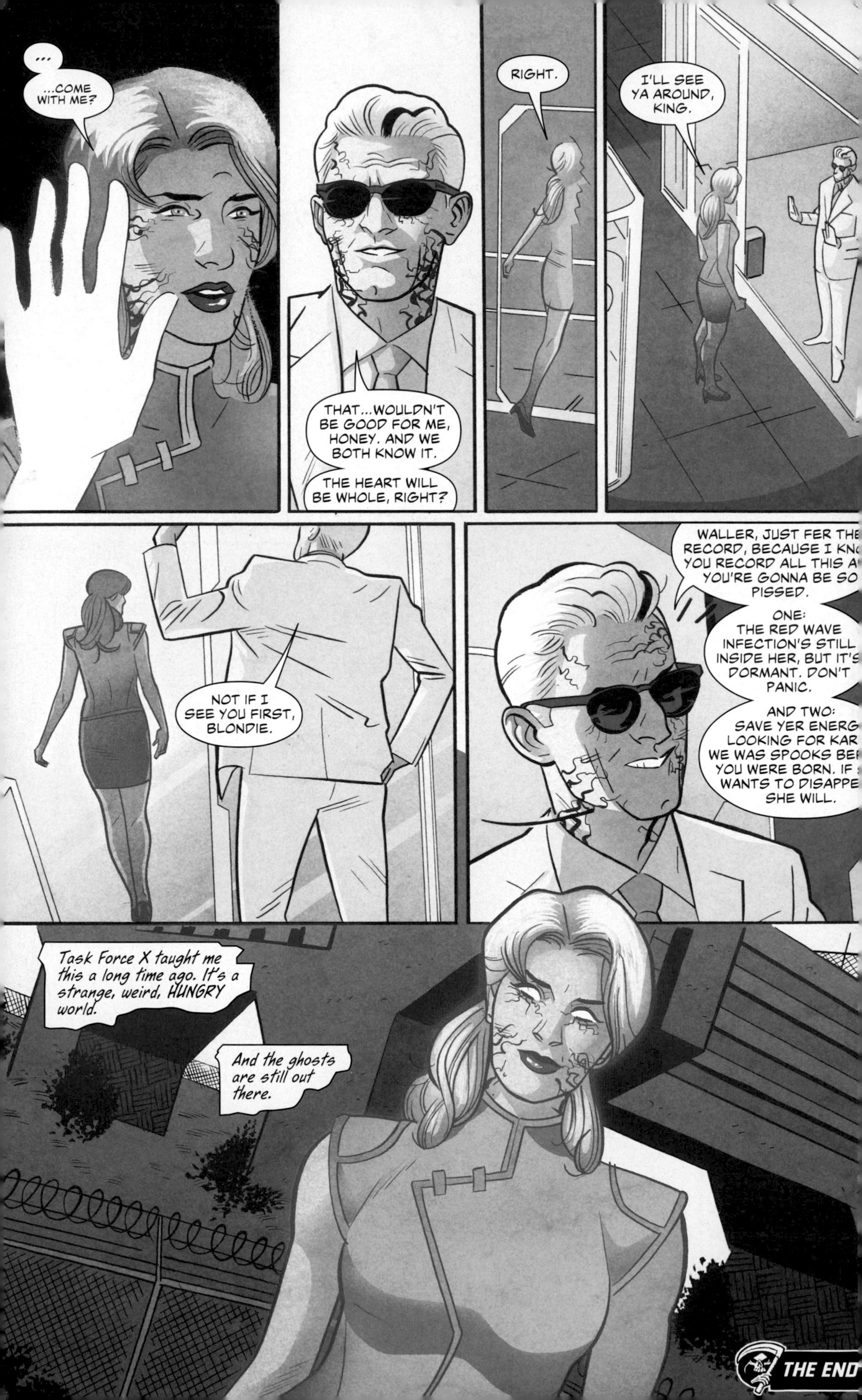
...
...COME WITH ME?
THAT...WOULDN'T BE GOOD FOR ME, HONEY. AND WE BOTH KNOW IT.
THE HEART WILL BE WHOLE, RIGHT?
RIGHT.
I'LL SEE YA AROUND, KING.
NOT IF I SEE YOU FIRST, BLONDIE.
WALLER, JUST FER THE RECORD, BECAUSE I KN YOU RECORD ALL THIS A YOU'RE GONNA BE SO PISSED.
ONE: THE RED WAVE INFECTION'S STILL INSIDE HER, BUT IT'S DORMANT. DON'T PANIC.
AND TWO: SAVE YER ENERG LOOKING FOR KAR WE WAS SPOOKS BE YOU WERE BORN. IF WANTS TO DISAPPE SHE WILL.
Task Force X taught me this a long time ago. It's a strange, weird, HUNGRY world.
And the ghosts are still out there.
THE END

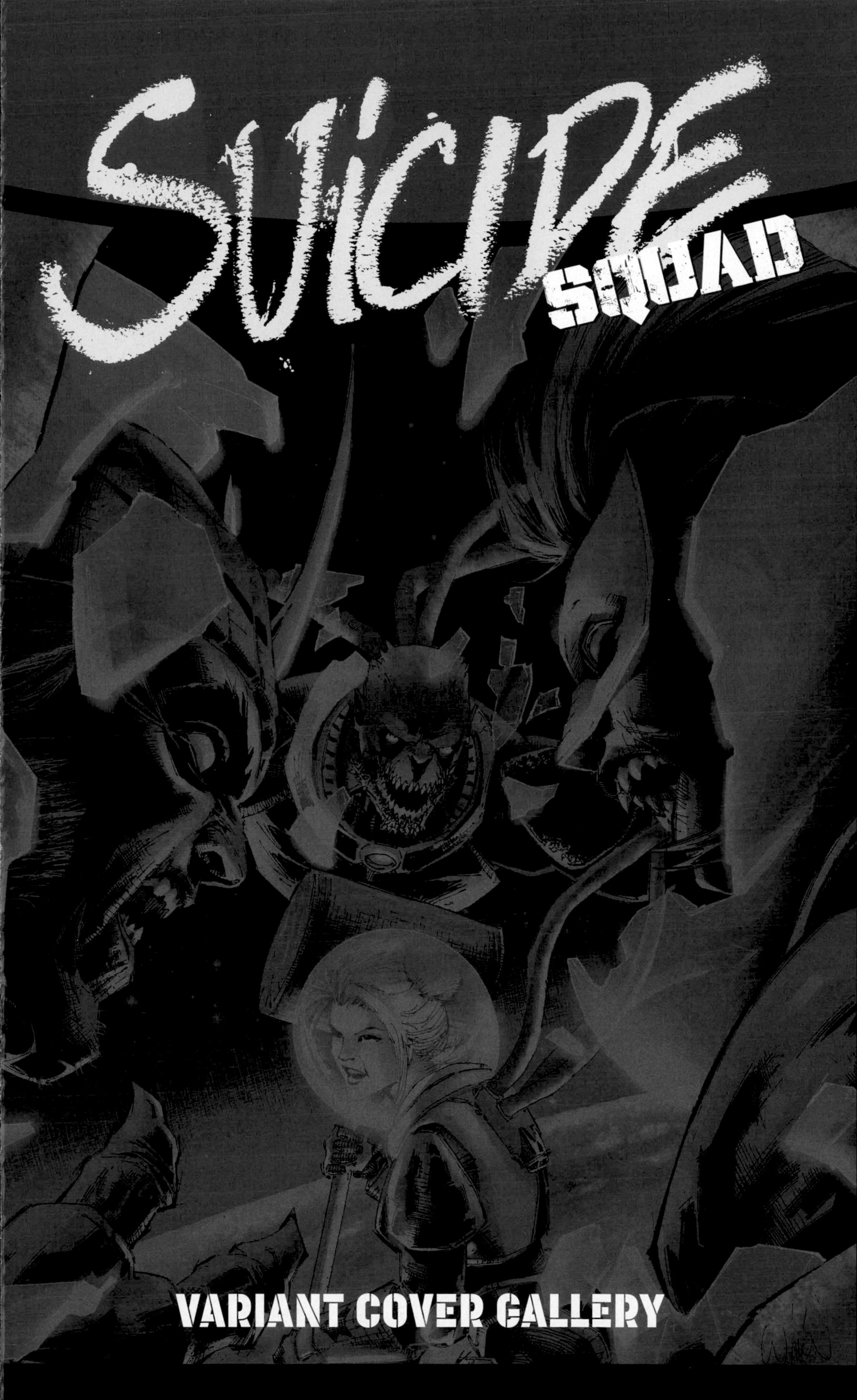
SUICIDE SQUAD
VARIANT COVER GALLERY

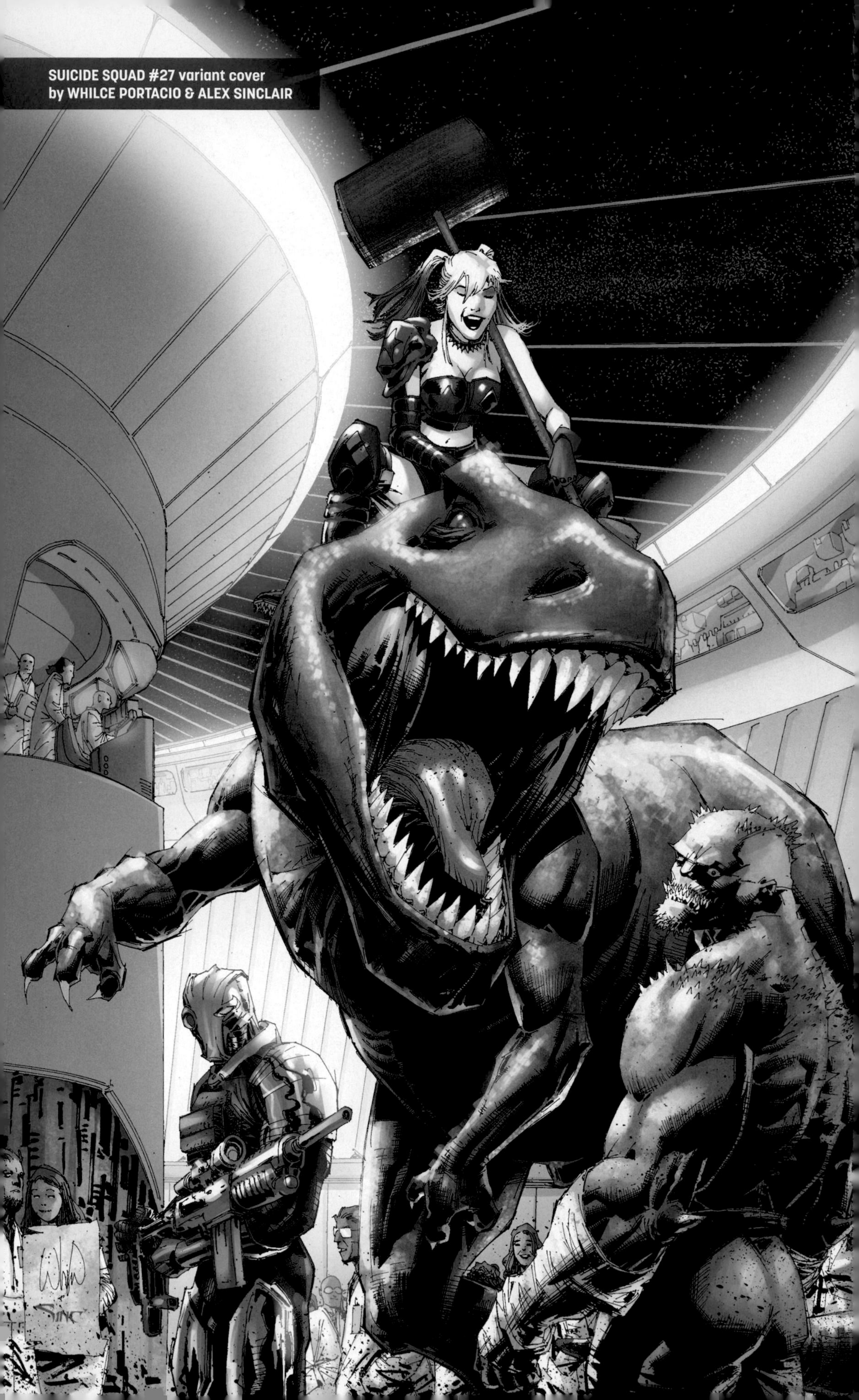

SUICIDE SQUAD #27 variant cover
by WHILCE PORTACIO & ALEX SINCLAIR

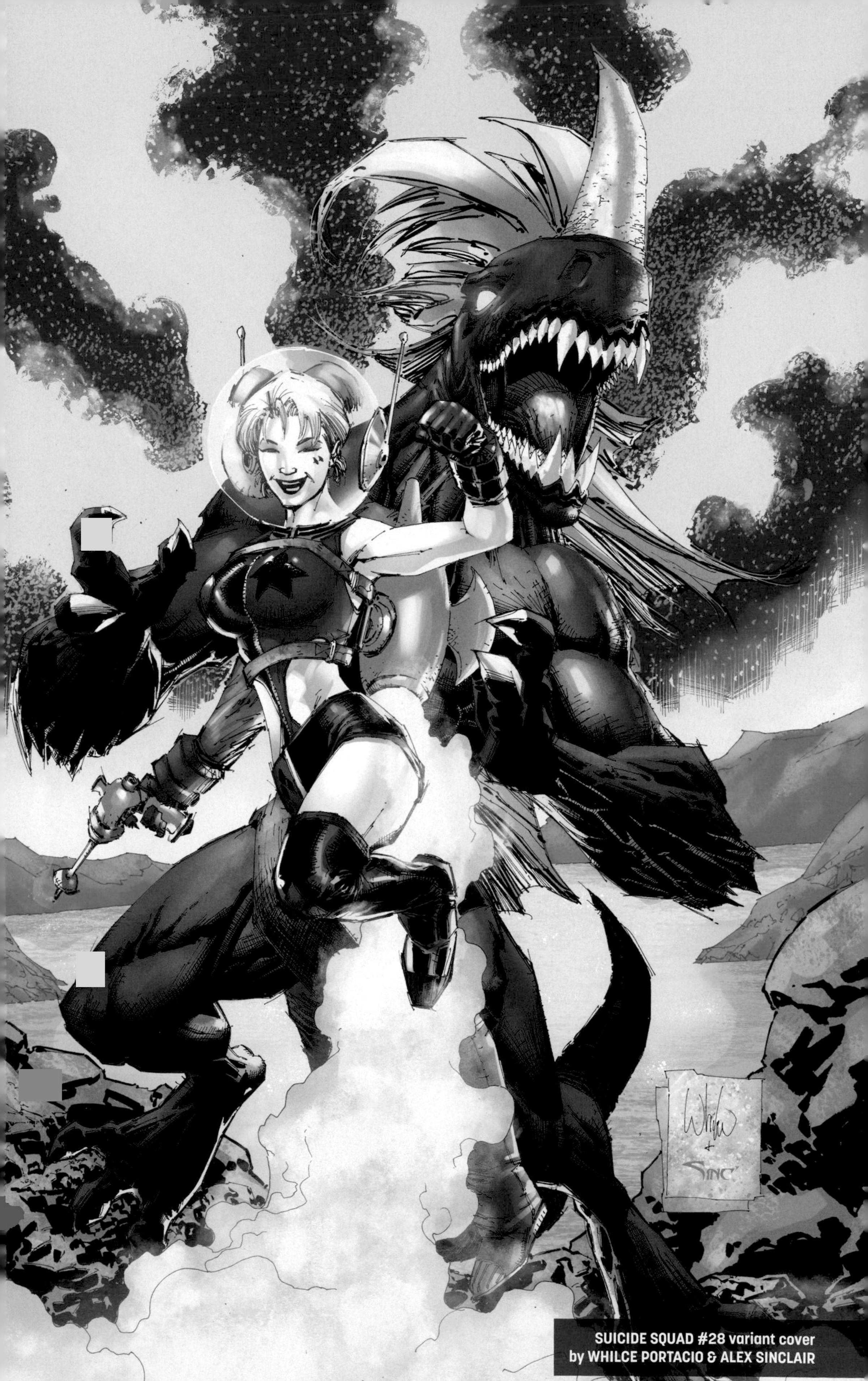

SUICIDE SQUAD #28 variant cover
by WHILCE PORTACIO & ALEX SINCLAIR

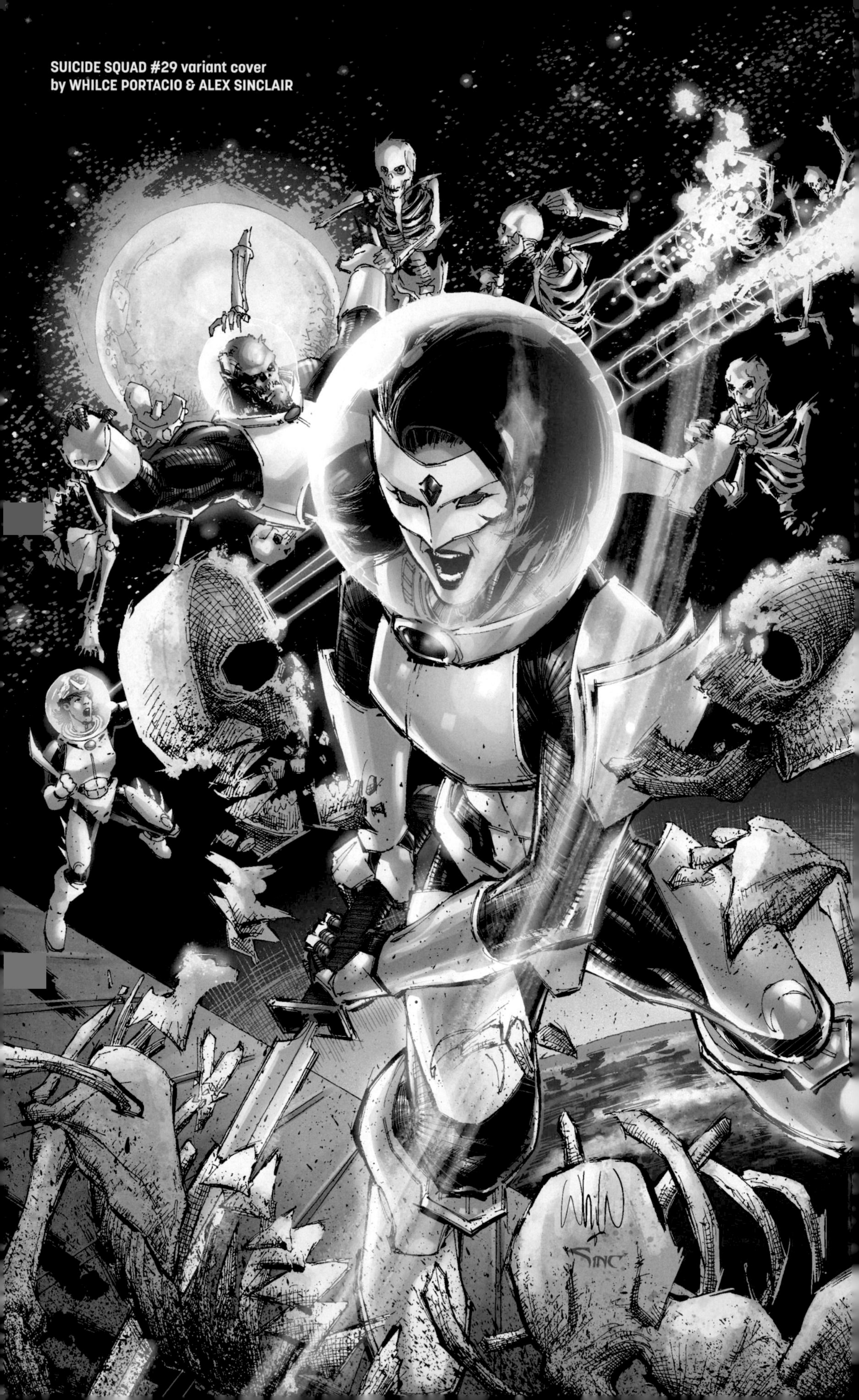

SUICIDE SQUAD #29 variant cover
by WHILCE PORTACIO & ALEX SINCLAIR

SUICIDE SQUAD #30 variant cover
by WHILCE PORTACIO & ALEX SINCLAIR

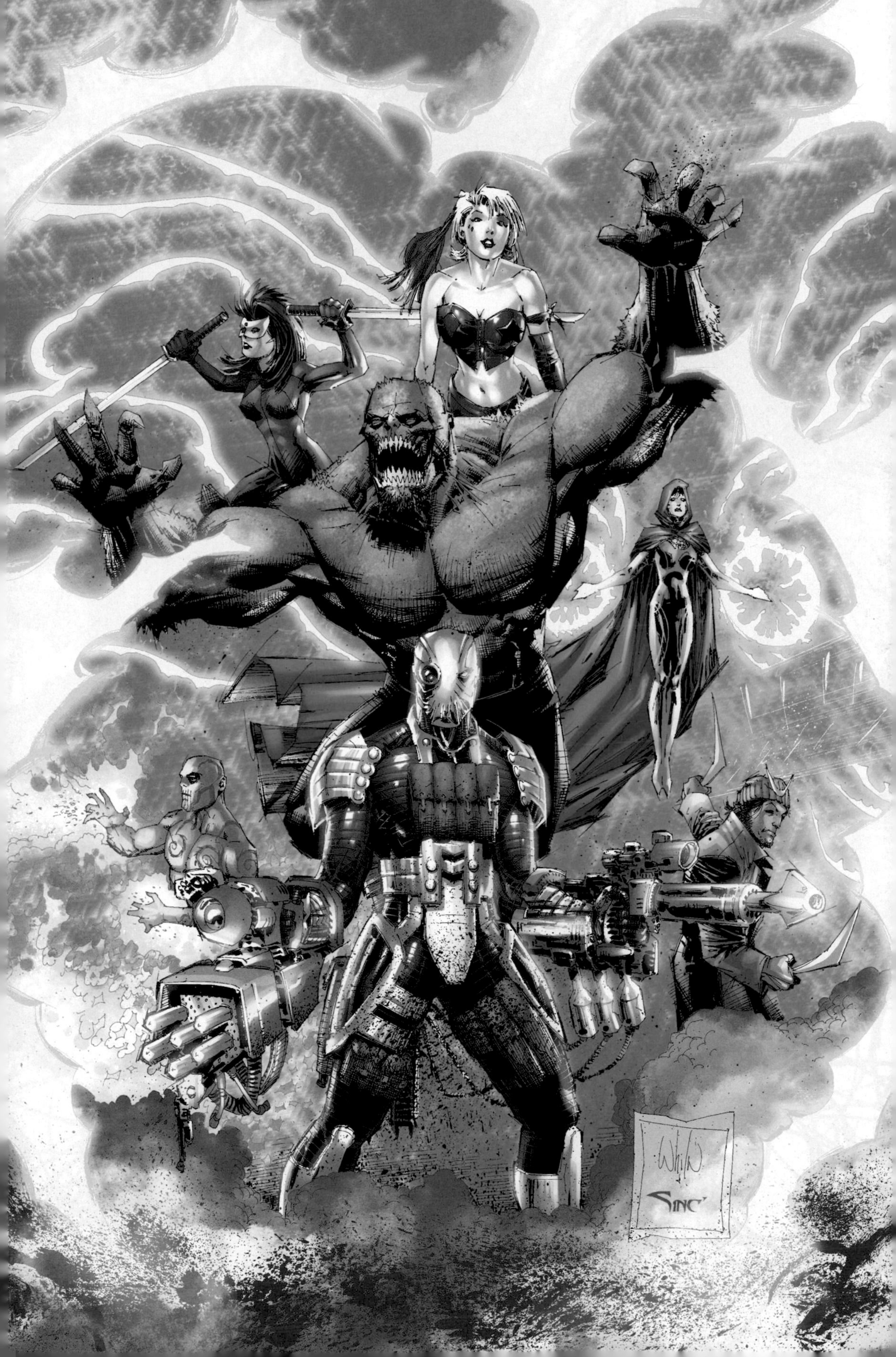

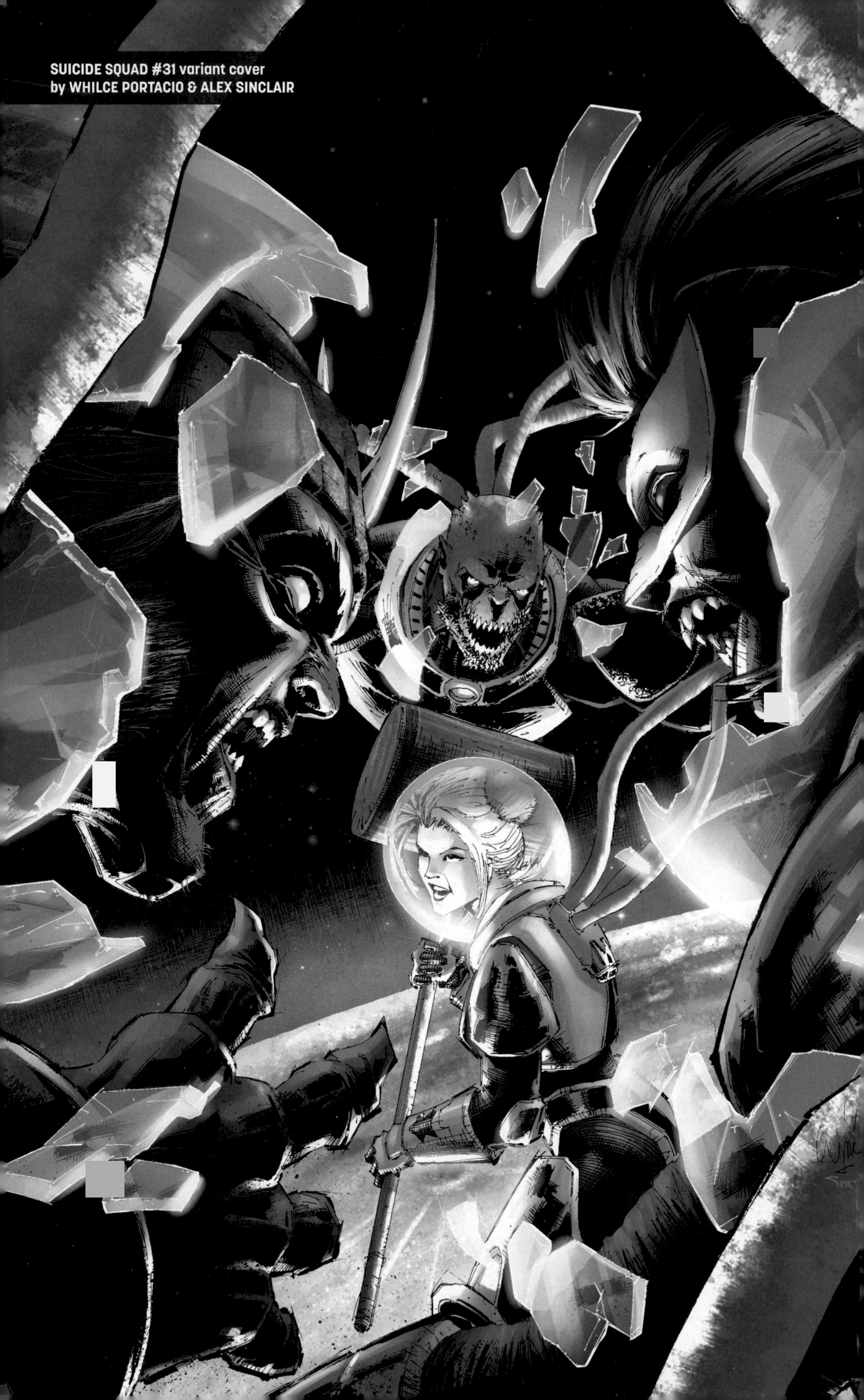

SUICIDE SQUAD #31 variant cover
by WHILCE PORTACIO & ALEX SINCLAIR

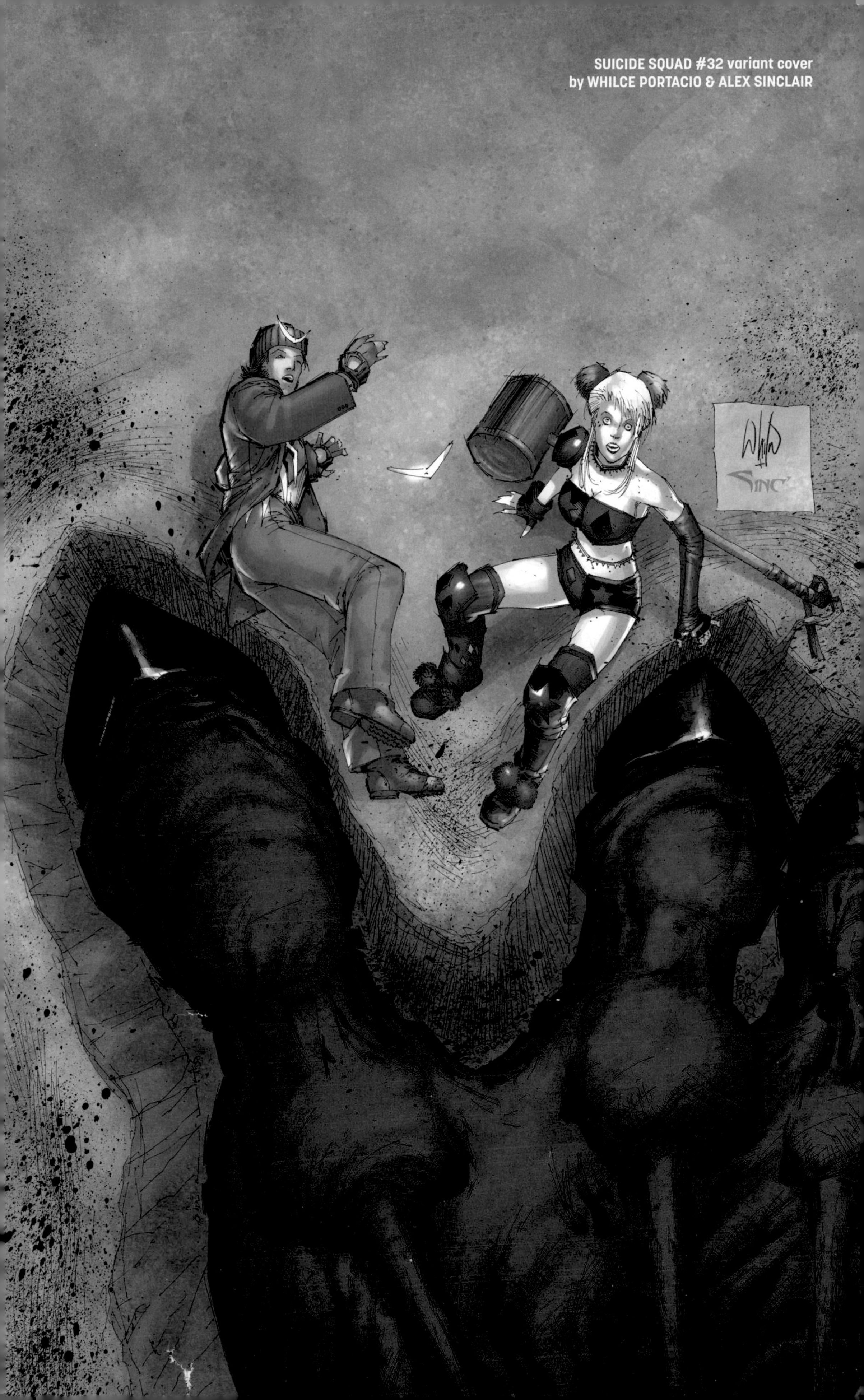

SUICIDE SQUAD #32 variant cover
by WHILCE PORTACIO & ALEX SINCLAIR

DC UNIVERSE REBIRTH

SUICIDE SQUAD

VOL. 1: THE BLACK VAULT

ROB WILLIAMS
with JIM LEE and others

VOL.1 THE BLACK VAULT

ROB WILLIAMS • JIM LEE • PHILIP TAN • JASON FABOK • IVAN REIS • GARY FRANK

**THE HELLBLAZER VOL. 1:
THE POISON TRUTH**

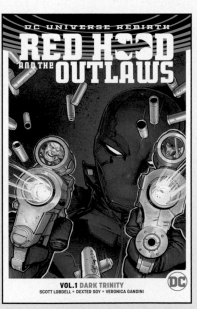

**RED HOOD AND THE OUTLAWS VOL. 1:
DARK TRINITY**

**HARLEY QUINN VOL. 1:
DIE LAUGHING**